Jazz™ Tips and Traps

Dick Andersen
Tim Barnhart
and
Janice M. Gessin

Osborne **McGraw-Hill**
Berkeley, California

Osborne **McGraw-Hill**
2600 Tenth Street
Berkeley, California 94710
U.S.A.

For information on translations and book distributors outside of the U.S.A., please write to Osborne **McGraw-Hill** at the above address.

A complete list of trademarks appears on page 268.

Jazz™ Tips and Traps

1234567890 DODO 898765

ISBN 0-07-881189-9

Cynthia Hudson, Acquisitions Editor
Kay Nelson, Technical Editor
Jean Stein, Senior Editor
Elizabeth Fisher, Editorial Assistant

Ted Gartner, Copy Editor
Judy Wohlfrom, Text Design
Yashi Okita, Cover Design

Dedicated to Dr. James S.B. Mackie.

Dick Andersen

Dedicated with gratitude to my father, Edward N. Barnhart, and my wife, Annie.

Tim Barnhart

Dedicated with love to the memory of Lillian, my grandmother, to Mom and Dad for their support, and to Laura for being so patient.

Janice M. Gessin

Contents

Acknowledgments

We would like to thank Jill Rollinson and Corvus Systems for the use of the OmniDrive hard disk. It performed perfectly and greatly increased our productivity. We are grateful as well to the Prentice Corporation for the use of their Popcom modems. Thanks to Marco Fuentes for his helpful contributions to the graphics chapter.

We also want to thank Pam Campagna, at Lotus Development Company, for her assistance in getting us rolling. Special thanks go to Cindy Hudson, Jean Stein, and Kay Nelson for their help with editing and keeping us on the straight and narrow. Also thanks to Janet McBeen and to Daniel Gasteiger.

D.A.
T.B.
J.M.G.

Preface

Why Tips and Traps? We've found it's hard to learn a program, even one as easy as Jazz, by simply reading the documentation or books that merely reiterate the material contained in the documentation. Why is this true?

Everyone is at a different level of expertise. The beginner feels it necessary to read almost everything in order not to miss something important, but without experience, what is really important cannot be easily distinguished from things that become self-evident when using the program.

On the other hand, experienced users must read a lot of superfluous information in order to find something that actually adds to their knowledge.

And both beginning and experienced users may find that being told how to do something may not at all explain why or when you would want to use it. The Tips and Traps format overcomes some of these limitations.

A Tip is a pointer on how to do a particular task in a quicker or more effective way. It often contains in itself the situation in which the Tip would prove useful, thus answering the question of why or when you might want to do something. A Trap is a warning about a difficult situation that can occur if you're not careful.

Tips and Traps expand on subjects that the documentation has not covered thoroughly, may not have covered at all, or that are so important that they should be mentioned again. They are connected with real situations encountered in using the program and are the result of real experience.

How to Use This Book

Each Tip or Trap entry consists of a descriptive heading followed by explanatory text. This means you don't have to read everything to get help with a problem. You can quickly skim over the headings to find the topic you're interested in. Consequently, *Jazz Tips and Traps* does not need to be read straight through, but can be kept at your side when you need it.

You can also get help quickly by using the Index. We have taken care to make the Index as thorough as possible, emphasizing common problems that can occur.

Is This Book for You?

The Tips and Traps format as well as the breadth of the subject matter covered lend themselves to use by beginner and expert alike.

Many chapters begin with a "Getting Started" section that contains basic Tips and Traps connected with the most common operations. In fact, the "Getting Started" sections have been designed to be useful in training sessions for beginning users. Later sections in each chapter focus on more advanced situations and problems.

Beginners can especially benefit from the Traps. It's easy to get bogged down in a confusing situation and not want to continue. Even the best documentation can't cover all situations.

More advanced users will find a wealth of useful material. Often a single Tip or Trap can prove worth the cost of the book because of the trouble it saves.

How the Book Is Organized

The following sections give a brief description of the contents of each chapter.

Chapter 1: The Jazz Environment

Jazz applications share features that are a result of the very thorough way Jazz has utilized the unique Macintosh environment. Chapter 1 focuses on using these features effectively and contains information on common operations, including file handling, disk handling, working with windows, memory management, and using Jazz with a hard disk.

Chapter 2: The Worksheet Environment

Chapter 2 covers entering and editing information in the Jazz Worksheet, moving around within it, working with ranges, memory management, recalculation, formatting, and printing. Because the Jazz Database is similar to the Worksheet by virtue of its rows and columns format, many editing tips in this chapter apply to the Database as well.

Chapter 3: Functions and Formulas

Chapter 3 contains detailed information on using the wide variety of formulas and functions used in both the Jazz Worksheet and Database. Even advanced spreadsheet users can benefit from the information covered in this chapter.

Chapter 4: Database

Chapter 4 discusses creating databases, entering and editing database information, and using the Query, Sort, Report, and Form features. Chapter 3, Formulas and Functions, also contains information useful for using formulas in the Database environment.

Chapter 5: Word Processing

This chapter on word processing discusses creating and editing documents, formatting text, and printing. Issues involving transferring data to the word processing function from other Jazz functions are discussed more fully in Chapter 8, Data Transfer.

Chapter 6: Graphics

Jazz Graphics allows creation of graphs from data contained in worksheets or databases. Chapter 6 discusses the issues of preparing data for use in a graph, creating and editing graphs, and enhancing them with formatting features. The subject of using graphs effectively is also covered.

Chapter 7: Communications

The features discussed include hardware and installation issues, transferring files from other computers, using Jazz to access information databases, and micro-to-mainframe communications.

Chapter 8: Data Transfer

One of Jazz's most powerful features involves transferring information between applications. Data can be transferred among the applications and can be dynamically linked to its source through a special feature called *HotView.* Chapter 8 discusses this as well as the topic of using Jazz with files from other programs, such as MacWrite, MacPaint, Lotus 1-2-3 and Symphony, and Microsoft Multiplan.

We hope you find *Jazz Tips and Traps* helpful. We know that you will discover Tips and Traps on your own and we encourage you to let us know about them. Please document them fully and send them to

Dick Andersen
Net 1
1280 Boulevard Way, #207
Walnut Creek, CA 94595

If we use them in subsequent editions of this book we will be happy to give you credit.

1

The Jazz Environment

The Tips and Traps in this chapter apply to all the Jazz functions: file and disk management, memory management, working with windows, printing, and so on. They also inform you of some additional topics, including using Jazz with a hard disk.

Like most chapters in this book, this chapter begins with a "Getting Started" section. The section contains a set of Tips and Traps that will help you start working with Jazz. It will be most valuable to those who are not completely familiar with the Macintosh.

In this chapter, as in the book as a whole, we assume that you have a basic knowledge of how the Macintosh environment works, including how to use the mouse, how to manipulate windows, and how to copy files and disks.

Getting Started

1.01 ***Tip:*** *Before you do anything, lock your Jazz Program disk and backup Program disk and make a copy of your Jazz Start-up disk.*

There is a small rectangular tab at the upper-left corner on the back side of every Macintosh disk. You can lock a disk by pushing this tab outward toward the edge of the disk as far as it will go. Locking the program disks will stop you from accidentally erasing part or all of the disks. It will also prevent you from saving any document files on these disks, but as we'll see later, you should never need to do this.

You should lock your Jazz Start-up disk, make a copy of it, put the original in a safe place, and then use it for nothing but making additional copies. Setting it aside will protect the Start-up disk against accidental changes.

To copy the original Jazz Start-up disk, first turn on the Mac, place the Start-up disk in the internal drive, and place an empty disk in the external drive. When you insert the empty disk, this is what you'll see:

After the initialization is finished, assign a name to the disk. You might call it "Start-up Copy 1", or you could leave it untitled until you know what you're going to use it for. Whatever you do, do not name it "Jazz Start-up". Doing so will produce two disks with the same name, and you may become confused about which is the original and which is the copy.

When you click on Initialize, the disk will be initialized. You can then proceed with the disk-copying operation by pointing to the Jazz Start-up icon, dragging it until it completely covers the icon of the new disk, and then releasing the mouse button. You'll then see the following dialog box:

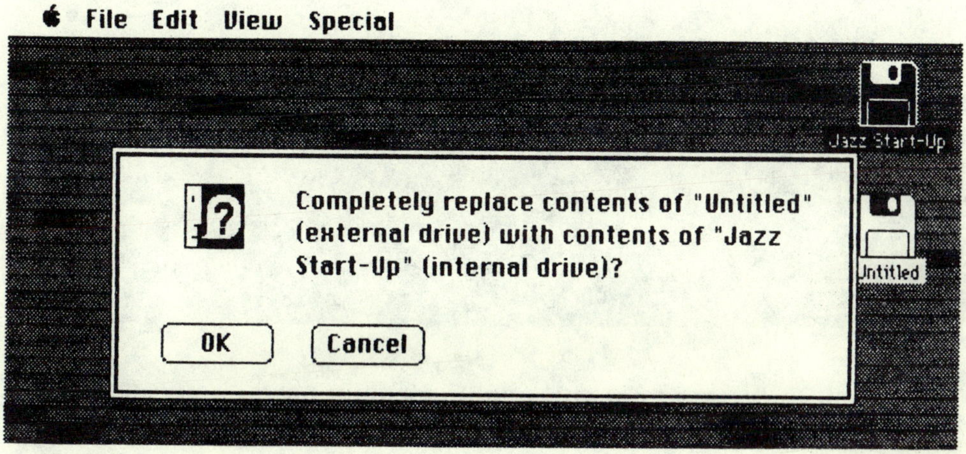

Since you do want to replace the contents of the new disk, you want to click on OK in the dialog box. The entire Start-up disk will then be copied to the new disk. When the copy operation is complete, eject both disks (see the following Tip), put the original Start-up disk away, turn off the Mac, turn it on again, and insert the Start-up disk copy in the internal drive to start a new session. If you don't turn the Mac off and on before inserting the new Start-up disk in the internal drive, you'll be asked from time to time to insert the original Start-up disk.

1.02 Tip: *To eject a disk from the Desktop, select the disk you want to eject and press COMMAND-E, or use the SHIFT-COMMAND key combination with either the 1 or the 2 key.*

You can eject a disk while you're on the Desktop by clicking on its name or icon to select it and then pressing COMMAND-E. (If its name or icon is already darkened, it's already selected.) You can also use SHIFT-COMMAND-1 to eject the disk in the internal drive or SHIFT-COMMAND-2 to eject the disk in the external drive.

1.03 Tip: *To start Jazz, turn on the Macintosh, put a Jazz Start-up disk copy in the internal drive, put a Jazz Program disk in the external drive, and double-click on the Jazz icon that appears on the Desktop.*

When you've inserted these two disks, you'll see the Jazz icon to the left of the Jazz Start-up icon:

Double-click on this icon to load Jazz and to get to the point where you can open a Jazz document. Do not try to open the Jazz disk itself; this will produce nothing.

1.04 Tip: *To start a new Jazz document, open an empty document by choosing New from the File menu and then double-clicking on the icon representing the document type you want.*

When you've just loaded Jazz by opening the Jazz icon, you'll see a screen with nothing but the top menu line. If you select New from the File menu, this is what you'll see:

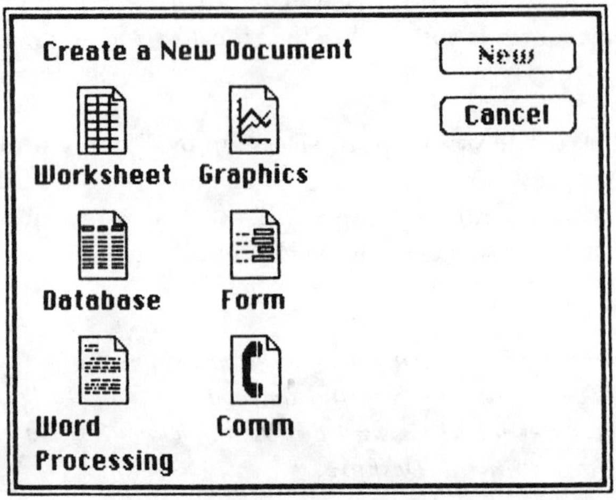

Double-click on the document type that you want and Jazz will open a new document for you. If you want to work in a new document when you already have one or more Jazz documents open, the procedure is exactly the same: select New and double-click on the icon for the type of document you want.

1.05 Trap: *If you don't save your documents frequently, or if you don't save both an original and a backup disk, you're liable to lose valuable information.*

You should never work longer than half an hour without issuing a Save command. Remember that Jazz saves only the currently active document. If you want to save an open document that's not currently active, you must first make it active (by clicking in its window or using the Window menu) and then select Save from the File menu. Occasionally someone pulls the plug, there's a power failure, or your system locks up because of a bug in the software. In such cases, you'll lose all the work you've done since you last saved the document.

It's also good practice to follow each Save command immediately with a Save As command to save a backup copy of the document on a backup disk. You can keep several disks handy for backups and label them accordingly. (They need not be Start-up disks.) When you choose Save As, you'll be presented with a dialog box. Click on Eject in this box. Replace the ejected disk with the backup disk and then click on Save. When the Save operation is complete, you can eject the backup disk and reinsert your original data disk. It's also possible to back up your documents from the Desktop after you quit Jazz by simply dragging the file icons to the backup disk icon. The problem with this approach, however, is that you often don't remember to do it. It's far better to use the Save As command to create a backup copy immediately after saving the original document.

You'll usually want each backup file to have the same name as its correponding original. In this way you will know what backs up what, and you won't have to change the file name in the Save As dialog box.

1.06 Tip: *When you need to insert another data disk, always insert it in the internal drive. Keep the Jazz Program disk in the external drive at all times.*

From time to time Jazz needs to read additional program code from the Program disk. If you've ejected it and placed a data disk in the external drive, chances are you'll be forced into annoying disk-swapping sequences.

1.07 Trap: *If you don't use a Start-up disk for storing data whenever possible, you'll waste time swapping disks.*

From time to time Jazz uses the Start-up disk you inserted when you turned on your machine at the beginning of the current session. If your document files aren't stored on the same disk, you'll be forced to interrupt your work to swap disks whenever Jazz needs information from your Start-up disk. To avoid this inconvenience, use the Start-up disk that holds the documents you are working on when you turn on your Mac.

The only problem with saving documents on Start-up disks is that about half of the available space is already used up by various system files and Jazz files, so some large documents will not fit on a Start-up disk. In such a case, you'll have to use the Save As command to save the document on a non-Start-up disk that you insert after ejecting the Start-up disk.

1.08 Trap: *If you don't give descriptive names to your disks and files, you'll lose track of the contents.*

Not knowing what is in a file can be a problem once you've accumulated many files on many disks. The names you give files should be as specific as possible. For instance, "Sales 85" is much better than "Sales," particularly if there could also be files named "Sales 84" or "Sales 86".

It's also a good idea to keep an up-to-date list of the files on the paper disk labels. This is how you can know what's on a disk without having to insert it in the Mac. When you actually need to make several lines of notes about the contents of a file or a disk, click on its name or icon from the Desktop, select Get Info from the file menu, and type in the notes.

1.09 Tip: *Print a copy of your work frequently.*

Even if you save both original and backup disk copies of your documents, you'll occasionally run into a situation where both the original and the backup files have been erased or altered. With important documents, therefore, it's best to print the work periodically so that you have a hard copy from which you can re-enter the data if all else fails. When printing a worksheet for this purpose, first select Show Attributes from the Style menu so you can print the actual formulas and not just their display results. (Make sure your columns are wide enough to print all your formulas without truncation.)

1.10 Tip: *To open an existing document on a disk already in the internal drive, select Open and double-click on the file name or icon you want.*

Remember that the New command is only for opening completely new documents for the first time. Always use Open for an existing document that is already on disk. If the disk you want is not already in the internal drive, you must, of course, eject the disk that's there by clicking on Eject in the Open dialog box.

1.11 Tip: *To end a Jazz session, select Quit, save all documents you wish to keep, and eject both disks.*

It's important to follow the correct procedure for ending a Jazz session so you can make sure that you save the latest work and you don't damage any disks. Turning the machine off with both disks still inserted is dangerous on both counts. The correct method is to select Quit and then respond as you wish to the Save Changes dialog box that you'll see for each open document. Once you've returned to the Desktop, eject both disks before turning off the Mac.

1.12 Tip: *COMMAND key combinations can eliminate pointing to commands with the mouse.*

If you look at the menu choices on the Desktop and in each Jazz function, you will notice the COMMAND key symbol and a letter to the right of many commands. You don't have to open the menu by pointing and then selecting the command if you press the COMMAND key and the appropriate letter instead. This feature allows an improvement in speed and may be preferred by some users, especially those familiar with command-driven programs for other computers.

Managing Files and Disks

1.13 Tip: *To record notes on a particular disk or file, select it from the Desktop and then select Get Info from the File menu.*

When the Get Info box appears, you'll see that it includes an area where you can add notes that will be saved on the disk. This can be a valuable way to add documentation in addition to what you can include in a file or disk name.

1.14 Tip: *To open an existing Jazz document quickly on start-up, open the disk on which the document resides and double-click on its icon or file name.*

When you open a document this way, both the Jazz program and the document you've chosen will be automatically loaded into memory. This method is slightly quicker than the alternative of double-clicking on the Jazz icon, selecting Open, and then opening the document you want.

1.15 Tip: *You can open several Jazz documents at once from the Desktop by using the SHIFT-click method.*

When you hold down the SHIFT key, every document icon you click on will be selected. If you then double-click on any of these icons, Jazz will open all the selected documents. You can also use the SHIFT-click technique to select groups of files for copying or deleting.

1.16 Tip: *To save a file with a new name or to save it onto another disk, select Save As from the File menu.*

The Save As dialog box gives you the opportunity both to eject a disk so you can insert another and to change the name of the file you're saving.

1.17 Tip: *To write over an existing file with a different name from* *the document you're saving, select Open to check its name first and then click on Cancel and select Save As.*

You may wish to write over an existing file with a different name as a way of erasing the file and reusing its disk space without quitting Jazz. You may also want to keep slightly different versions of a document under different names. Whatever the reason, if you want to use Save As to save the current document under the name of another existing file, there's no way of finding out what that existing file name is once the Save As dialog box is on your screen. If you select Open first, you can write down the name, select Cancel, and then select Save As.

1.18 Tip: *Select Revert to Saved from the File menu to reload a document from the disk when you've corrupted the version in memory.*

Sometimes you mistakenly delete something or perform some other operation that you can't undo. Such an error may force you to continue working with the last saved version of the document. A quick way to reload this latest version from disk is to select Revert to Saved; but before you do so, be aware that the document in memory will be completely replaced. If there are some parts in memory that you want to retain, you might want to cut and paste them to a temporary work document before choosing Revert to Saved. You can then cut and paste them back in after the Revert to Saved if you wish.

1.19 Tip: *Protect individual files from being erased or from having their names accidentally changed by clicking the Lock box in the Get Info window.*

If you try to erase or change the name of a file locked in this way, Jazz reminds you that this is a protected file. Locked files can still be opened and saved.

1.20 Trap: *If you don't always keep an empty disk handy, you may get into trouble when a file is too large to save on its original disk.*

Seldom does a document get so large that it takes up an entire disk. However, you'll often store several documents on a disk, make a change to one of the documents, and then find that you haven't enough room on the original disk to save the updated document. Since there's no standard way of freeing more disk space on the current disk without quitting to the Desktop and losing the documents in memory, you could be at a loss unless you have another disk handy that contains a lot of empty space. If you do have the extra disk, just eject the current one, insert the new one, and save the file.

1.21 Tip: *Select By Size from the Window menu to check the disk space usage of each file on your data disk at the very beginning of each Jazz session.*

If you habitually check the remaining disk space, you'll know when you're running out of space. You'll also be able to monitor which files on the disk are no longer needed. As soon as you're sure that a file is no longer needed, drag it to the trash immediately. Then choose Empty Trash if you're absolutely sure you can get rid of it. In this way you keep your data disks clear of out-of-date material and you avoid the surprise of a disk filling while you're within Jazz.

1.22 Tip: *If you've saved data files on a Start-up disk and need more disk space on it, there are several files that you can erase.*

As mentioned in the "Getting Started" section, it's convenient to be able to save documents on Start-up disks, because doing so minimizes disk swapping. However, if you open a Start-up disk, you'll see that much of it is already taken up with two Jazz files and the System Folder:

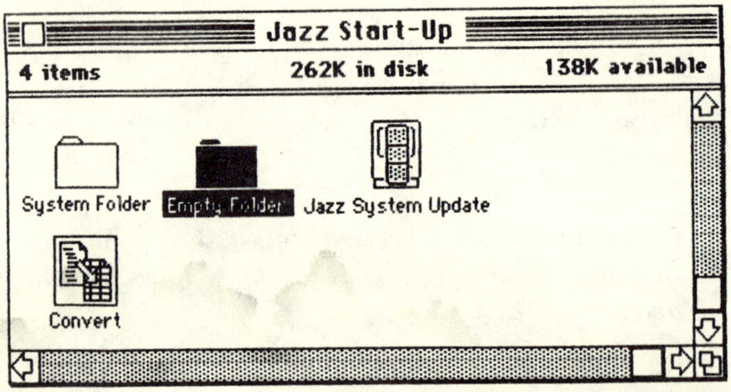

If you open the System Folder, you'll see that it contains a number of different files:

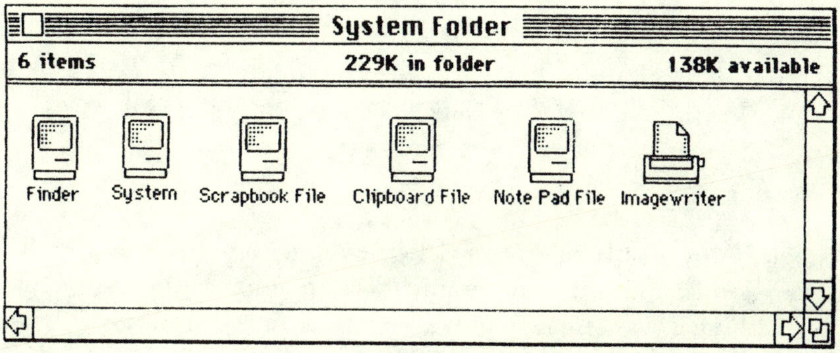

You can trash any or all of these files to free disk space and still have a usable data disk. However, the disk may not continue to work as a Start-up disk. The files you may want to trash first are the Note Pad, Scrapbook, Clipboard, or Convert file (visible in the Start-up disk directory window). If you need still more space, you might wish to trash all the others as well.

1.23 Tip: *If you try to save a document to disk and get the message "There isn't enough space on this disk," try saving the file under the same name as a file that you don't need.*

You may try to save a file and find there is no more room on the disk. You might not have another disk handy. One way to save the file is to try saving it under the name of a file that you no longer need on the same disk. Your new file will completely overwrite the old file and its contents will be lost, so be careful to choose a file you really don't need. Remember, to save the file, select Save As and type the name of the old file in the box. Then select Save.

1.24 Tip: *Free space on your disk by saving a document with nothing in it under the name of a document that you don't need on the same disk.*

You can open a new document and, without entering any information in it, save it under the name of a document already on your disk. Because the new document has nothing in it, it will take up little disk space. If the document on the disk had taken up, for example, 40K of space, saving an empty document, which averages

2 or 3K, would free approximately 37K of space. Make sure you don't need the document on the disk. It will be completely replaced by the empty document. You will then have some space to save the document you need.

1.25 Tip: *You can create more space on your Jazz Start-up disk by using the Font and Desk Accessory Mover in Finder 4.1 to remove unneeded fonts and desk accessories.*

With the release by Apple of Finder 4.1, there are some new desk accessories, Desktop commands, and utility programs that can enhance the use of Jazz. This version of the Finder was released along with version 4.5 of MacWrite, and both are available free of charge to Macintosh owners at Apple dealers.

Along with the Finder is a document file entitled *What's New,* which explains in detail the new features of the Finder and how to use them. This is a MacWrite document, and to open it you will need the new version of MacWrite on the same disk. It's a good idea to print out the document.

What's New gives instructions on installing the new Finder on disks containing the System Folder files. These instructions apply to your Jazz Start-up disk. Read the document carefully.

One utility provided with the new Finder is the Font and Desk Accessory Mover. With it you can remove both unneeded fonts and desk accessories (the commands that appear in the Apple menu). Because every font or desk accessory takes up space, you can remove ones you are sure you won't need. If you have a hard disk, this is not a problem.

With the Font and Desk Accessory Mover, you are able to add different fonts and desk accessories made by third parties. There is a host of new products, including financial calculators, appointment books, telephone dialers, and special fonts. You can add these to your Jazz Start-up disk and other Macintosh programs with the Font and Desk Accessory Mover, and they will then be available to you in the Apple or Font menu. Be careful to follow the installation instructions accompanying these products.

1.26 Tip: *If the system hangs up and you can't use either the keyboard or the mouse to get out, you can eject your disks with a bent paper clip.*

Poke the end of a bent paper clip into the small hole at the lower right of each disk drive opening, and the disk will pop out. Under no circumstances should you do this when the disk drive is whirring or you may damage the disk.

1.27 Tip: *To copy disk A to disk B without replacing disk B, open a window for the target disk and use the SHIFT-click technique to select all the files on disk A and drag them as a group to the target.*

If you copy disk A by dragging its icon onto the top of disk B's icon, you'll of course replace the entire contents of B. If you want to just add the contents of A to the contents of B, you can use the technique described here.

Memory Management

1.28 Trap: *If you don't check your memory availability often, you might find that you don't have sufficient memory to perform some necessary operations, such as saving a file, printing, or copying.*

Jazz requires a relatively large amount of memory for all of its operations. This limitation is especially critical when you need to save a file. With this in mind, use About Jazz from the Apple menu to check the memory availability often, or you might not have sufficient memory to save the document you are working on.

The Jazz program itself requires about 256K of Macintosh memory, depending on the Jazz functions in use at the time, and another 256K or so is available for storing the documents you create. The amount of memory needed to save a document depends on its size and complexity. For example, more memory is required to save a worksheet that contains several complex formulas than one of equal size with simple formulas. In a word processing document, some print fonts and styles also require additional memory. There are no hard and fast rules regarding memory requirements, but you can be sure that if you create a document that requires almost all of the available memory, you won't have sufficient memory to save it. Check your memory availability frequently.

1.29 Tip: *If you find you can't complete an operation because you* *don't have enough memory, try using the Disable Undo command to free memory.*

When you use Cut, Copy, or Clear, Jazz automatically holds the data that you have operated on in case you wish to undo the action. Naturally, this uses memory. When you select Disable Undo you stop this process. But be careful. You will no longer have the Undo option; and if you select Clear while Disable Undo is selected, your data will be gone forever. See the following Tip.

1.30 Tip: *If you get a message that there isn't enough memory to complete an operation, try closing unnecessary HotViews or other documents, or emptying the Clipboard.*

You can do several things when you run out of memory when working in Jazz. You can use the Freeze command to close HotViews, you can close other files you may have open, or you can cut some small piece of data to replace any larger piece being held in the Clipboard. See the previous Tip for one other method.

Window Management

1.31 Tip: *Use the Size box to resize windows for optimum viewing of several windows.*

Figure 1-1 shows the Size box, which can be used to resize a window both horizontally and vertically. Suppose you are working with two documents simultaneously and need to cut and paste between them. Resizing the windows and positioning them one above the other, as seen in Figure 1-1, simplifies the process. You can easily switch between windows while viewing the contents of both.

1.32 Tip: *You can bring a window to full size by using the Zoom Up command in the Window menu.*

When you first open a document, its window does not fill the entire screen. You can use the Zoom Up command in the Window menu (or press COMMAND-Z) to

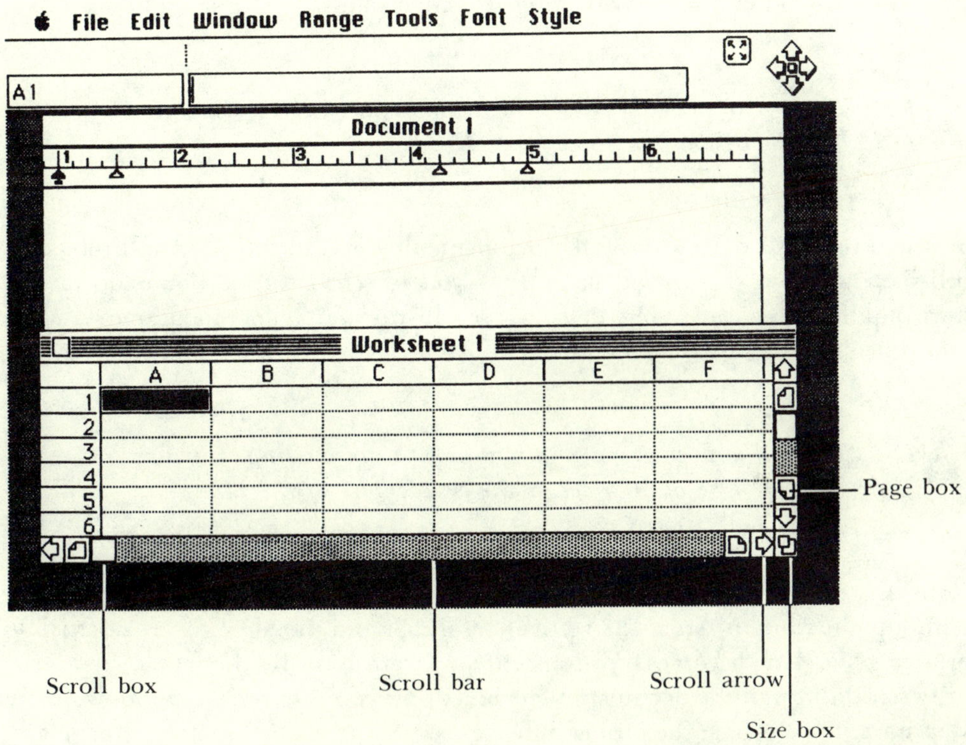

Figure 1-1. Sizing windows

enlarge the active window to fill the entire screen. When the window is at its maximum size, this command becomes Zoom Down, which will return the window to its original size. You will find this command useful when you are working with several windows that have been resized.

1.33 Tip: *You can reposition windows without activating them by holding down the* COMMAND *key and dragging the Title bar.*

When a window is activated, it is placed on top of all other open windows. There are times when you might want to reposition a window without activating it.

Remember, clicking anywhere in a document window makes it the active window. However, if you hold down the COMMAND key and drag the Title bar, you can move a window without affecting its active status.

1.34 Tip: *If you can't view the entire contents of a window, use the Scroll bars or Page box.*

You will usually be working with documents that exceed the viewing limits of a full-sized window. The Scroll bars allow you to scroll through your document horizontally or vertically. The Page box scrolls through a document one window at a time.

1.35 Trap: *If you don't resize a window before moving it, you may not be able to access the Scroll bars or the Size box.*

Consider the active window in Figure 1-2. The window was moved to the right without adjusting the size. The vertical Scroll bar and the Size box are not visible or accessible. This becomes a nuisance if you want to resize the window or vertically scroll through the document. The best approach is to resize a window before you move it. To correct the problem in Figure 1-2, move the window to the left by dragging the Title bar.

Using Jazz With a Hard Disk

1.36 Tip: *If you can afford a hard disk for your Mac, buy it.*

There is no question that a hard disk can make using Jazz easier. Since you can store a large number of files on a hard disk, you eliminate a lot of disk shuffling. Hard disks also open and save files much more quickly than floppies. Though hard disks can be a great time-saver, there are a few points to remember when using them.

Sometimes a hard disk can malfunction in ways that prevent you from recovering files from it. Because of this, become habitual about backing up onto floppy disks important files stored on the hard disk.

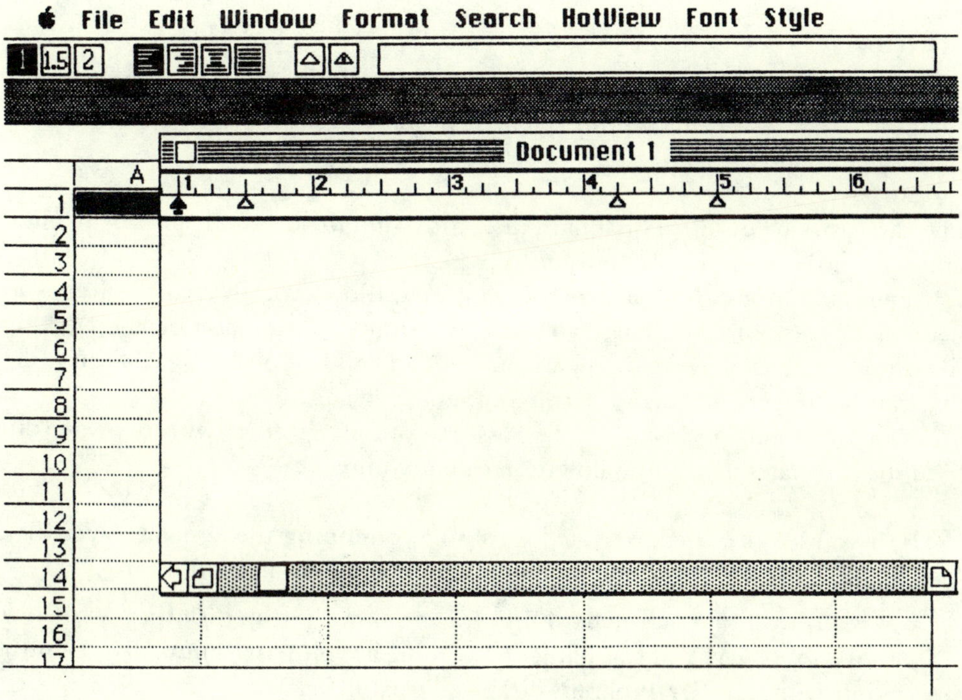

Figure 1-2. Positioning windows

A hard disk also needs to be handled very carefully to prevent the read and write heads from banging against the metal disk. Manufacturers usually provide a utility program that will hold the heads stationary when you move the drive.

There are several hard disks on the market. Read the reviews in Macintosh magazines and try as many as you can before making a choice. One point to consider is that some of the drives hook up to the printer or modem port of the Macintosh, causing the obvious problem of how to use a printer or modem while using the drive. Some of the manufacturers have addressed this problem by putting a printer port for the Mac's printer on the back of the hard disk.

Each hard disk drive manufacturer provides software that initializes the disk, creates volumes to organize files stored on it, backs up files, and performs other "housekeeping" chores. The better software harmonizes with the Desktop menus and the way the Finder functions. What is important is that you find software that is easy to use and that doesn't prevent any Finder commands from working.

1.37 Tip: *Install Jazz on a hard disk by placing all the Start-up files as well as the Jazz icon in the same volume or drawer.*

Jazz can easily be installed on a hard disk, although the original Jazz documentation does not mention how.

Each brand of hard disk has software that allows you to create volumes in which to store your files. These volumes, or "drawers," function on the Desktop like floppies. They have their own icons, which can be opened by clicking; files that can be dragged to them for copying; and other features.

Our comments on installing Jazz assume you are familiar with the way your hard disk operates and know how to create a volume.

- If you haven't already created a volume containing the System Folder files, follow the hard disk manufacturer's directions on how to do it.
- Create a volume on the hard disk for the Jazz Start-up disk files, which we will copy later. You can name the volume as you wish, but to avoid confusion with the Jazz Program disk, don't name it "Jazz."
- Open the window to your new volume.
- Make sure the Jazz Program disk is locked to prevent any accidental erasure.
- Place the Jazz Program disk in a drive.
- When the Jazz logo appears on the Desktop (this is not the same as the disk icon), drag the logo into the window of your new volume. Some material will be copied from the Jazz Program disk.
- Eject the Program disk.
- Insert the Jazz Start-up disk.
- Drag the icons of the Convert file and the Jazz System Update file into the window of your new volume to copy them. You don't need to copy the System Folder.
- Eject the Jazz Start-up disk.
- Double-click on the Jazz System Update icon. This will run the Update program, which will automatically update some material in the System files in the other volume.

- You can then drag the Jazz System Update file from your Jazz volume window to the Trash to save some space.

You now have installed Jazz on your hard disk. When you want to start Jazz, insert the Program disk and double-click on the Jazz logo in your Jazz volume window, not the Jazz logo on the Desktop that appears when you insert the Jazz Program disk. If you double-click on the Jazz logo on the Desktop, Jazz will run off the floppy, which defeats the purpose of using your hard disk. The Jazz Program disk must always be in a floppy drive while Jazz is running, although some copy programs advertise that they can copy the entire Jazz program to the hard disk and eliminate the need of keeping the floppy in a drive the whole time.

1.38 Tip: *When using a hard disk, use your external drive to make backups of important work as you go.*

If you have a hard disk and an external drive, use the external drive for a storage disk. As you work on a document, save your file both to the hard disk and to the external disk by using the Save As command's Drive option to alternate the disk being saved to. Doing this means that you don't have to copy files to a backup floppy from the Desktop, which is more time-consuming.

Printing

1.39 Tip: *You can control where a document's printed left margin appears by aligning the paper with the red line on the Imagewriter's paper bail.*

You often need to know where a margin will actually appear on paper when printing starts. Since Jazz allows you to set very specific margins for printing, if you align the left perforated line on computer paper or the left edge of a sheet of paper with the red line on the paper bail, you will know that a margin setting of zero will actually begin printing at the edge, a margin setting of one inch will be indented one inch, and so forth. (On some Imagewriters, this red line does not exist. You can make a mark there if you wish, once you determine where the zero margin point actually is.)

1.40 Tip: *You can print your entire screen or just the active window by using* COMMAND *key combinations.*

At times you want to be able to print the information on the screen. You do this by depressing the CAPS LOCK key and pressing COMMAND-SHIFT-4 simultaneously. This prints the entire screen.

You can print just the contents of the active window by pressing the COMMAND-SHIFT-4 without having CAPS LOCK depressed.

1.41 Tip: *To keep the printer from moving to the top of the next page after printing a selected area, turn the printer off as soon as the last desired character has been printed.*

Sometimes you want to print several different areas separately and have them stay on the same page. Jazz will normally not allow this, since it automatically sends a form feed to the printer at the end of each print operation. You can fool the printer, however, if you're very quick and are able to turn it off before it receives the form feed. When you turn it on again, the print head will be positioned right after the end of the range you just printed, instead of at the top of the next page.

2

The Worksheet Environment

The Tips and Traps early in this chapter pay special attention to the features of the Jazz Worksheet that involve entering information in cells, moving within the worksheet, editing information, selecting ranges, formatting, and printing. (See Chapter 3 for Tips and Traps related to the actual formulas and functions you'll use in a worksheet document.) As you progress through this chapter, you'll find more advanced Tips and Traps about such topics as memory management, worksheet recalculation, cell protection, and manipulating ranges.

When specifying techniques for entering information into cells, the Tips and Traps in this chapter will use the word *enter* to refer to the use of either the ENTER, RETURN, or TAB key. (See Tips 2.01 and 2.02.)

Figure 2-1 shows a Jazz Worksheet window with a simple worksheet. You can refer to the various labeled elements in this figure whenever you encounter an unfamiliar term in any Tip or Trap in the following sections.

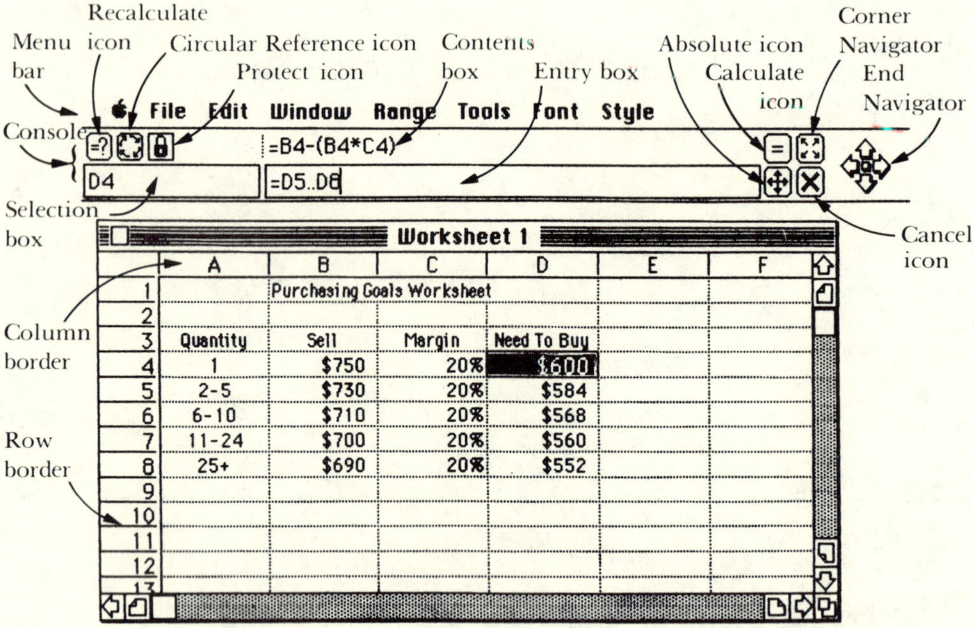

Figure 2-1. The Jazz Worksheet

Getting Started

2.01 *Tip:* *To place data in a cell, click on the cell to make it active, type a number, text, or formula, and press* ENTER.

Once you've made a cell active, it displays in black with a white border. (See cell B2 in the following illustration.)

When you begin typing numbers or text, they appear in the Entry box above the worksheet grid. Here the number 750 has been typed, but it appears only in the Entry box. It will not appear in the active cell until you press ENTER, RETURN, or TAB.

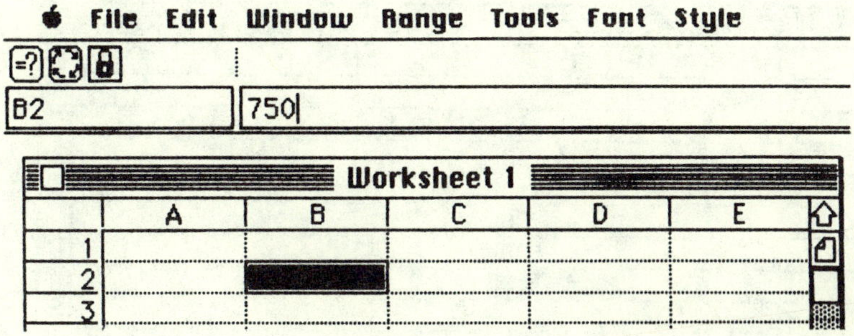

A cell is referred to by the column and row in which it resides. The active cell in this example is B2. Notice that its address is reflected in the Selection box at the upper left of the screen.

When you press ENTER, RETURN, or TAB, the contents of the Entry box are placed in B2. The Contents box, located just above the Entry box, always shows what is in the active cell:

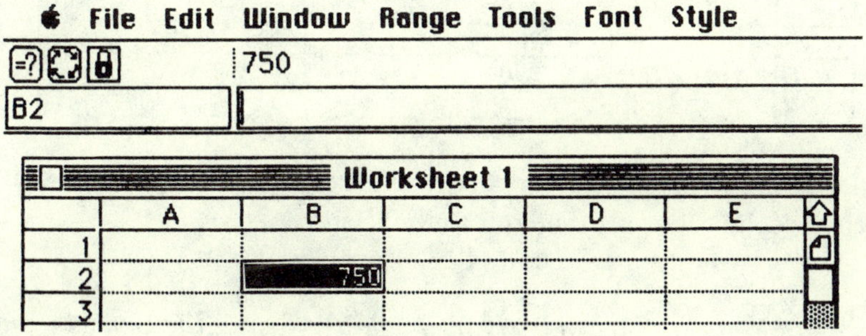

2.02 Tip: *To enter information into a series of cells in a column or row, use the RETURN key or the TAB key instead of the ENTER key.*

When you're entering data in a column, using the RETURN key places your current entry in the current active cell and moves the active cell to the next cell below. Here's the result of entering four more numbers below cell B2 while using the RETURN key after each entry:

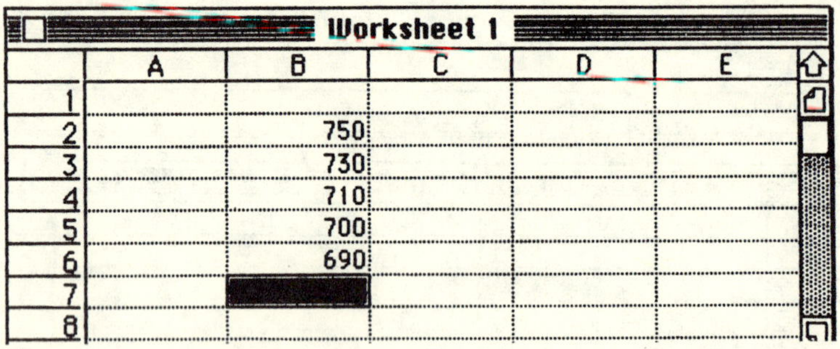

When you're entering data in a row, using the TAB key places your current entry in the current active cell and moves the active cell one cell to the right. Here the labels were entered from left to right using the TAB key:

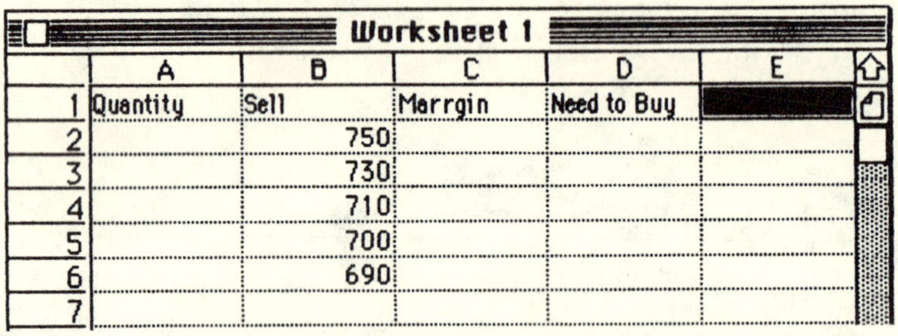

Using SHIFT along with RETURN moves the active cell up one cell; using SHIFT along with TAB moves the active cell one cell to the left.

2.03 Tip: *You can start an entry over again by using the Cancel icon.*

While you're entering data in a cell or editing a previous entry, you can make Jazz forget what you've just entered and return the cell to its previous state by clicking on the Cancel icon, shown in Figure 2-1 as the X at the upper right of the figure.

2.04 Tip: *If you're working with a large worksheet, you can view off-screen sections by scrolling or by using the Page icon.*

The Jazz Worksheet provides a lot of room to work with. In fact, if the worksheet were on paper, it would extend approximately 21 feet to the right of your computer and somewhere around 128 feet beneath your desk.

You can look at any section of your worksheet by using the scroll arrows to move one column or row at a time, by using the Page icon to move one screen at a time, or by dragging the Scroll box to take you to any location horizontally or vertically. Clicking in the Scroll bar above or below the Scroll box will also move you up or down one screen at a time.

See the section on "Memory Management" in this chapter to find out just how much of this workspace you can effectively use.

2.05 Trap: *The active cell does not move when you scroll.*

When you scroll to another section of the worksheet, the active cell remains where it was last placed. If you type an entry and press ENTER, it will, of course, appear in the active cell. This may surprise you if you expected the active cell to move when you scrolled. Remember to relocate the active cell by clicking or by using the following method.

2.06 Tip: *Use the End Navigator to move the active cell to the end of continuous work areas.*

The End Navigator icon is illustrated in Figure 2-1. If you click on one of its arrows, the active cell moves in that direction. Just how far it moves depends on the contents of the cells it moves over.

If in Figure 2-1 cell A3 were the active cell, clicking on the End Navigator's right arrow would move the active cell to cell D3, but clicking again would move it to the very end of row 3, 252 columns to the right. Clicking on an End Navigator arrow moves the active cell to the last non-empty cell in a series of non-empty cells, or to the first non-empty cell in the next series of non-empty cells, or to the edge of the worksheet.

2.07 Tip: *You can quickly replace cell contents by selecting and retyping.*

The fastest way to replace the contents of a cell is to select the cell and then type the new entry. Pressing ENTER, RETURN, or TAB or clicking in the worksheet area replaces the old contents with the new.

2.08 Tip: *Delete or insert characters in an active cell by going into Edit mode by double-clicking.*

You can insert or delete one or more characters in a cell without retyping the entire contents. In Figure 2-2 the contents of cell C1 have been mistyped but placed in the cell. You can remove the extra "r" by double-clicking on the cell to place the contents in the Entry box.

Now you can edit the cell's contents. If you want to insert one or more characters, click at the insertion point and start typing. If you want to delete one or several characters, click at a point just to the right of the unwanted characters and use the BACKSPACE key as many times as you need. If you want to delete many characters at once, point to the first one and drag the highlight to the right until you've highlighted the entire area you want to get rid of. In all these cases, you finish the operation by pressing ENTER.

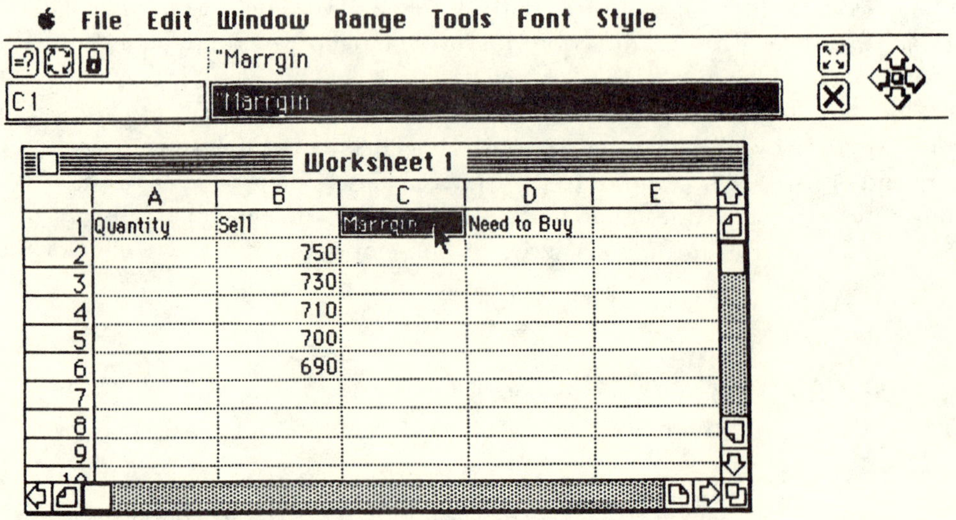

Figure 2-2. Using Edit mode

2.09 Tip: *You can quickly move the active cell to any cell, range, or range name by double-clicking the Selection box and entering the address.*

The Selection box always contains the address of the active cell. Placing a new address in the Selection box moves the active cell to that location. If you enter the address or range name of a range of cells (for example, A1..A10), the cell in the upper-left corner of that range (in this case A1) becomes active, and the entire range is selected and highlighted. This is a convenient way both of getting to a range and selecting it in one step.

Entering and Editing Data

2.10 Tip: *You can delete and insert characters at the same time by using Edit mode.*

Double-clicking on a cell to place it in Edit mode allows you to edit in several ways. Any characters in the Entry box selected by pointing and dragging are automatically removed when you type in new data. Pressing the BACKSPACE key when characters are selected also removes them but does not replace them with anything.

2.11 Tip: *You can quickly erase the contents of a single cell by activating it, pressing the SPACEBAR, and pressing ENTER.*

While you can also erase a cell by selecting it and choosing Clear from the Edit menu, pressing the SPACEBAR and ENTER is usually quicker.

2.12 Tip: *Edit a cell when a range is selected by using Open Cell.*

When a range of cells is selected, you can change the contents of any cell without deselecting the range. Move the active cell within the range by using the RETURN or TAB key or the Corner Navigator. Then select Open Cell from the Edit menu. This places the cell's contents in the Entry box for editing and retains the current selection.

2.13 Trap: *If you don't type an equal sign (=) first when entering a formula, Jazz may treat the entry as text.*

If you start with a number, Jazz will treat it as a number, but if you start with a cell reference or a function, you'll get text unless you begin with =.

When you type a formula into a cell by using the equal sign first and then pressing ENTER, the cell shows the result of calculating the formula. If you forget to enter the =, you'll see the formula itself in the cell as text.

2.14 Tip: *To see what formula a cell contains, click on the cell and look in the Contents box.*

When a cell contains a formula, it will display the result of the formula and not the formula itself. To see the formula, click on the cell and look in the Contents box.

2.15 Tip: *You can enter a cell address or the entire range address in a formula by pointing and clicking.*

When you type a parenthesis or an operator (such as =, +, −, *, or /) in a formula and then want to refer to a cell, you can click on the cell and its address will be automatically placed in the formula.

You can also place a range of cells in a formula where Jazz expects a range by pointing and dragging across it.

Once you get used to it, you may find that this method of specifying cell addresses in formulas is quicker than actually typing them in. It is also often less error-prone, as long as you're careful to point to exactly the range you wish. Furthermore, it's only in this mode that the Absolute icon is available to you. Using the Absolute icon is by far the safest way of entering absolute cell addresses; if you use the alternate method of typing in dollar signs, you can easily make mistakes.

2.16 Trap: *If you enter a number in a cell formatted previously as text, Jazz will convert it to text on entry, and it will not function as a number in any formulas that refer to that cell.*

If a cell has been formatted as text from the Range Format menu, a number entered in it will automatically be turned into text. The danger here is that if only a few numbers were accidentally placed in text-formatted cells, you might not notice that they are not included in calculations. If you ever see a number in the Contents box that is preceded with the " label prefix character, this may be a tip-off that you've mistakenly formatted that cell as text. When you're entering one or more numbers, you should use the Range Format command to make sure the cell or range of cells is formatted correctly before you actually make the entries.

2.17 Tip: *You can enter numbers in a cell previously formatted as text by typing an equal sign first.*

If you type an equal sign first when typing numbers in a cell previously formatted as text, you don't have to use the Format command to reformat the cell to hold numbers. The equal sign will cause the numbers to be treated as numbers, but they will still observe the justification that the text had.

2.18 Tip: *If you enter text wider than the cell will display, it will be displayed in the adjacent cells to the right if they are empty.*

Text wider than a cell will spill over into adjacent cells if they are empty.This is handy if you want to add a long label.If the adjacent cells are not empty, the text will only display up to the width of its own cell, with the display truncated after that point. The cell will of course retain its full contents, even though not all those contents are displayed.

2.19 Tip: *When you've made a mistake, the Undo command might be able to help.*

The Undo command in the Edit menu is helpful for replacing material that you have cut or cleared from the worksheet. As long as you have not pasted the cut material into the worksheet or cut or copied something else onto the Clipboard, Undo Cut or Undo Clear will place the material back into its original spot. If you have already chosen Paste and you want to undo the operation, you can of course cut and paste the range back to its original position.

Undo can also help by removing your last cell entry as long as the cell is still the active cell. If you have moved the active cell by clicking, the Undo Entry command will not work.

2.20 Tip: *To insert a new column or row, click on the margin at the column letter to the right of or at the row number above where you want it to go.*

Each column and row has a letter or number in the margin of the worksheet grid. Clicking on the letter or number highlights the entire column or row. When a column or row has been selected, the Edit menu offers the option of inserting a new one at that point. You can also use the COMMAND-I key combination instead of the Edit menu. To insert more than one column or row at once, either select the number of columns or rows you wish to insert or use the COMMAND-I key combination as many times in succession as you need to.

2.21 Tip: *To delete a column or row, click on its letter or number in the margin; then select Clear.*

Selecting an entire column or row by clicking on its letter or number prepares it for several possible operations. If you select Clear, the column or row is removed and the rest of the worksheet moves to fill in the empty space.

Selecting Cut also removes the column or row but places it in the Clipboard. Selecting Copy leaves the contents in place but places a copy in the Clipboard.

To delete more than one column or row at once, select the column or row labels by pointing and dragging; then select Clear.

2.22 Tip: *Avoid retyping by copying a cell or range of cells.*

Copying the contents of a cell to another location lets you avoid retyping a cell entry or formula.

Even if you copy only one cell, you can duplicate it into as many cells as you want. In the following illustration, cell B9 contains a formula totaling cells B5 . . B7:

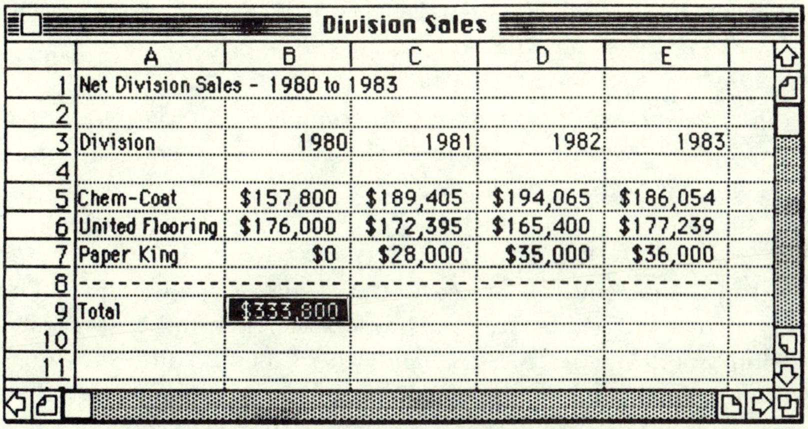

	A	B	C	D	E
1	Net Division Sales - 1980 to 1983				
2					
3	Division	1980	1981	1982	1983
4					
5	Chem-Coat	$157,800	$189,405	$194,065	$186,054
6	United Flooring	$176,000	$172,395	$165,400	$177,239
7	Paper King	$0	$28,000	$35,000	$36,000
8	----------	--------	--------	--------	--------
9	Total	$333,800			
10					
11					

Because cell B9 contains a formula, although it actually only displays the answer, copying and pasting it into cells C9 through E9 copies the formula. If cell B9 contained text or numbers, the text or numbers would also have been duplicated.

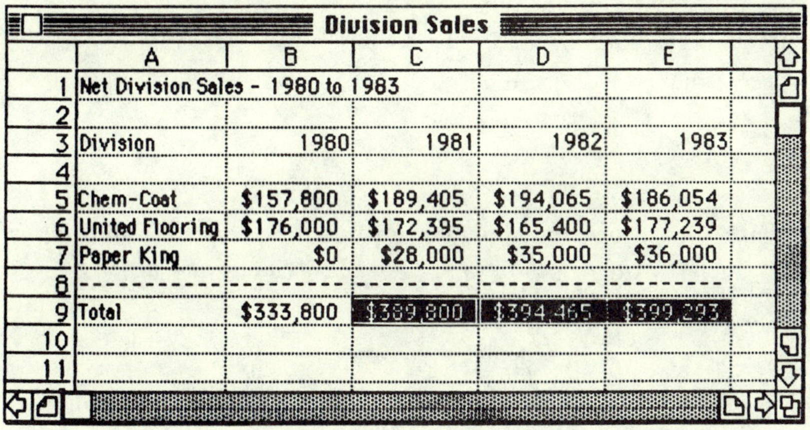

	A	B	C	D	E
1	Net Division Sales - 1980 to 1983				
2					
3	Division	1980	1981	1982	1983
4					
5	Chem-Coat	$157,800	$189,405	$194,065	$186,054
6	United Flooring	$176,000	$172,395	$165,400	$177,239
7	Paper King	$0	$28,000	$35,000	$36,000
8	----------	--------	--------	--------	--------
9	Total	$333,800	$389,800	$394,465	$399,293
10					
11					

2.23 Tip: *If you forget what range you have just cut or copied, look at the Clipboard.*

Between the time when you cut or copy and select the cell or range into which you want to paste, it's easy to forget what you've done. You can remind yourself what material was selected by looking at the Clipboard.

2.24 Trap: *Don't select the Cut or Copy command without selecting the source range first, and don't select Paste without selecting the target range first.*

In Jazz the source range must be selected before Cut or Copy is chosen. The target range must then be selected before you choose Paste. Some other spreadsheet programs (including 1-2-3 on the IBM PC) handle these steps in a different sequence and actually prompt the user for the source and target ranges. If you've used one of these other programs, you'll have to forget the habits you formed in copying and moving ranges or you'll be confused about what Jazz expects. To summarize, these are the steps to perform if you want to copy or move a range:

1. Select the source range.
2. Select Cut (to move) or Copy (to copy), or use COMMAND-X or COMMAND-C.
3. Select the target cell or range.
4. Select Paste or use COMMAND-V.

2.25 Tip: *To cut or copy just one copy of a range of cells and then paste them, you only need to select the upper-left cell of the target area.*

In fact, if you select more than one cell as the target range,you may get more than one copy of the source. See the following Tip.

2.26 Tip: *To create more than one copy of a Cut or Copy source range, simply expand the target selection beyond one cell.*

Jazz will make as many copies of the source range as it can in the range you select as a target. For instance, if you select two cells as the source range and then select a target range of either four or five cells, Jazz will make two copies of the source range in the target area.

2.27 Trap: *Lack of accuracy in selecting a target range may cause a Cut or Copy command to overwrite valuable data.*

Be careful when you select a target cell or range. If you paste into a range, everything in the range will be replaced. If you paste into a single cell, an area equal to the size of the source range will be replaced. Get in the habit of checking the results of a paste immediately. If it looks wrong, you can always select Undo Paste if you catch the problem immediately.

2.28 Tip: *You can empty a cell or a range of cells of both content and format by selecting the cell and then selecting Clear.*

The Clear command removes both contents and formatting. There is no way to clear the cells of contents and still retain formatting. (Cutting a range to the Clipboard also removes the formatting.) What you can do is individually clear each cell of its contents by making the cell active, pressing the SPACEBAR, and then pressing RETURN, SHIFT-RETURN, TAB, or SHIFT-TAB to go to the next cell.

2.29 Trap: *When clearing the contents of a column or row, do not select the column or row heading, or you'll delete the entire column or row.*

When you want to clear a column or row of data but leave the column or row intact, be careful not to include the heading in your selection. Clicking on the column or row heading and selecting Clear removes the column or row as well as all the data. Select only the cells you wish to empty.

Selecting Cells and Ranges

2.30 Tip: *There are several ways of selecting a cell or a range of cells.*

You may often need to select more than one cell at a time when formatting, moving, copying, and deleting groups of cells. A selected range can contain as many rows and columns as you need.

There are several ways to select ranges:

- By pointing and dragging
- By using SHIFT-click (see the following Tip)
- By entering the address of the range or its range name in the Selection box
- By using Select All.

When you type a range in the Selection box, place a period between the first and last cell in a range; for example, B3.D9. If you make a mistake, use the BACKSPACE key to correct errors as you type. You can also edit the contents of the Selection box after pressing ENTER by double-clicking on the Selection box and clicking to place the Insertion bar for deleting or inserting new characters.

When you choose Select All from the Edit menu, all the cells in the current active area are selected. This command is useful when you want to apply a format to the entire worksheet, print an entire worksheet, or move a worksheet to another document.

2.31 Tip: *You can expand a selection by using SHIFT-click or SHIFT-End Navigator*

When you have selected a range but need to expand it, you can do so by pointing to the end of the new area, holding down the SHIFT key, and clicking. Sometimes you can speed up the process by holding down the SHIFT key and clicking on an End Navigator arrow. In this mode, End Navigator moves the active cell in the direction chosen in its usual manner (to the last non-empty cell, to the next non-empty cell, or to the worksheet border). But in doing so it extends the range selected over the entire area it traverses.

2.32 Trap: *Using the End Navigator while a range is selected will deselect the area.*

If you want to view another section of the worksheet when a range is selected, use the Scroll arrows, Scroll box, Page boxes, or type the address in the Selection box. Using the End Navigator will deselect the range.

Formatting

2.33 Tip: *Control the justification of cell contents by using the Format options from the Range menu.*

In the following illustration, the worksheet uses the preset justification settings; numbers are right-justified and text is left-justified.

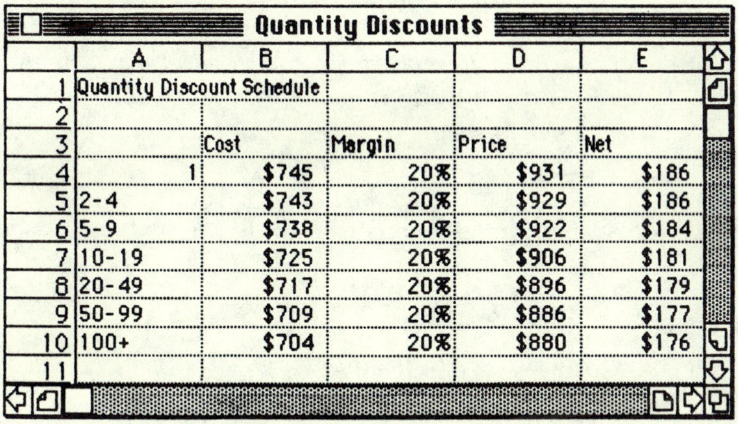

Quantity Discounts

	A	B	C	D	E
1	Quantity Discount Schedule				
2					
3		Cost	Margin	Price	Net
4	1	$745	20%	$931	$186
5	2-4	$743	20%	$929	$186
6	5-9	$738	20%	$922	$184
7	10-19	$725	20%	$906	$181
8	20-49	$717	20%	$896	$179
9	50-99	$709	20%	$886	$177
10	100+	$704	20%	$880	$176
11					

The labels in column A and row 3 would look better if they were centered. First select the range and open the Format command from the Range menu. Select Text and then Center. The format will be applied to the selected range:

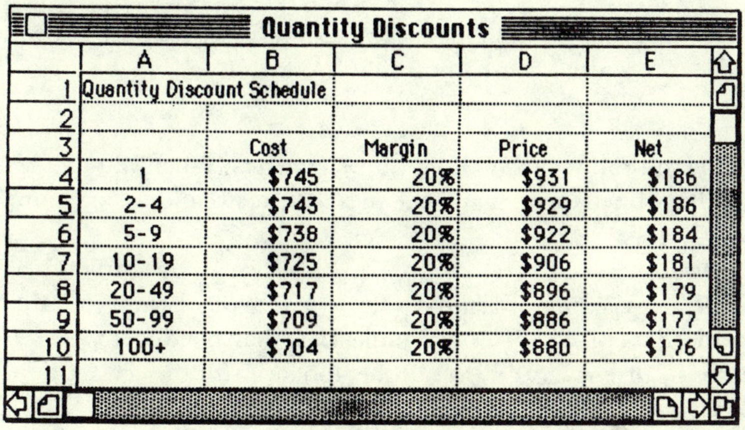

Quantity Discounts

	A	B	C	D	E
1	Quantity Discount Schedule				
2					
3		Cost	Margin	Price	Net
4	1	$745	20%	$931	$186
5	2-4	$743	20%	$929	$186
6	5-9	$738	20%	$922	$184
7	10-19	$725	20%	$906	$181
8	20-49	$717	20%	$896	$179
9	50-99	$709	20%	$886	$177
10	100+	$704	20%	$880	$176
11					

2.34 Tip: *If you don't format cells containing dollars and cents with Currency format, you won't be able to display their contents as dollars and cents.*

If you type dollar signs and commas to enter numbers as dollars and cents, you will find that the numbers appear without them. You need to apply the Currency format to that range. Numbers typed within that range will have dollar signs and commas added automatically.

2.35 Tip: *You can remove formats from cells by selecting them and using Clear from the Edit menu or by reformatting the cells using Range Format.*

Using Clear, of course, removes all contents from the selected range as well as the formats.

2.36 Tip: *When you copy cells, the formats go with them.*

When you copy cells formatted by the Range Format options, their formats are copied also. If, for instance, you copy centered text, the centered format still remains. If you type a new entry into the cell, it too will be centered.

2.37 Tip: *You can fit more material into a cell's display by expanding the width of its column.*

Jazz presets the column widths to hold nine characters. When you type a numerical entry longer than nine spaces, it appears in scientific notation. For example, ten 7's will appear as 7.777778E9.

If you have formatted the cells with Currency format, still only nine characters, including dollar sign, comma, decimal point, decimal places, and your numbers, can fit. With two decimal places set, only numbers less than or equal to $9,999.00 will fit. When a cell has Currency format, a number too large for the cell will only show as three little periods.

You can easily widen columns, however. Move the pointer to the top of the worksheet, to the margin row containing the column letters. When the pointer is exactly between columns, it becomes a vertical bar with a left- and a right-pointing arrow. Position it at the right boundary of the column you wish to widen, drag it to the new width you want, and release the mouse button to set the new width.

When the column is wide enough, the contents will be displayed in full. It is a good idea to keep your columns only as wide as they need be. Having columns too wide lets you see less of your worksheet.

Printing

2.38 Tip: *Print any area of a worksheet by selecting it and then using the Print Selection command in the File menu.*

When you need to print a specific range of the worksheet, you can select it and choose Print Selection in the File menu. To print the entire current active area of the worksheet, select Print Document.

2.39 Trap: *Preset margins in the File menu's Page Setup box are in inches, not in character positions.*

You might expect margin settings to be expressed in numbers of characters. But Jazz expresses margins in inches or fractions thereof. You can enter fractional inches as decimal numbers; 0.50 equals 1/2 inch, for instance. The default settings are 1/4 inch for all margins except the bottom margin, which is set at 1 inch to accommodate the default footer. If you add a header, you must set the top margin to at least 1 inch to accommodate it.

2.40 Tip: *Be sure you understand the rules Jazz follows in printing a range that is wider or longer than what your margin and paper settings allow.*

Suppose you have a worksheet whose active area extends from A1 through L69. With standard margins and 8 1/2 by 11-inch paper, you will need four pages to print this range. Starting at the upper left of the range, Jazz first prints as many rows and columns as it can on the first page; in this case A1 through H47 would be printed. Next, Jazz prints the remaining columns in the range (I through L) and as many rows as it can (47). Jazz then prints the remaining rows (starting with 48), first for the first set of columns (A through H) and then for the second set (I through L).

In some cases, this pattern may give you just what you want. If not, you may want to consider using Print Selection to print separately different portions of the entire range.

2.41 Tip: *To print a multipage range with the same titles at the top or at the left of each page, use Range Set Titles before you print.*

When you have a worksheet that can't all be viewed on the screen, you can freeze one or more title rows at the top of the screen (starting with row 1) or one or more title columns at the left of the screen (starting with column A) by first selecting the rows or columns containing the top or left titles and then selecting Set Titles from the Range menu. This allows you to scroll left and right and up and down, still keeping your titles on the screen for reference.

As the previous Tip suggests, you run into a similar problem when you try to print a range that won't fit on one page. In such a case, you'll frequently want to have the top or left titles print on every page. Let's say you have titles that you'd like to have printed at the top of every page in rows 2 through 3 of the worksheet. You first select rows 1 through 3 (you must include row 1) by pointing and dragging on the row numbers at the left margin. Then select Set Top Titles from the Range menu. You set left titles in the same way, except that in the first step you select columns (starting always with A) by clicking or pointing and dragging on the column letters in the margin.

When you select Print Document or Print Selection after setting titles, the top or left titles will print on every page.

2.42 Tip: *Form the habit of printing the page number and date at the top of every page you print.*

You can ask Jazz to print the page number automatically at the top or bottom of each page by including the # character in a header or footer on the Page Setup screen. Similarly, the @ character in a header or footer causes Jazz to print the current date at the top or bottom of each page. It's a good idea to use both of these options as a matter of course so your printed work is properly documented. Otherwise, you and others are likely to become confused about which printed page goes with which others and when they were created. A header specification that included both these options plus a report title might look like this:

Page #|Net 1 Projected Revenue|@

Inserting the vertical bar characters as shown causes Jazz to print each part of the specification as a separate string with spaces in between.

2.43 Trap: *Jazz will always print the worksheet borders and grid along with your data unless you hide one or both using the Style menu.*

When you print a worksheet, you usually don't want to print the borders (the column letters at the top and the row numbers at the left) or the actual spreadsheet grid. To turn one or both off, select Hide Borders or Hide Grid from the Style menu before printing.

Memory Management

The topics covered in this section are specific to the Jazz Worksheet environment. Chapter 1 includes several Tips and Traps related to the topic of memory that apply to all the Jazz environments.

2.44 Trap: *If you expand your active area unnecessarily, you may run out of memory.*

The active area is the area bounded by cell A1 at the upper left and the last filled, formatted, or protected cells in the other corners of the worksheet. The Tip that follows explains how to determine the size of the active area. You can assign cell-formatting or protection attributes to cells that do not contain text or numeric entries, so it is possible to have an active area larger than is apparent. Jazz allocates a minimum amount of memory (about 4 bytes) for each cell in the active area, regardless of whether it contains any data. Since the active area always starts in A1, keep your work in the upper-left corner of the worksheet as much as possible for maximum memory efficiency. You can also conserve memory by minimizing blank rows or columns, and by keeping empty cells formatted with General format, the default format setting.

2.45 Tip: *To determine the actual size of the active area, use the Select All command or the Corner Navigator icon with the* COMMAND *key.*

The Select All command highlights the active area of your worksheet. When you have chosen Select All, the Selection box shows the active area in terms of cell coordinates. In Figure 2-3 the active area is A1..D9, with a single entry in D9. Once you've chosen Select All, you can then identify each of the corner cells of the worksheet's active area in turn by clicking on the Corner Navigator icon several times; this moves the active cell in a counterclockwise direction to each corner of the active area. There's a small trap here, however: if you used Set Top Titles or Set Left Titles from the Range menu to freeze titles, the frozen titles will not be included in the range highlighted by Select All. Jazz does it this way to prevent double printing of titles. You'll still get the information you need, however, if you remember that the upper-left corner of the active area is always A1.

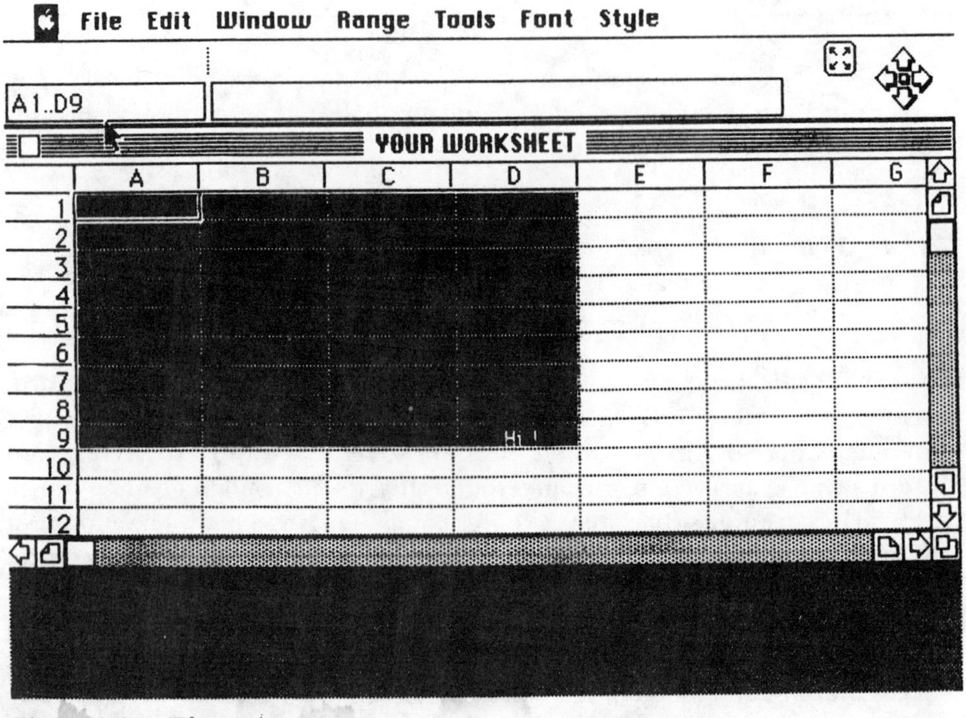

Figure 2-3. The active area

You can bypass Select All entirely by simply clicking several times on the Corner Navigator icon while holding down the COMMAND key. This moves the active cell to each corner of the active area in turn.

The primary reason for examining your active area is to determine if you have inadvertently assigned formatting or protection attributes to, or entered data into cells outside of, your actual work area, resulting in inefficient memory use. See the next Tip for what you can do to shrink the size of your active area and reclaim memory.

2.46 Tip: *There are several ways to shrink the size of the active area and reclaim memory.*

If your active area is too large because you've formatted or protected cells unnecessarily, use Range Format to set the format back to the default or Range Protection to turn off protection for those cells. In both cases, you'll reclaim the memory saved by shrinking the size of the active area.

If your active area is too large because you have unnecessary data in certain cells, use Clear to clear it out and reclaim the memory used by those cells. If your active area is too large because you have too many empty rows or columns, use Cut and Paste to squeeze the work as much as possible into the upper-left corner of the worksheet. For some reason, you will not always reclaim all reclaimable memory by clearing and cutting and pasting. Sometimes holding down the COMMAND key and clicking on the Corner Navigator icon several times will reclaim more. If you think you need to reclaim still more, try saving the worksheet document, closing it, and opening it.

Recalculation

2.47 Trap: *Data entry will be slow in a large worksheet unless you set recalculation to Manual by changing the Range Recalculation settings.*

The default recalculation setting is Automatic. This means that every time you make a change in the worksheet, all formulas are recalculated. With large worksheets, complex formulas, or both, the process of entering numbers can be speeded up significantly by setting recalculation to Manual. But see the following Tip.

2.48 Tip: *When recalculation is set to Manual, be sure to look for the Recalculate icon to remind you when to recalculate your formulas.*

Since it is easy to forget that your worksheet has been set to Manual recalculation, when entries are made that may change calculated results, Jazz displays the Recalculate icon in the upper-left corner of the console:

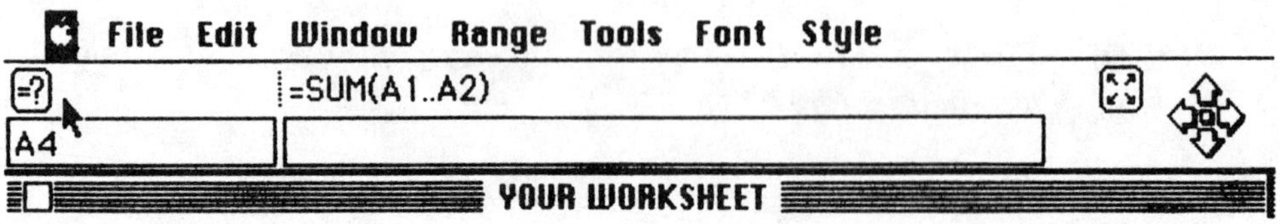

When you want to recalculate your worksheet, just click on this icon; the formula cells display the recalculated results and the Recalculate icon disappears.

2.49 Tip: *The Recalculate command affects your entire worksheet, regardless of which cells are highlighted when it is selected.*

Recalculation is not a selective process when you use the Recalculate icon. With large worksheet applications, this limitation can be troublesome. The next Tip suggests a technique to get around this limitation.

2.50 Tip: *When recalculation is set to Manual, you can recalculate selected worksheet ranges by copying a range to itself.*

By copying and pasting a range of cells to itself, you can selectively recalculate one or more cells without having to wait for a large worksheet to recalculate. For example, the following worksheet shows a small section of a large sales projection model; you are looking at the projections for one product during the second quarter of the year. The unit price of the product is entered in cell O35, and the projected monthly sales in cells P36, Q36 and R36. The total sales (P38. . R38) are derived from the formula =$O$35*P36. Cell O35 is an absolute reference because the unit price is a constant value, and you don't want relative adjustment when the formula is copied.

SELECTIVE RECALC

	N	O	P	Q	R	S
33	Sales Projections					
34	Product #7		April	May	June	
35	Product Price	$29.95				
36	Product Sales		5000	8000	8500	
37						
38	Total Sales		$149,750	$239,600	$254,575	
39						
40						

Suppose you want to evaluate the impact on monthly sales of a $0.50 increase in the price of one product. With a large worksheet, recalculation could take a long time; selective recalculation would be more efficient. Below is the same worksheet with the increase in the unit price (cell O35). Notice that the sales totals have not been affected; recalculation is currently set to Manual. To recalculate the sales totals, highlight the range P38 . . R38 and select Copy. Then highlight just P38 and select Paste. Row 38 now reflects the price increase, and the operation was completed in just a few seconds.

SELECTIVE RECALC

	N	O	P	Q	R	S
33	Sales Projections					
34	Product #7		April	May	June	
35	Product Price	$30.45				
36	Product Sales		5000	8000	8500	
37						
38	Total Sales		$149,750	$239,600	$254,575	
39						
40						

There is a trap associated with this useful technique, however. When Recalculation Order is set to the default Natural Order, Jazz recalculates the entire worksheet correctly, regardless of whether a formula in one column (column O, for example) refers to a cell in a later column (column P, for example). Jazz is smart enough in this mode to recalculate formulas in their "natural order," regardless of their physical location on the worksheet. However, when you try to recalculate a range by copying it to itself, Jazz uses the Columnwise order of recalculation, regardless of what the Recalculation Order setting is at the time. Columnwise order means that Jazz first recalculates the first column in the range, then the second, and so forth. As a result, recalculating rows O and P by copying that range to itself might not bring the results in column O up to date. Why? Because row O depends by formula on the results of row P, and in Columnwise recalculation, row P has not yet been recalculated and brought up to date at the time that row O is recalculated. You can usually correct this problem by copying a range to itself a second time; occasionally, you need to copy it to itself more than twice. The bottom line is that recalculating a range to itself is a useful way to perform a quick partial recalculation of the worksheet, but you must be prepared to do it more than once in cases where you may have forward references of the type we've described.

2.51 Trap: *When recalculation is set to Manual, don't forget to recalculate before saving or printing.*

If you save a worksheet before recalculating, it will be in the same uncalculated state when it is reloaded. You should recalculate before saving because formula results can be misleading when the worksheet is used later. It is equally important to recalculate before printing your worksheet.

2.52 Tip: *When you see the Circular Reference icon, click on it to find out which cell is causing the circular reference.*

Here three formulas have been entered in cells S1 . . U1, with cells S3 . . U3 displaying the actual formula entries:

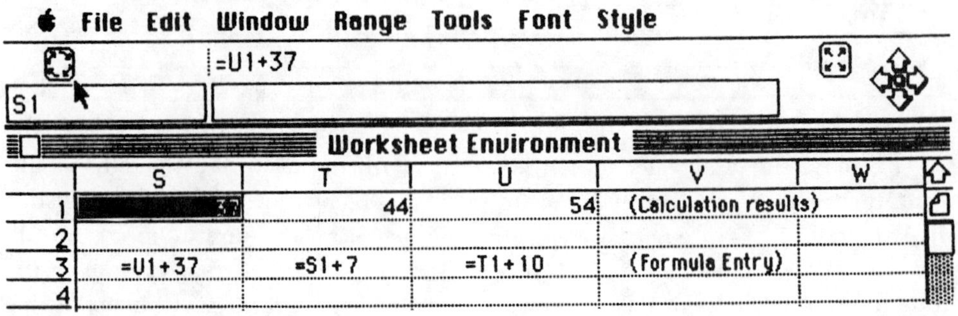

The formula in S1 depends on U1, and U1 is dependent on T1, which depends on S1. This results in mutual dependency between S1 and U1. This type of reference usually occurs accidentally, requiring you to identify the formulas that caused the circular reference so that they can be changed. When a circular reference occurs, Jazz displays the Circular Reference icon in the upper-left corner of the console. If you click on it, Jazz selects a cell containing a formula that is part of the circular reference. If, after you correct the formula, the Circular Reference icon is still visible, click on it again to identify any additional formulas that need to be changed.

For some applications where two variables depend on each other, a circular reference is just what you want. In these situations, recalculating the worksheet or a particular area (see Tip 2.50) a number of times will give you the desired result. The exact number of times you'll have to recalculate to converge to the result you want will vary with the circumstances. If you know what that number is, you can set the Recalc Settings Iteration Count accordingly. Jazz will then recalculate the worksheet the specified number of times during each recalculation pass.

Manipulating the Worksheet

2.53 Tip: *If you want a change to affect your entire worksheet, use the Select All command first.*

You can perform editing and formatting procedures on the entire active area of a worksheet if you first use the Select All command to highlight all active cells.

2.54 Tip: *You can sort selected ranges in your worksheet by keying on as many as three sort ranges and choosing Ascending or Descending order.*

The sort utility can be used in the Worksheet as well as the Database environment. Sorting reorders the information in a range either alphabetically or numerically. In selecting a sort range, it's usually best to select the desired range in the worksheet before choosing Set Sort Ranges from the Tools menu. You can then click on the Use Selected box to set the range you already selected. If you don't use this method, you often forget what range you wanted to sort by the time you choose Set Sort Ranges; you then have to go back to the worksheet to pinpoint the sort range and then choose Set Sort Ranges a second time. (Refer to Chapter 4 for Tips and Traps related to sorting.)

2.55 Trap: *Be careful when cutting and pasting ranges; if you wipe out a cell referenced in a formula, Jazz displays a "REF" notation instead of the calculation result.*

You will see the notation "REF" displayed in a formula cell if a Cut procedure affects a cell referenced in the formula. Figure 2-4 shows three examples of the same procedure: getting the sum total of a column of numbers. The =SUM function was entered in cell A9 and copied to C9 and E9. In Example 2, the entry in C2 was eliminated by the Cut command. This resulted in wiping out one of the cells in the range referenced in the formula, =SUM(C2..C7). Jazz responds with the REF notation to inform you of an incorrect cell reference in your formula. [This formula has now actually become =SUM(REF), wiping out the range specification completely.] Using the Undo command before performing another operation will cancel the REF and restore your formula to its original state. If it's too late to restore the "REF" entry with the Undo command, reenter or edit your formula, specifying the appropriate original cell references. In Example 3, the entry in E2 was eliminated using the Clear command. Jazz considers the =SUM formula to still be accurate since none of the cells it refers to has been cut, so the formula remains as is and the results are accurate.

One way to prevent this Trap is to do a Copy/Paste to "move" the range you wish to relocate and then Clear the contents of the original location. When you do it this way, however, remember that Jazz will adjust relative formula references in the target area after the Copy/Paste.

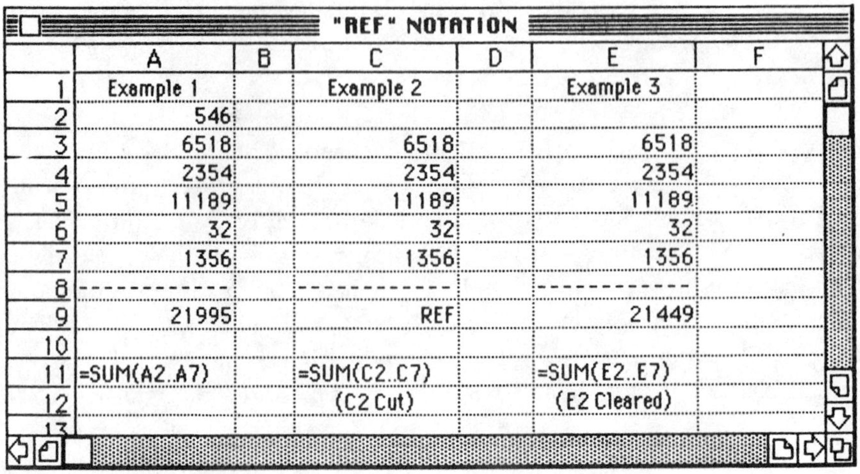

"REF" NOTATION

	A	B	C	D	E	F
1	Example 1		Example 2		Example 3	
2	546					
3	6518		6518		6518	
4	2354		2354		2354	
5	11189		11189		11189	
6	32		32		32	
7	1356		1356		1356	
8	------------		------------		------------	
9	21995		REF		21449	
10						
11	=SUM(A2..A7)		=SUM(C2..C7)		=SUM(E2..E7)	
12			(C2 Cut)		(E2 Cleared)	

Figure 2-4. Three ways to sum a column

2.56 Trap: *When working with two or more worksheets on the Desktop, make sure to click twice on the destination worksheet when performing a Cut or Copy and Paste procedure from one to the other.*

The first time you click on a worksheet window, you are activating the window, not selecting a specific cell. It isn't until you click a second time that a cell is highlighted and selected. Forgetting this can be problematic if you attempt a Cut/Copy and Paste procedure from one worksheet window to another; you will not be pasting into the cell you intended unless you've explicitly selected it.

2.57 Tip: *After you've entered a formula or function, you can convert it to a value with the Calculate icon.*

You can use the Calculate icon to convert a formula to its current value. The worksheet in Figure 2-5 has the same formula entered in two cells, H7 and H9. The displayed results are identical; however, the cell contents are different. The formula in H7 was entered in the usual way; should numbers in cells referenced by the

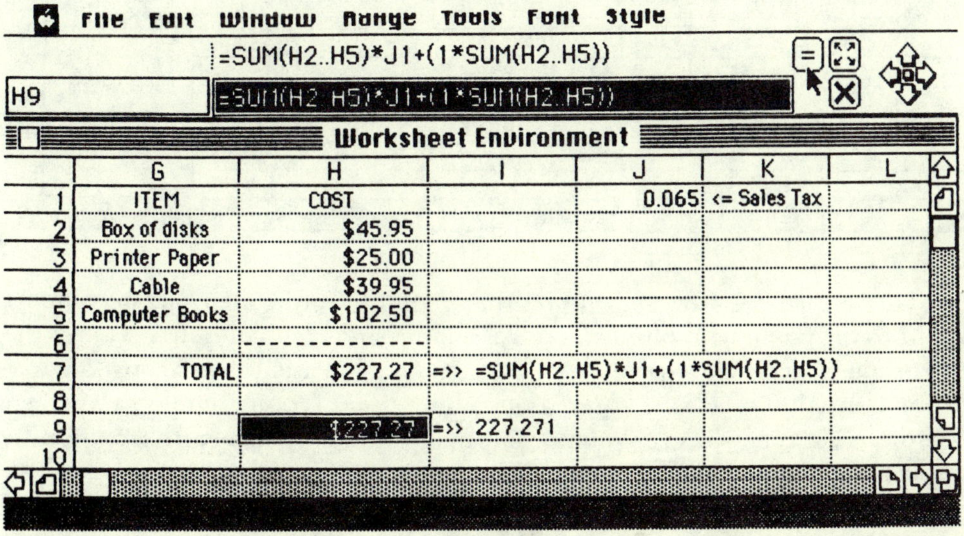

Figure 2-5. Using the Calculate icon to convert a formula to a number

formula be changed, the results will also change. The same formula was entered in cell H9. To convert it to its current value, double-click on H9 to display the formula in the Entry box, and then click on the Calculate icon. The formula has been replaced with a number equal to the current value of the formula, and you lose the formula. Recalculation of the worksheet will no longer affect this cell.

You can use this technique to freeze the current result of a formula. It's common to want to do this with the =NOW function in cases where you want to keep it from being recalculated every time the worksheet is recalculated.

2.58 Tip: *To copy just values instead of formulas, use Paste Value.*

This copy option allows you to copy a range of cells, converting all formulas into their current values. This feature is useful for applications involving accumulation and consolidation of numbers. Jazz pastes the current values of the cells on the Clipboard, not the formulas, into the selected worksheet range. The contents of the Clipboard are not changed; if you want to follow Paste Value with a regular Paste, the formulas are still contained in the cells on the Clipboard.

Consider the following worksheet for a typical use of the Paste Value function:

PASTE VALUES

	A	B	C	D	E	F	G	H
1		MONTHLY					QUARTERLY	
2	1st Month	2nd Month	3rd Month	Qtr Sum		1st Qtr	2nd Qtr	3rd Qtr
3	------	--------	--------	--------		-------	-------	-------
4	2563	3471	81736	$87,770				
5	416	56732	13482	$70,630				
6	1098	67889	9438	$78,425				
7	22218	1234	22349	$45,801				
8								
9								

This is an "end-of-period" application; monthly entries are made in columns A-C, the sum function in column D returns quarter sums, and columns F-H store the quarter totals. At the close of a quarter, we use Copy and Paste Value to copy values of the totals in column D to the appropriate column (in this case, column F). We then clear the monthly entries in columns A-C to make way for the new entries for the next quarter.

With a Copy and a regular Paste, the formulas in column D would be copied to column F, which would not give the desired result of "freezing" the end-of-quarter totals. Here is the same worksheet after performing the Paste Value operation and clearing monthly entries; you can now make monthly entries for the next quarter:

PASTE VALUES

	A	B	C	D	E	F	G	H
1		MONTHLY					QUARTERLY	
2	1st Month	2nd Month	3rd Month	Qtr Sum		1st Qtr	2nd Qtr	3rd Qtr
3	-------	--------	--------	--------		-------	-------	-------
4				$0		$87,770		
5				$0		$70,630		
6				$0		$78,425		
7				$0		$45,801		
8								

2.59 Trap: *In some situations you'll get wrong results on a Copy unless you use absolute references.*

You can save time when you enter a formula once and then copy it to other locations on the worksheet where the same mathematical relationship exists. Cell N7 in the following worksheet contains the formula =SUM(N3..N5).

Worksheet Environment

	M	N	O	P	Q	R
1	The Bear Shop					
2	Inventory	April #	% of Total	(Formulas)	July #	
3	Steiff Collection	224	67.47%	<< =N3/N7	621	
4	Dakin	43	ERR	<< =N4/N8	713	
5	Cuddlees	65	ERR	<< =N5/N9	117	
6		========			========	
7	=SUM(N3..N5)>>	332			1451	<< =SUM(Q3..Q5)
8	(Formula)					(Formula)
9						
10						

What isn't obvious is the fact that Jazz records this formula in terms of relative positioning: "Take the value four cells above, add it to the value three cells above, add that value to the value two cells above, and place the result in cell N7."

This process is known as *relative addressing* and is in effect unless absolute addressing is indicated. With relative addressing, cell coordinates are automatically adjusted when formulas are copied to other cells in the same worksheet. The formula in N7 was copied to Q7, and Jazz automatically adjusted the cell references to reflect the change in columns. In this instance, this was the desired effect.

Now consider the formulas in column O of the figure. The formula in cell O3 calculates "percent of total" for the number in N3 (=N3/N7). When this formula is copied to cells O4 and O5, the cell references are adjusted and the results show ERR (error). The reason is that the denominator in P4 and P5 has become N8 and N9, respectively, instead of remaining as N7. Since N8 and N9 are empty, Jazz considers them to have a value of zero; the division by zero results in ERR.

To get accurate results, the reference to cell N7 needs to be absolute, which prevents adjustment of references when the formula in O3 is copied to O4 and O5. Consider the formula in O3 below:

Worksheet Environment

	M	N	O	P	Q	R
1	The Bear Shop					
2	Inventory	April #	% of Total	(Formulas)	July #	
3	Steiff Collection	224	67.47%	<< =N3/$N$7	621	
4	Dakin	43	12.95%	<< =N4/$N$7	713	
5	Cuddlees	65	19.58%	<< =N5/$N$7	117	
6		========			========	
7	=SUM(N3..N5)>>	332			1451	<< =SUM(Q3..Q5)
8	(Formula)					(Formula)
9						
10						

The dollar signs ($) are used to make the references to N7 absolute references, which are permanent references to a particular cell. The dollar sign in front of the column letter makes the column's cell references absolute, and the dollar sign in front of the row number makes the row's cell references absolute. An absolute address refers to the same cell, regardless of the cell to which you copy the formula. You can specify an absolute reference either by typing in the dollar signs as you type the formula or by selecting the Absolute icon when you specify cell references during formula entry by clicking or pointing and dragging with the mouse. (See the next Trap.)

You can have both relative and absolute addresses in a single formula. Because a cell address has both a row and a column reference, it is possible to have one component fixed as an absolute, while leaving the other relative. This is known as *mixed cell addressing.*

2.60 Trap: *Don't expect the Absolute icon to be visible unless you use the mouse to select cell addresses when entering a formula or function.*

The Absolute icon can be used to convert a cell reference to an absolute or mixed reference if you've entered that reference by clicking in the appropriate cell while entering the formula. If you type in the cell reference instead of using the mouse, the icon will not be visible.

If you need to specify both endpoints of a range of cells as absolute references, you must first highlight the entire range and then click on the Absolute icon. The icon isn't visible until the range of cells has been highlighted.

2.61 Tip: *To specify a mixed reference, simply click a second time to freeze just the column; click a third time to freeze just the row. Clicking a fourth time makes the address relative again. As soon as you type another character, the Absolute icon disappears.*

Be sure to check your entries for accuracy; make sure that you have the right number of dollar signs and their placement is correct. All it takes is one extra click and you could end up with cell references that produce strange results.

2.62 Tip: *To copy a formula without adjusting relative addresses, convert it to a label first, copy it, and then turn it back into a formula.*

Normally, if you want to copy formulas without adjusting relative addresses, you would assign absolute references. However, there might be instances when you have relative references that you want to behave like absolutes during a Copy and Paste procedure. You can convert formulas to labels by inserting a label-prefix character before the equal sign (=). First, double-click on the formula cell to display the contents in the entry box, insert a label prefix, and then press RETURN. When copied to other cells, these formulas-turned-labels will not be adjusted (see Figure 2-6). The last step is to display the cell contents of the copied formula label in the entry box and delete the label prefix you inserted. It's a formula again, without any adjustment of relative addresses.

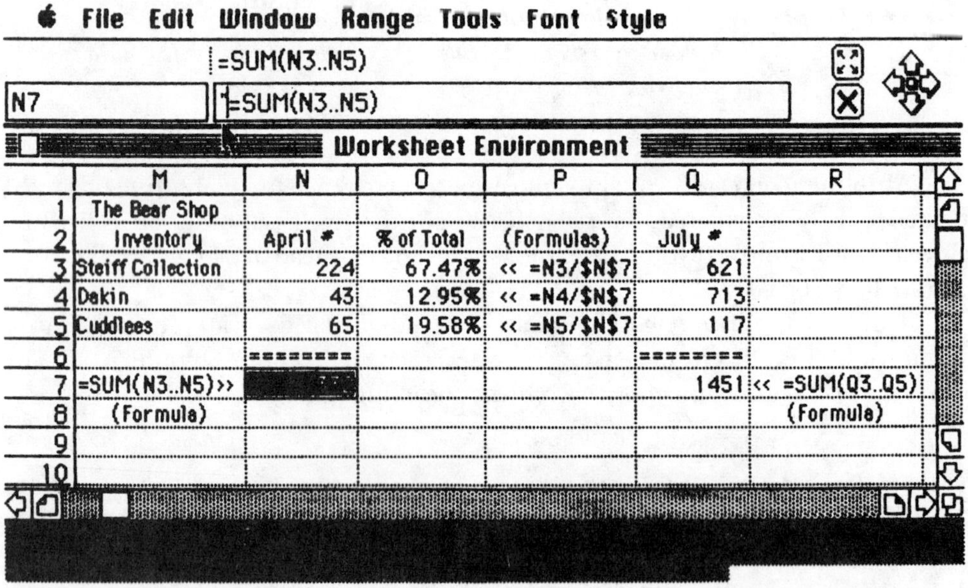

Figure 2-6. Adjusting formulas with worksheet wraparound

2.63 Trap: *If you get a cell reference like A8192 or IV1 after a Copy/Paste, you've copied a range containing relative references to the wrong location.*

Consider the formula =SUM(N3..N5) entered in N7 in this illustration:

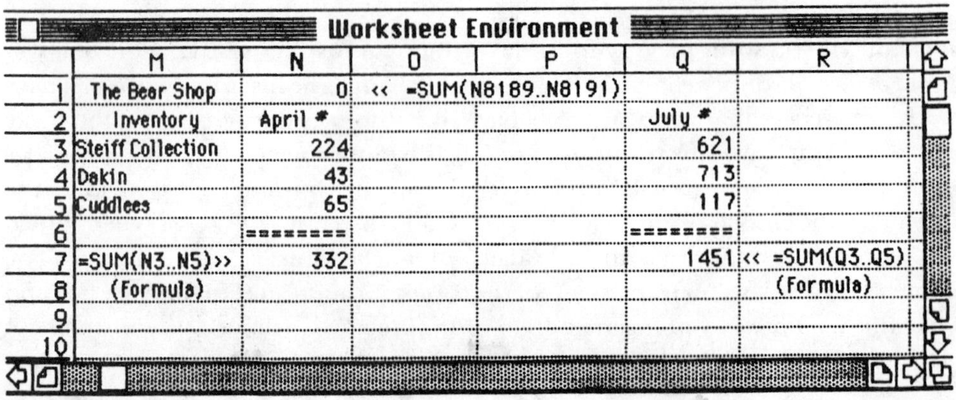

This formula does not have absolute references, so copying it to other cells will cause cell addresses to adjust. This is the normal desired effect. But suppose we mistakenly copy N7 to N1. The formula in N1 will adjust to read =SUM(N8189. .N8191). This happens because for purposes of relative cell reference adjustment, Jazz considers each edge of the worksheet to be connected to the opposite edge. Therefore, the row just before row 1 is row 8192, the row at the other end of the worksheet. Similarly, the column just before column A is column IV, the last column in the worksheet.

If you get strange cell references like this, it's probably a tip-off that you've copied a range containing relative references to the wrong location.

2.64 Trap: *The column and row headings in the Clipboard usually won't match the column and rows of the range cut or copied from the worksheet.*

When you cut or copy a range of cells, the contents are placed on the Clipboard. The example in Figure 2-7 shows a range of cells in a worksheet, S1. . S7. When we copied this range, Jazz placed the contents on the Clipboard, where they were stored in the range A1..A7. The Clipboard always stores entries beginning at A1, regardless of the

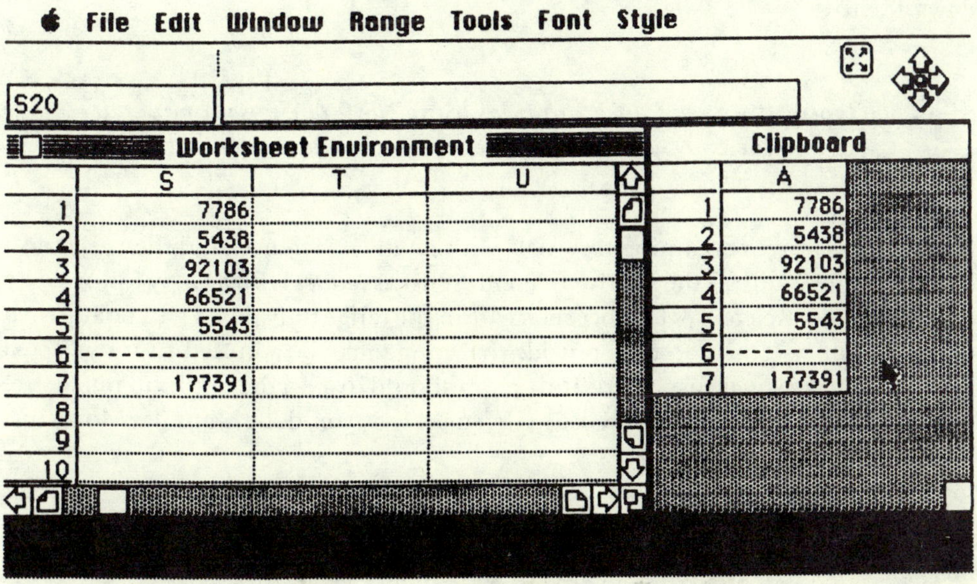

Figure 2-7. Copying ranges to the Clipboard

cell references in the original worksheet. Therefore, to check the original location of a range when you copy, look at the source worksheet range, not the Clipboard.

You can't view formulas when they are on the Clipboard; only the value is displayed. Entries on the Clipboard can't be displayed in the Entry box. This means that only the results, and not the actual formula, can be seen. Look at the worksheet source range to examine formulas. You also can't edit Clipboard entries, so if you notice while examining information on the Clipboard that something needs to be changed, you'll have to go back to the worksheet to edit the original source and then repeat the Cut or Copy.

2.65 Tip: *You can easily change columns into rows in a worksheet by selecting Transpose from the Edit menu under Paste Special.*

Use the Transpose command to rotate the contents of the Clipboard 90 degrees and paste the contents into the selected destination range. This redefines columns as rows and rows as columns. Relative addresses are appropriately adjusted for accurate references. The Transpose Values option works the same way, except that only the values, not the formulas, of cells on the Clipboard are pasted.

When would you want to transpose a range? Suppose that you have set up a worksheet with sales figures entered by columns and years by rows. You may need to print your worksheet on a form that requires the years across the columns instead of down the rows.

2.66 Trap: *If you've copied formulas using the Transpose command, Jazz may adjust relative references in ways you don't expect.*

If you copy a range containing formulas with relative references and then execute a Transpose, Jazz adjusts the relative references just as it does with a Copy followed by a regular Paste. References to other cells within the range transposed will be adjusted correctly, but references to cells outside that range may be adjusted in unexpected ways. Whenever you transpose formulas, you should inspect the results to make sure they're what you wanted. Those cell references that you don't want Jazz to adjust should be expressed as absolutes.

2.67 Tip: *Use Set Titles to freeze selected rows or columns that contain important labels.*

Worksheets frequently fill more than one screen. Scrolling to the right and down often causes column and row titles to disappear from view. Unless you have a photographic memory, it is hard to remember exactly what information is contained in those titles. You can get around this problem by first selecting one or more rows (starting with row 1) as top titles or one or more columns (starting with column A) as left titles and then selecting either Set Left Titles or Set Top Titles from the Range menu.

When selecting top titles rows, you must include row 1, and you must select entire rows by clicking or pointing and dragging on the row numbers in the worksheet border. Similarly, when selecting left titles columns, you must include column A, and you must select entire columns by clicking or pointing and dragging on the column letters in the worksheet border.

Advanced Formatting

2.68 Tip: *You can easily change the font or style attributes for your entire spreadsheet in one operation.*

All font and style options can be used in the Worksheet environment. However, you can't be selective; all cells will be affected by changes. You can get around this limitation by copying your entire worksheet and pasting it into a document window, where selective changes can be made. Font and style attributes are lost, however, when you execute a transfer from the Word Processing environment back to the worksheet.

2.69 Tip: *If you want to fill a cell with a pattern that repeats a given character or characters, using the BACKSLASH key (\) is quicker and easier than using the =Repeat function or assigning the Repeat format to the cell.*

The easiest way to enter repeating labels is to press the BACKSLASH (\) key and then enter the characters you want repeated in the cell. Figure 2-8 shows five examples. Column X shows the display that results from entering the repeat codes shown in column Z.

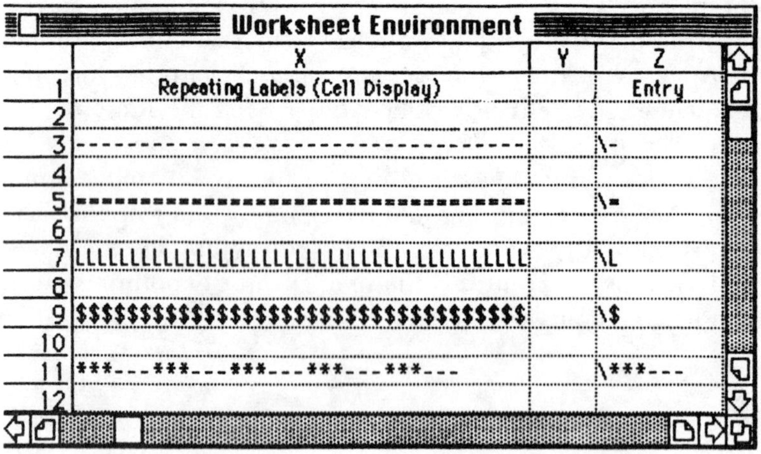

Figure 2-8. Repeating labels

2.70 Trap: *When you use the BACKSLASH key to repeat a character or string of characters, you are actually assigning a format that will stay in effect until you either change the format or use the Cut command.*

This has the same effect as formatting the cell with the Repeat format. This means that new entries made in cells that were previously used to display a repeated pattern of characters will also be repeated, even if you don't preface your new entry with a backslash.

2.71 Tip: *If you want to identify a cell's current format or Protection setting, highlight the cell and select the Format or Protection command.*

You can use these two commands both to identify current settings and to assign new attributes.

2.72 Tip: *To display on the screen all the attributes of every cell in your worksheet, use the Show Attributes command from the Style menu.*

With this command, worksheet cells are enlarged so that all format and protection attributes can be noted. Some formats, such as Currency and Percent, are easily identified in the worksheet, while others, such as Fixed and General, are not always obvious. Figure 2-9*a* shows a worksheet with cells displayed in the normal way; Figure 2-9*b* shows the same worksheet after the Show Attributes command has been selected. All cells are affected by this command; it is not possible to see attributes of only certain ranges.

2.73 Trap: *If your columns aren't wide enough, you won't be able to decipher cell contents after using the Show Attributes command.*

The formula in C8 (Figure 2-9*b*) has been truncated because the cell is not wide enough to display the entire entry. Column D has been widened, making it possible to display the entire formula. If you need to widen all of your columns, choose Select All from the Edit menu; then select Column Width from the Style menu. Otherwise, widen each individual column as necessary by pointing and dragging on its right-hand column divider line in the column border at the top of the worksheet.

2.74 Tip: *Using the Show Attributes command before printing a worksheet can be useful in documenting your formulas and detecting errors.*

By first selecting Show Attributes and then printing, you can get a detailed account of your cell formulas and attributes in hardcopy form. This is one of the best ways to both detect errors in formulas and provide you and others with documentation that shows the formulas you've used. Make sure that your columns are wide enough to display all formulas; otherwise the formulas will be truncated on printing. The best approach is to scroll through the worksheet after choosing Show Attributes but before printing, making necessary adjustments in column widths as you go.

A printed copy of your formulas is much more valuable if you've assigned range names to key ranges in your worksheet. For instance, the formula =PRINCIPAL * *a.*

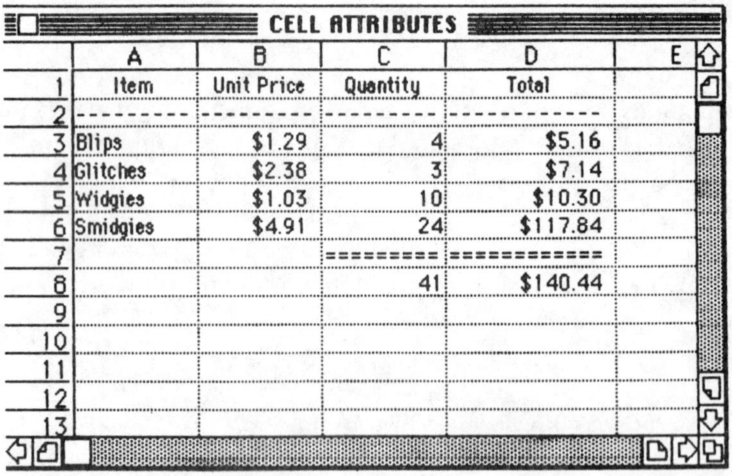

CELL ATTRIBUTES

	A	B	C	D	E
1	Item	Unit Price	Quantity	Total	
2	---------	---------	---------	------------	
3	Blips	$1.29	4	$5.16	
4	Glitches	$2.38	3	$7.14	
5	Widgies	$1.03	10	$10.30	
6	Smidgies	$4.91	24	$117.84	
7			=========	============	
8			41	$140.44	
9					
10					
11					
12					
13					

b.

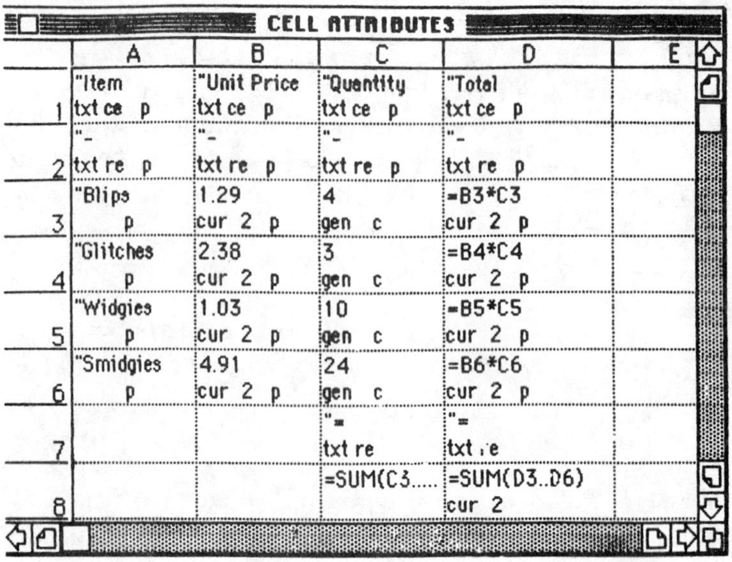

CELL ATTRIBUTES

	A	B	C	D	E
1	"Item txt ce p	"Unit Price txt ce p	"Quantity txt ce p	"Total txt ce p	
2	"- txt re p	"- txt re p	"- txt re p	"- txt re p	
3	"Blips p	1.29 cur 2 p	4 gen c	=B3*C3 cur 2 p	
4	"Glitches p	2.38 cur 2 p	3 gen c	=B4*C4 cur 2 p	
5	"Widgies p	1.03 cur 2 p	10 gen c	=B5*C5 cur 2 p	
6	"Smidgies p	4.91 cur 2 p	24 gen c	=B6*C6 cur 2 p	
7			"= txt re	"= txt re	
8			=SUM(C3.....	=SUM(D3..D6) cur 2	

Figure 2-9. Displaying cells normally (a) and with Show Attributes (b)

INTEREST is much more understandable on a printout than the formula =A12∗B15.

2.75 Trap: *Don't expect changing the format default to affect previously entered text.*

Setting the format to one of the default options (Default Numeric or Default Text) will not affect previously entered text. Only future entries will be displayed in the new format. If you need to change existing entries, highlight cells and select the Format command to reformat the highlighted range.

2.76 Tip: *Use Range Protection settings to ensure that essential areas of the worksheet are not inadvertently changed.*

You can protect worksheet cells from inadvertent entries or deletions. This is an important option when you are creating a worksheet into which others will enter data, and you want to make sure that labels and formulas are not changed. Protection can be selectively set for ranges as small as one cell or as large as the entire active area. (See the following Trap.)

2.77 Trap: *Selected protection settings are not enforced until you select the Enforce Protection Settings option.*

When you choose protection settings for a selected range, you are only assigning an attribute to the highlighted cells. Protection is not actually in effect until you select the Enforce Protection Settings option at the bottom of the Protection Settings dialog box. When Jazz is enforcing protection settings, you will see the Protect icon displayed in the Console at the upper left. The default for Jazz does not enforce protection in the worksheet.

2.78 Tip: *You can make sure that you and others are entering data of the proper type by employing the Check Entry Format option of the Range Protection settings.*

By selecting this protection option, you can have Jazz verify the format of data entries. This can prevent you from making a data entry that does not match a previously defined display format. Jazz verifies date, time, numeric, and text formats. A warning box appears if you attempt to make an entry that does not match the assigned cell format.

2.79 Tip: *You can hide cell entries from view by using Hide Values followed by Enforce Protection.*

If you select the Hide Values option, Jazz hides the contents of the selected cells from view. Why would you want to hide entries? There are times when you must hide sensitive data from view. For instance, you may not want an employee to see the salaries of other employees.

You may also want range names in cells for purposes of documenting your worksheet, but you probably don't want to print them on a report. Use the Hide Values option to suppress their printing. Remember, even though a cell entry may be hidden from view, it is still there and can still be referenced in a formula.

Since Hide Values is a Protection setting, it will not be activated unless you choose Enforce Protection at the bottom of the Protection Settings dialog box.

2.80 Tip: *If your hidden values are hiding from you, use the Show Attributes command to locate them.*

If you can't remember where your hidden values are, use the Show Attributes command to identify them. You will not see the actual cell entry, but rather an "h" that Jazz uses to denote a hidden value.

Range Names

2.81 Tip: *Assigning a name to a cell or range of cells often has several advantages.*

Jazz allows you to assign one or more names of your own choosing to any cell or range of cells in a worksheet. You assign a range name using the Range Name command. Once you've created a range name, you can change it, delete it, or change the cells to which it refers by using the Range Review Names command. See the following Tips for examples of why range names are useful.

2.82 Tip: *You can use descriptive range names to document formulas so that you know the meaning of the ranges they refer to.*

When you assign a name to a range, you can use the name thereafter in constructing formulas. As the Selection box in Figure 2-10 shows, the name Principal has been assigned to cell I4. When you enter the formula in I7 that refers to I4, you can enter the range name Principal instead of just the cell reference I4, as in the Contents box at the top of Figure 2-11. Note that range names have also been given to other cells that appear in this formula. It's a good idea to make the range names you assign as descriptive as possible; that is, they should describe well what the cell or range of cells is really about. When you assign descriptive names, your formulas become much more understandable to both you and others, and it's much easier to spot an error in a formula that was once correct but has been inadvertently corrupted. We recommend assigning range names to all key variables. In our example, that would obviously include the variables Principal, Rate, Years, and Payment.

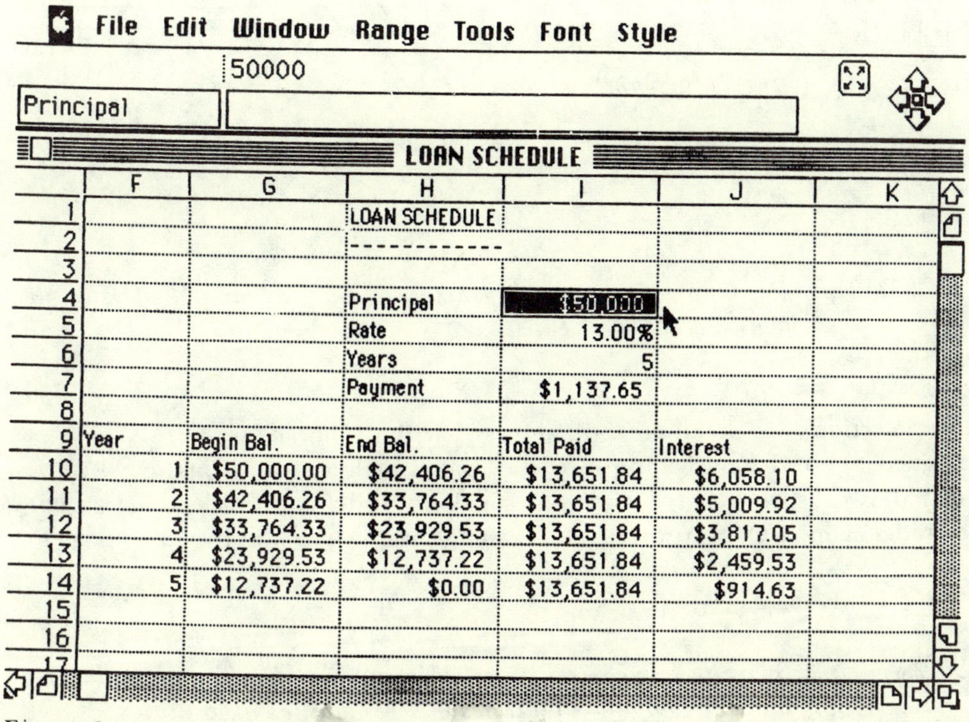

Figure 2-10. Assigning range names

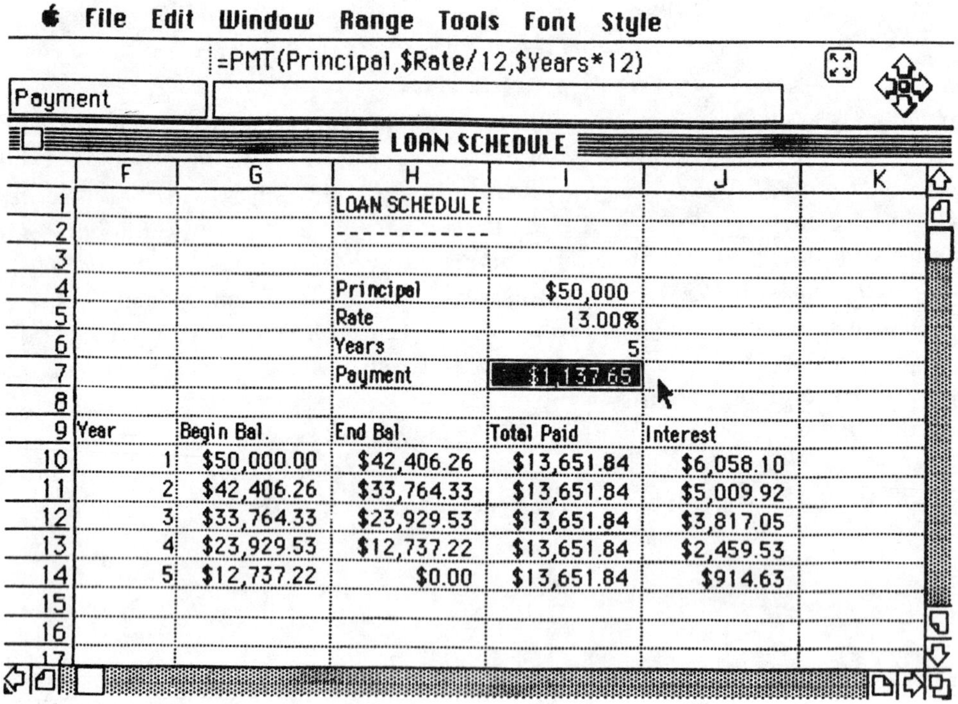

Figure 2-11. Using range names in formulas

2.83 Tip: *Use range names for quick access to a particular area of your worksheet.*

The Selection box in Figure 2-12 shows that the range name LOAN has been assigned to cell F1 at the beginning of the Loan Schedule area. No matter where you are in the worksheet at a given time, you can double-click on the Selection box, enter the range name LOAN, press RETURN, and go immediately to the Loan Schedule area.

2.84 Tip: *By using range names, you can avoid mistakes when entering the same range several times in several different formulas.*

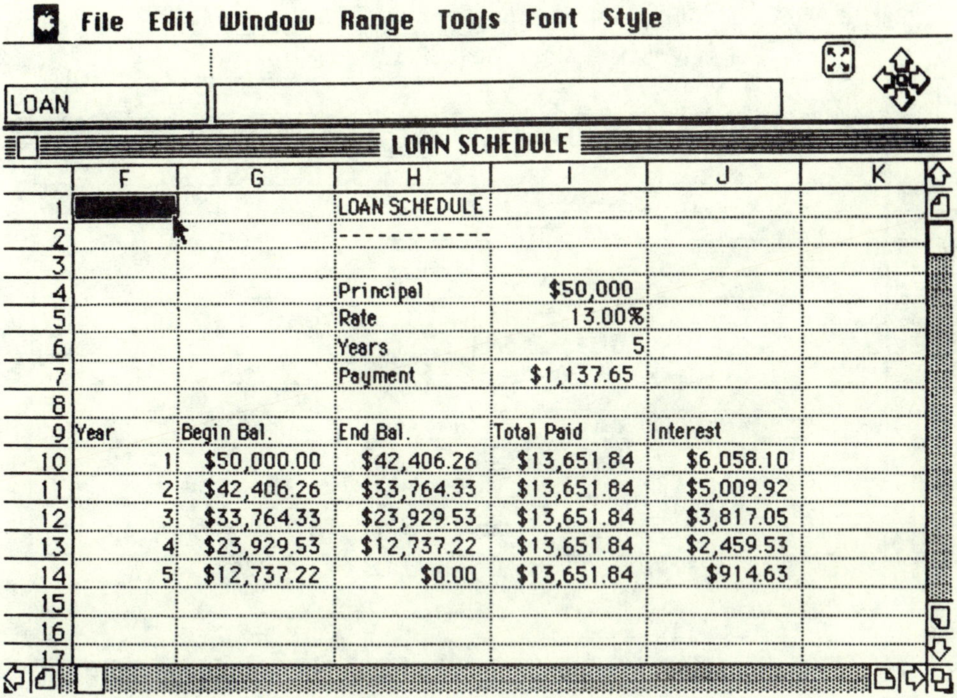

Figure 2-12. *Using range names to move around the worksheet*

As the Contents box in Figure 2-13 shows, the formulas in H10 through H14 refer to the same fields, Rate and Year, as the formula in I7. If only the cell addresses I5 and I6 had been entered in constructing these two formulas, we could easily have made a mistake (for example, entered I4 instead of I5 in one of the formulas). But when range names are entered, there is little chance of error. Jazz even allows you to enter a range name into a formula by clicking on an existing range name instead of typing in the name. Any time you're in entry mode on a cell, choose Enter into Formulas from the Edit menu and click on the Range Names option. Jazz then gives you a menu of existing range names. If you click on one, it'll appear in the formula in the active cell at the current insertion point.

2.85 Trap: *Don't fail to observe the absolute versus relative reference distinction when assigning range names.*

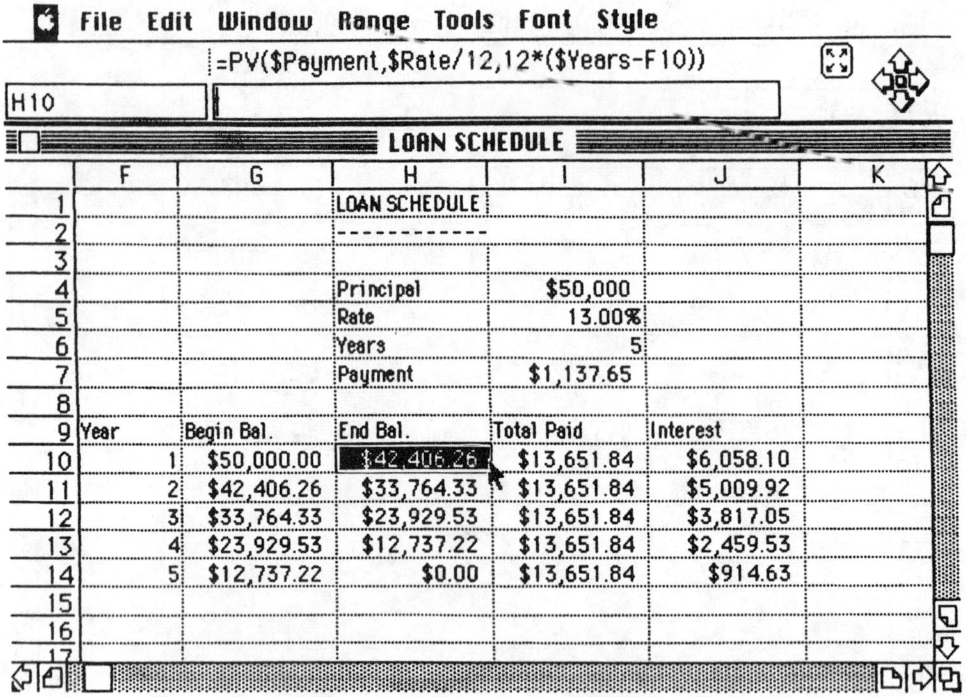

	F	G	H	I	J	K
1			LOAN SCHEDULE			
2			------------			
3						
4			Principal	$50,000		
5			Rate	13.00%		
6			Years	5		
7			Payment	$1,137.65		
8						
9	Year	Begin Bal.	End Bal.	Total Paid	Interest	
10	1	$50,000.00	$42,406.26	$13,651.84	$6,058.10	
11	2	$42,406.26	$33,764.33	$13,651.84	$5,009.92	
12	3	$33,764.33	$23,929.53	$13,651.84	$3,817.05	
13	4	$23,929.53	$12,737.22	$13,651.84	$2,459.53	
14	5	$12,737.22	$0.00	$13,651.84	$914.63	
15						
16						
17						

Figure 2-13. *Using a range name in several formulas*

Normally, when you copy a Jazz formula, the cell references are adjusted automatically. As the Contents box in Figure 2-13 shows, cell H10 contains a formula that refers to F10. We copied this same formula into cells H11 through H14. Since the reference to F10 is relative, the Jazz Copy/Paste sequence automatically adjusted this reference to F11 in H11, F12 in H12, and so on. This is just what we want, since the formula should refer to the Year column in the current row. But notice that we preceded all the range names in the formula in H10 with a dollar sign. This turns them into absolute references and ensures that the associated cell references will not be adjusted by a Copy/Paste operation. We do not want such an adjustment in this case because we want the End Balance formula in each row to refer to the same fields in our original "parameter" area in I4 through I7.

When you want a range-name reference to be absolute, type a dollar sign before specifying the range name. If you're actually typing in the range name, enter $ before typing it. If you're clicking on it or using the Range Name option of Enter into Formula, enter $ before doing that. (If you're clicking on it, you also have the option of clicking on the Absolute icon that appears in the Console as soon as you click on the cell you want to include in the formula.)

2.86 Tip: *To delete a range name, use the Discard option in the Names Review dialog box.*

When this dialog box appears, you will see a scrollable list of currently assigned range names. Simply select the ones you wish to delete and then click on Discard.

What-If Tables

2.87 Tip: *Use a what-if table to compare how a series of different changes to one or two "assumption variables" affects the results of one or more formulas.*

Jazz lets you build either a one-way or a two-way what-if table. A one-way table displays formula results that compare the results of changes to one assumption (input), cell, or variable. A two-way table compares the results of changes to two input cells. This comparative process is sometimes called *sensitivity analysis* and is one of the most useful applications of worksheets.

Suppose you want to borrow $70,000 to buy a house, and according to your budget, can't exceed a $750 monthly house payment. To determine whether you can afford a loan at this time, you need to know the maximum interest rate that yields a monthly payment less than $750. Figure 2-14 is a one-way what-if table with a range of interest rates and the corresponding monthly payments. In order to set up a what-if table, you need to select the table range (in this case B9..B16), choose Tools/Set Table Ranges/Use Selected, then select the input cell (in this case C2), choose Tools/Set Table Ranges/Use Selected, and finally click on Compute in the Set Table Ranges dialog box. (See the *Jazz Handbook* for full details.) The formula in C9 uses the =PMT function to calculate the monthly payment. When you compute the what-if table, Jazz substitutes into the input cell (C2) each of the values in turn in the first column (B) of the what-if table, computes the result, and places it in the second column (C). In this case, you can see that if the current interest rate exceeds 12.5%, you can't afford the loan.

Let's consider a different scenario: You don't know exactly how much you need to borrow; the range is $70,000 to $85,000. Again, you can't exceed a $750 monthly payment. Figure 2-15 shows a two-way table that compares a series of paired changes in both interest rate (column B) and principal amount (row 8). In this case we defined the table range as B8..F16 and the two input cells as C1 and C2. Cell B8 contains the =PMT formula that's used to calculate all the results (see the Contents box). When

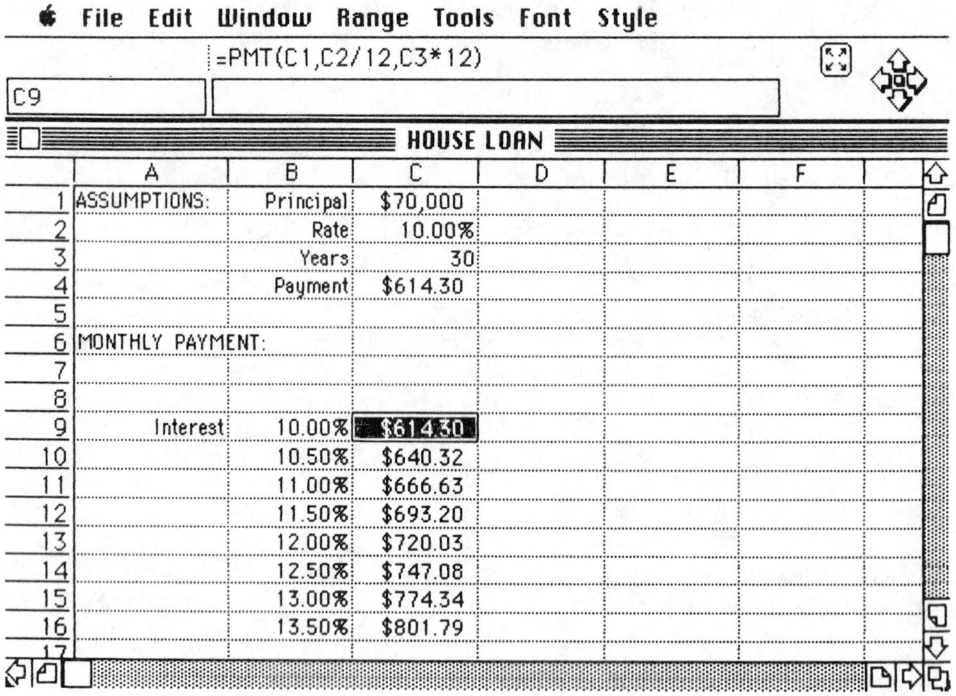

	A	B	C	D	E	F
1	ASSUMPTIONS:	Principal	$70,000			
2		Rate	10.00%			
3		Years	30			
4		Payment	$614.30			
5						
6	MONTHLY PAYMENT:					
7						
8						
9	Interest	10.00%	$614.30			
10		10.50%	$640.32			
11		11.00%	$666.63			
12		11.50%	$693.20			
13		12.00%	$720.03			
14		12.50%	$747.08			
15		13.00%	$774.34			
16		13.50%	$801.79			
17						

Figure 2-14. One-way what-if table

we compute the table, we get the results of each pair of input values in C9..F16. The results show that at a Principal of $70,000 you can afford an interest rate of 12.5%, at $75,000 you can afford only 11.5%, and so on.

2.88 Trap: *Don't forget to select Compute Table from the Tools menu if you change one of the parameters of a what-if table, or the results won't be brought up to date.*

Figure 2-16 shows the same what-if table constructed in Figure 2-15, except that the loan term has been increased to 40 years; however, table results are unchanged. A table recalculates only when you select Compute Table from the Tools menu, and Jazz does not remind you to recompute when you change a formula or value. Figure 2-17 shows what the table looks like after selecting Compute Table and thereby recomputing the entire table.

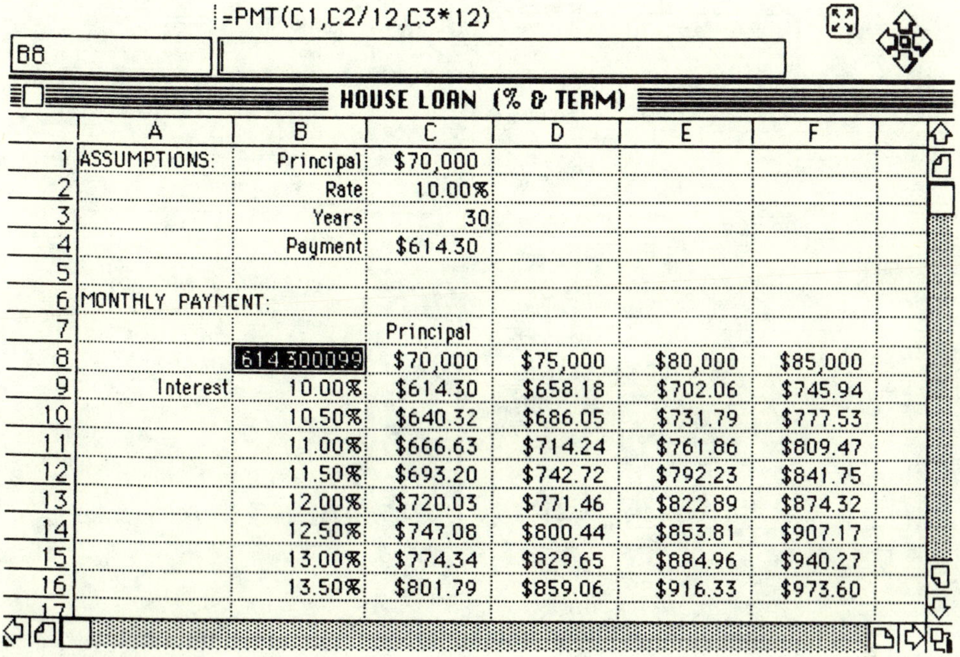

=PMT(C1,C2/12,C3*12)

B8

HOUSE LOAN (% & TERM)

	A	B	C	D	E	F
1	ASSUMPTIONS:	Principal	$70,000			
2		Rate	10.00%			
3		Years	30			
4		Payment	$614.30			
5						
6	MONTHLY PAYMENT:					
7			Principal			
8		614.300099	$70,000	$75,000	$80,000	$85,000
9	Interest	10.00%	$614.30	$658.18	$702.06	$745.94
10		10.50%	$640.32	$686.05	$731.79	$777.53
11		11.00%	$666.63	$714.24	$761.86	$809.47
12		11.50%	$693.20	$742.72	$792.23	$841.75
13		12.00%	$720.03	$771.46	$822.89	$874.32
14		12.50%	$747.08	$800.44	$853.81	$907.17
15		13.00%	$774.34	$829.65	$884.96	$940.27
16		13.50%	$801.79	$859.06	$916.33	$973.60

Figure 2-15. Two-way what-if table

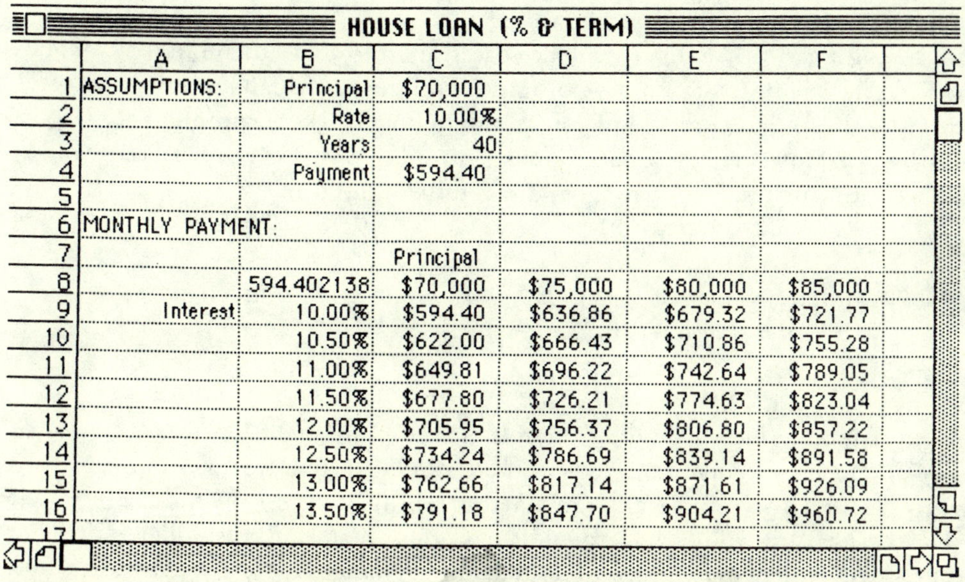

HOUSE LOAN (% & TERM)

	A	B	C	D	E	F
1	ASSUMPTIONS:	Principal	$70,000			
2		Rate	10.00%			
3		Years	40			
4		Payment	$594.40			
5						
6	MONTHLY PAYMENT:					
7			Principal			
8		594.402138	$70,000	$75,000	$80,000	$85,000
9	Interest	10.00%	$594.40	$636.86	$679.32	$721.77
10		10.50%	$622.00	$666.43	$710.86	$755.28
11		11.00%	$649.81	$696.22	$742.64	$789.05
12		11.50%	$677.80	$726.21	$774.63	$823.04
13		12.00%	$705.95	$756.37	$806.80	$857.22
14		12.50%	$734.24	$786.69	$839.14	$891.58
15		13.00%	$762.66	$817.14	$871.61	$926.09
16		13.50%	$791.18	$847.70	$904.21	$960.72

Figure 2-16. Changing the assumptions in the two-way table

HOUSE LOAN (% & TERM)

	A	B	C	D	E	F
1	ASSUMPTIONS:	Principal	$70,000			
2		Rate	10.00%			
3		Years	40			
4		Payment	$594.40			
5						
6	MONTHLY PAYMENT:					
7			Principal			
8		594.402138	$70,000	$75,000	$80,000	$85,000
9	Interest	10.00%	$614.30	$658.18	$702.06	$745.94
10		10.50%	$640.32	$686.05	$731.79	$777.53
11		11.00%	$666.63	$714.24	$761.86	$809.47
12		11.50%	$693.20	$742.72	$792.23	$841.75
13		12.00%	$720.03	$771.46	$822.89	$874.32
14		12.50%	$747.08	$800.44	$853.81	$907.17
15		13.00%	$774.34	$829.65	$884.96	$940.27
16		13.50%	$801.79	$859.06	$916.33	$973.60
17						

Figure 2-17. The recalculated table

2.89 Tip: *Use Range Fill to fill in the input values of a what-if table.*

You can automatically enter a sequence of values into a specified range. Consider Figure 2-17. The interest rates in Column B and the principal amounts in Row 8 were entered using the Range Fill command. In both cases, the numbers step up in value by equal intervals. Step values can be formulas, positive numbers, or negative numbers (in which the sequence goes down rather than up).

2.90 Trap: *If you don't specify the appropriate input cell, a what-if table will return identical values.*

In a one-way table, identical values in a column indicate that the formula at the top of the column isn't dependent on the specified input cell. In a two-way table, having identical values in a column tells you that the formula isn't dependent on Input Cell 1. Having identical values in a row tells you that the formula isn't dependent on Input Cell 2. In all three cases, you need to either change one or both input cells or change the formula so that it depends on the appropriate input cell.

2.91 Tip: *Make your what-if table assumptions separate entries in the worksheet rather than building them into your what-if table formulas.*

By doing this, you can change your assumptions easily and instantly see the results of those changes. The worksheet in Figure 2-17 shows the entry cells for the assumptions in the upper-left corner. Since they're separate from the what-if table formula in B8, you can specify any one of them as a what-if table input cell. Designing your worksheet with a separate assumption section is usually the best approach for all worksheet models, regardless of whether you intend to use what-if tables.

3

Functions and Formulas

Formulas and functions can be employed in many of the different Jazz environments. Though the most obvious of these areas is the Worksheet environment, formulas and functions offer increased facility and flexibility when working with databases and database reports. See Chapter 4 for specific tips on using formulas and functions in the Database environment.

General Hints

3.01 Tip: *Use Enter Into Formula (Edit menu) when you enter functions to prevent syntax errors and remind you of required arguments.*

There are about 100 different functions available to Jazz users, and it's difficult to remember the proper syntax and necessary arguments. To use Enter Into Formula, first highlight the cell where you want to enter the formula. Then select Enter Into

Formula from the Edit menu and make sure Functions is selected in the dialog box Jazz presents you. Double-click on the name of the function you wish to enter. Jazz then presents you with the function and a set of highlighted "dummy" arguments in the Entry box at the top of the screen. You can now replace these dummy arguments with the ones you really want either by typing them in or by selecting the desired ranges in the worksheet by using the mouse. The dummy arguments are handy because they remind you of the number and type of arguments Jazz requires for a particular function.

You can enter a range name into a formula in the same way by clicking on Range Names instead of Functions in the Enter into Formulas dialog box. Jazz will present you with a menu of existing range names in the current worksheet. You can double-click on the one you want and have it entered automatically into the formula in the active cell at the current insertion point.

3.02 Trap: *When you type a formula into a cell, Jazz will interpret it as a label unless you begin with a number or an = sign.*

This Trap is particularly significant for experienced spreadsheet users who are familiar with programs that use other symbols. With most other spreadsheet programs, you begin a function with an @ sign (@SUM in 1-2-3, for example). Jazz does not use this prefix, so when you begin a formula entry with a function, you must let Jazz know that it's a function (and not a text label) by preceding it with an = sign, as in =SUM. If you start the entry with a number, the = sign is not necessary.

One reason to use Enter into Formula (Edit menu) when you begin an entry with a function is that Jazz automatically begins the entry with an = and you don't have to worry about it.

3.03 Trap: *If you don't count the first column as column number 0 when a Jazz function demands a column number argument, you'll get unexpected results.*

Certain Jazz functions (notably VLOOKUP, HLOOKUP, INDEX, and the Data Range functions) require an argument specifying the column number in a range. It's important to remember that in such cases Jazz considers the first column in the range to be number 0, the second number 1, and so on. For instance, if you want to do a vertical lookup into the second column of a two-column table, you want a function that looks something like this: VLOOKUP(A1,H1...I10,1). The 1 in the third argument points to the second column in the table. Don't make the mistake of entering VLOOKUP(A1,H1..I10,2) in a case like this, or you'll point to the wrong column and get unexpected results.

***3.04 Trap:** Forgetting to enclose literal text in quotes will cause Jazz to reject your formula entry.*

If you forget to enclose literal text with double quotes, Jazz presents a dialog box telling you the formula is invalid. When you click OK, Jazz returns you to the Entry box so you can edit your entry. The following formula is incorrect and will be rejected by Jazz: =IF(COST<1000,OK,COST OVERRUN). The correct form would be =IF(COST<1000,"OK","COST OVERRUN"). This will cause the text OK to appear in the cell if COST is less than 1000; otherwise, the text COST OVERRUN will appear.

***3.05 Tip:** When a long formula returns ERR (error) or an unexpected result and you're not sure why, make the formula a temporary label and copy it to several other cells to analyze it.*

The Entry box in Figure 3-1 shows a fairly typical formula (in C14) that uses an IF function to determine the profit-sharing percentage that applies to an employee with a certain number of years of service (cell A4). As you see, the result of this formula is currently ERR. The question is whether it's the second or the third argument of the IF function that is at fault. Sometimes the answer is not immediately obvious just from an inspection of the formula. This is particularly true when the argument of one IF function is yet another IF function. Here's a technique for breaking apart the formula to determine which part of it is causing the problem:

1. Double-click on the offending cell (C14) to place it in the Entry box for editing, place the insertion point at the very beginning of the formula, and enter a text prefix character (a single quote is best) at the very beginning of the formula. Press ENTER to turn the formula temporarily into text.

2. Copy/Paste the cell that now contains your formula in the form of text to an empty target area. Select a target range with a number of cells equal to the number of possible offending arguments in your formula (in this case 2). The fact that we turned the formula into text first means that Jazz will not adjust address references

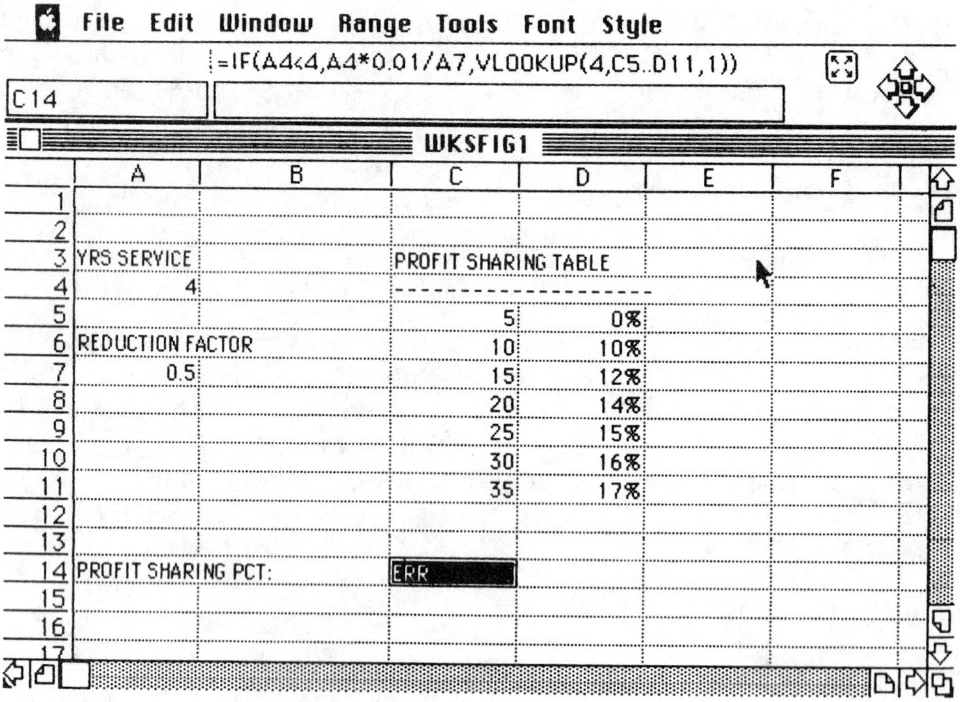

Figure 3-1. Detecting errors in long formulas

during the Copy/Paste. Figure 3-2 shows the result of copying the temporary text entry in C14 to C16..C17.

3. Edit each of the target cells in turn so that each contains only one portion of the original formula. As the text labels in D16 and D17 of Figure 3-3 indicate, we've edited C16 and C17 so that the first contains only the expression that was in the first argument of the original formula and the second contains only the expression that was in the second argument. Don't forget that when you edit these cells, the last thing you have to do is to delete the label prefix from the beginning of the entry and make sure that the entry in each cell begins with an = sign; otherwise you won't end up with formulas.

4. As C17 in Figure 3-3 shows, you'll now be able to see which portion of the original formula caused the problem. In this case, it was the VLOOKUP formula in the second argument. Close examination of the arguments of this VLOOKUP function reveals that the first argument (4) is less than the smallest value in the index column (the first column) of the table in C5..D11. Jazz will return an ERR in this situation. One way to correct the error would be to change the =IF(A4<4 at the beginning of the offending formula in C14 to =IF(A4<=4.

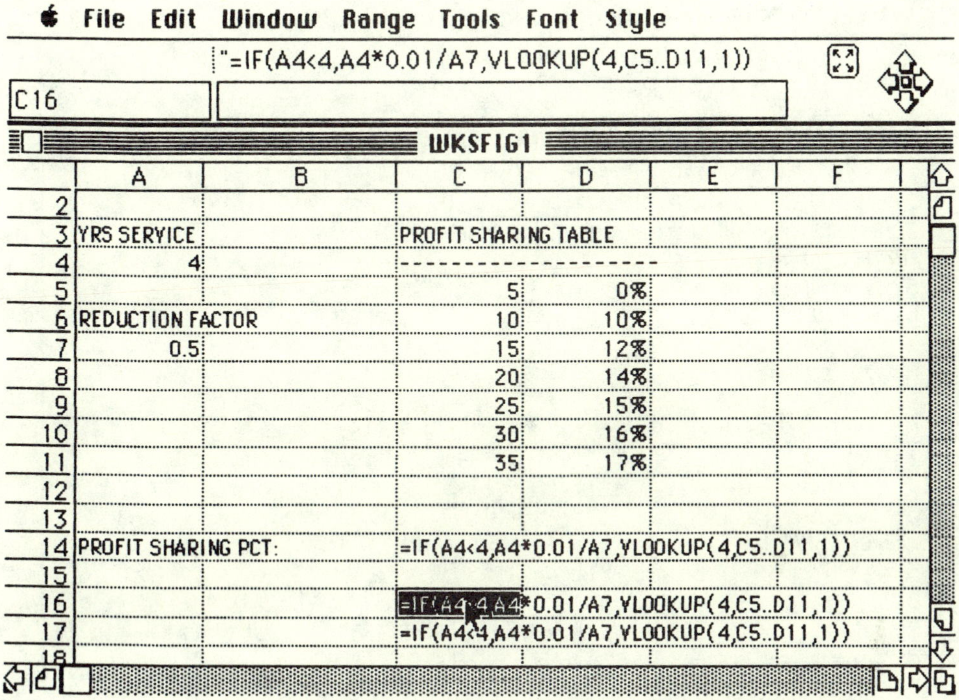

Figure 3-2. Converting a formula cell to a label and copying it to other cells

5. Finally, turn the original formula-become-text back to a formula again by deleting the text prefix character. Make sure you retain the = sign at the beginning of the formula.

***3.06 Trap:** If you include a cell containing text in an arithmetic expression, you'll get an ERR result in the cell.*

Sometimes you'll end up with a formula that references a cell containing text as part of an arithmetic expression. Cell D5 in Figure 3-4 shows such a situation. The formula shown in the Entry box (=D4+C5) adds the New Sales for the current account to the Balance Forward for the previous account. We used Copy/Paste to copy this same formula to D6 and D7. As the figure shows, all three cells in column D evaluate to ERR. The reason is that the formula in D5 refers to a cell (D4) that contains text. The cure for this type of problem is to make sure that the offending cell

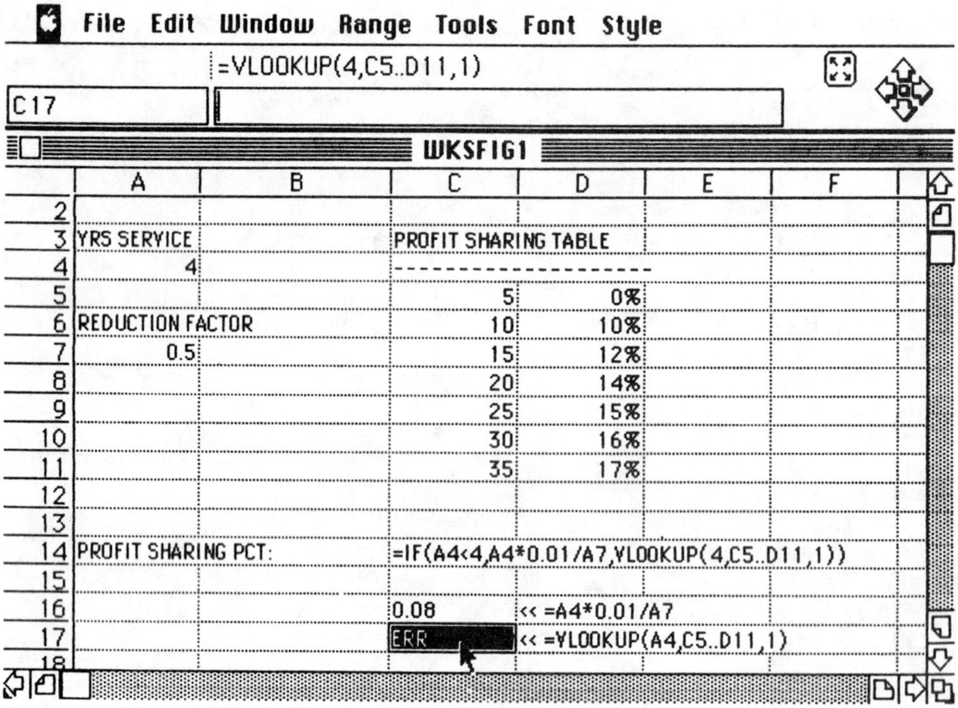

Figure 3-3. Editing cells to break formulas into logical parts

is completely empty. You can accomplish this in this case by copying the heading line in row 4 up to row 3 and clearing it from row 4. Figure 3-5 shows the result. All the formulas in column D now evaluate correctly because Jazz considers an empty cell to have a value of 0.

This is a particularly dangerous Trap for those who are familiar with 1-2-3 or other spreadsheet programs that treat all text as having a value of 0 and therefore do not return ERR in this type of situation. (See Chapter 8, Data Transfer, for more on this and other possible problems in converting files from other spreadsheet programs to Jazz files.)

If you supply a range containing text as an argument for an arithmetic function, Jazz has no problem with it. For instance, if we had placed the formula =SUM(C4..C7) in cell C9 in Figure 3-4, Jazz would have returned the result 122000 even though C4 contained text.

3.07 Trap: *If your formulas aren't balanced correctly, you will get wrong results.*

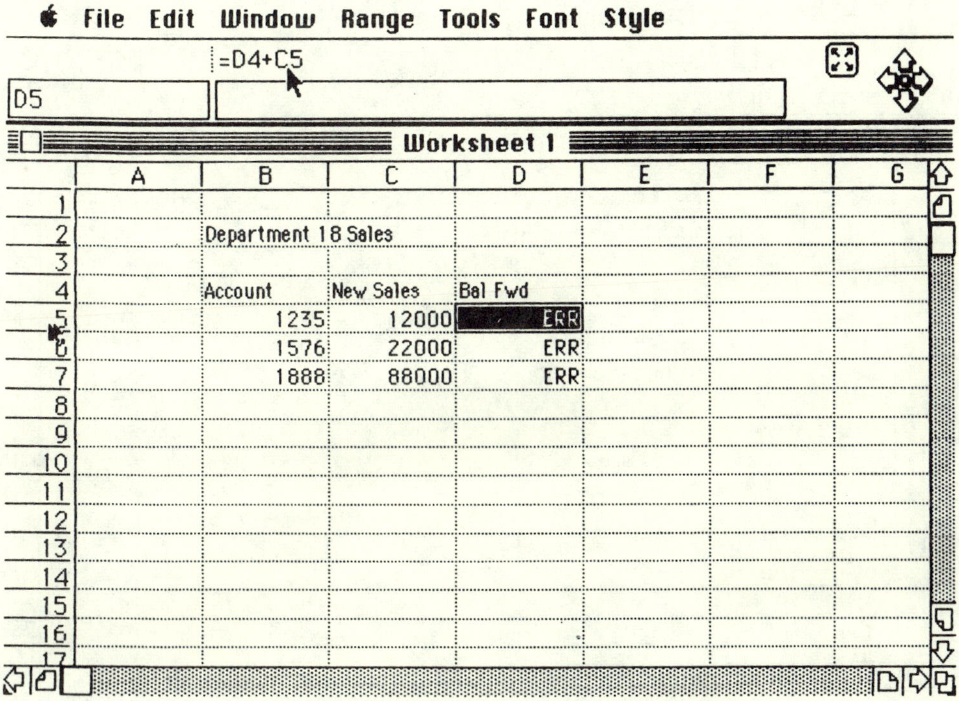

Figure 3-4. Formulas referencing text cells return ERR

A balanced formula has the same number of open parentheses and closed parentheses. Jazz won't let you enter a formula unless it is balanced. However, it is possible to enter a formula that is balanced incorrectly. A formula is correctly balanced when its related parts are grouped together by parentheses: functions with their corresponding arguments and formulas with the cells they reference. This is more likely to occur with complex formulas that need several sets of parentheses, such as nested IF functions. If a formula is suspect, print it out on paper. Check first to be sure that the formula cell is wide enough to display the entire entry. Then draw connecting lines between paired parentheses, starting first with the smallest and innermost groupings. It will look something like this:

```
IF(A7<MIN(B1..B10),37,VLOOKUP(ABS(C2),TABLE,2))
```

3.08 Trap: *If you need to nest several functions in one long formula, be careful not to confuse yourself and others.*

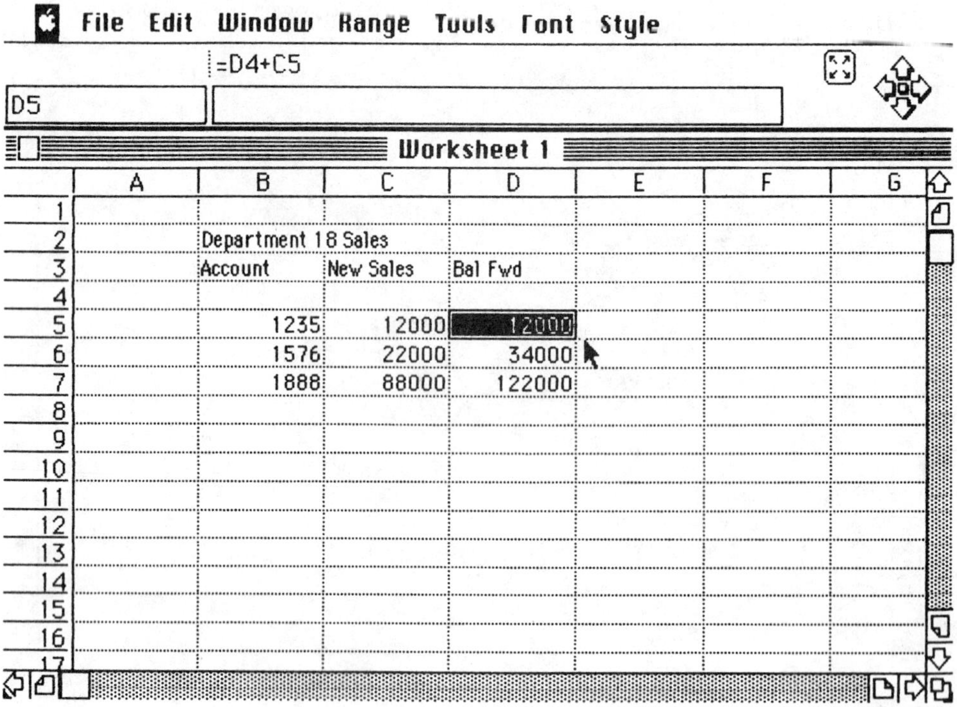

Figure 3-5. Empty cells are assigned a value of 0

Functions can be used wherever a number is called for, making it possible to nest several functions in one, often unwieldy, formula. It is easy for you to get confused in this process long before Jazz decides your formula is too long. Consider =IF(A4<MIN(B2..B10),0,VLOOKUP(ABS(C23),D1..D7,2)).

You should try to keep formula entries workable and understandable. The best way to do this is to break up complex formulas and enter the parts in separate cells where possible. The lookup function, =IF(A4<MIN(B2..B10),0,SERVCHRG), has been placed in a separate cell named "SERVCHRG".

3.09 Trap: *If you don't understand the rules of precedence, you will get the wrong results from your formulas.*

Mathematical operations (such as addition, multiplication, and so forth) are ranked according to an established order of precedence. When Jazz encounters a formula, mathematical operations take place from left to right unless other considerations intervene. These "other considerations" have to do with what is called "order of precedence" for mathematical operations. Use your Jazz manual as a reference when you need to know the precedence order of a particular operator.

When in doubt, use parentheses to force the precedence of operators. Suppose you entered the formula =6+4/2. You might be expecting the formula to return a 5; however, division has precedence over addition, and the result would be 8. You can use parentheses to offset a particular mathematical operation and change the order of operations: =(6+4)/2. The result would now be 5.

In general, your formulas will be more accurate if you enclose formula segments in parentheses whenever appropriate. There are no restrictions on the number of sets of parentheses you can use; however, be careful to balance your parentheses correctly. Refer to Trap 3.07.

3.10 Trap: *If you inadvertently enter a formula with "mixed" absolute and relative references, you'll get unexpected results when you copy it to other cells.*

Refer to Chapter 2 for a general discussion on the topic of "mixed" formula references. Cutting and pasting such formulas causes the relative part to adjust to the new cell location, but the absolute part will remain unchanged. For example, copying a cell containing the formula reference B$1 and then pasting it down three rows and over six columns will result in the reference H$1; the row, defined as absolute, remains 1, while the column, defined as relative, adjusts by six columns.

3.11 Trap: *Don't assume that two numbers that look the same necessarily have the same values, and don't confuse the =ROUND function with the Fixed format option.*

A cell's display and its actual contents are different concepts and can best be explained by discussing the difference between using the =ROUND function and assigning the Fixed format option to a cell. Both cause numbers to appear with a specific number of decimal places.

Consider the following illustration:

A	B	C	D	E	F
737.123	<<	Number entered without formatting (Cell A1)			
737.12	<<	=ROUND(A1,2) (Cell A3)			
737.12	<<	=A1 entered and formatted FIXED,2 (Cell A4)			
0	<<	=IF(A3=A4,1,0) (Cell A6)			

Cell A1 contains the unformatted number 737.123. A3 uses the =ROUND function to round off the number in A1 to two decimal places. Cell A4 displays the number in A1 in fixed decimal format (Fixed format option with two decimal places). Although these numbers are displayed identically, they are, in fact, different. When the =ROUND function rounds the number off to two decimal places, all remaining digits are dropped. Formatting a number, on the other hand, affects the display of the value and no digits are dropped; you just don't see them.

3.12 Trap: *If two results that you expect to be equal are not of equal precision, they may not compare as equal in a Jazz formula.*

This has major implications for logical tests in Jazz formulas. Consider the numbers in column A of Figure 3-6; the entries are formatted Fixed,2 and appear to be identical. Column C is not formatted and all digits are visible.As you can see, the numeric entries in A3 and A4 are, in fact, not identical past the third decimal place. The formula in B5 compares the entries in A3 and A4: the =IF function returns a 0, indicating that the entries don't compare equally. Both A8 and A9 use the =ROUND function to round the numbers in A3 and A4 to the second decimal place. The formula in B10 compares these rounded figures and returns a 1, indicating that they are of equal precision. Use the =ROUND function on both sides of a logical test should you question whether they're of equal precision.

3.13 Trap: *If you don't use =ROUND for all numbers with decimals, formula results may not be accurate.*

A	B	C
[Col A format=FIXED,2]	[Logical Test]	[Formulas/Numbers entered in Col A]
713.33		713.33333333348
713.33		713.33300004378
	0	=IF(A3=A4,1,0)
713.33		=ROUND(A3,2)
713.33		=ROUND(A4,2)
	1	=IF(A8=A9,1,0)

Figure 3-6. Using the ROUND function to test precision of formula results

This is particularly important if you work with dollar values and want accuracy to the penny. In Figure 3-7 the numbers in column D are the unrounded results of multiplying the entry in column B by the entry in column C. The formula in D10 rounds off the sum: =ROUND(SUM(D5..D8),2). The calculation result is $508.91, one penny less than expected.

The solution to this problem is seen in Figure 3-8. The =ROUND function is used to round each entry in column D. The formula in D10 sums the column of individually rounded numbers, and the result is accurate. When a rounding error

ROUNDING ACCURACY (1)

	A	B	C	D	E	F	G
1	SOMMA MATERIALS COST SHEET						
2	======================						
3		Amount	Unit Cost	Total			
4	Materials	------	---------	---------			
5	Foam	127	2.111	$268.10	<< =B5*C5 (D5)		
6	Thread	12	1.008	$12.10	<< =B6*C6 (D6)		
7	Fabric	78	2.176	$169.73	<< =B7*C7 (D7)		
8	Binding	53	1.113	$58.99	<< =B8*C8 (D8)		
9				=========			
10				$508.91	<< =ROUND(SUM(D5..D8),2) (D10)		
11							

Figure 3-7. Formula results inaccurate because of rounding error

ROUNDING ACCURACY (2)

	A	B	C	D	E	F	G
1	SOMMA MATERIALS COST SHEET						
2	======================						
3		Amount	Unit Cost	Total			
4	Materials	-------	-------	---------			
5	Foam	127	2.111	$268.10	<< =ROUND(B5*C5,2)		(D5)
6	Thread	12	1.008	$12.10	<< =ROUND(B6*C6,2)		(D6)
7	Fabric	78	2.176	$169.73	<< =ROUND(B7*C7,2)		(D7)
8	Binding	53	1.113	$58.99	<< =ROUND(B8*C8,2)		(D8)
9				=========			
10				$508.92	<< =SUM(D5..D8)		(D10)
11							

Figure 3-8. Formula results accurate when ROUND function is used

like this might occur, it is advisable to employ the =ROUND function for all numbers with decimals.

3.14 Tip: *Use the =ROUND function with a negative number for the argument to round off to a specified place to the left of the decimal point, such as rounding a dollar amount to the nearest $100.*

If you want the value of $113.02 to be rounded off to the hundredths place, enter =ROUND($113.02,−2).

The result of this function will be $100 since the −2 in the argument tells Jazz to round off to the hundredths place.

3.15 Tip: *When you need the remainder of a division, use the =MOD function.*

Suppose you have 183 Macintosh computers that you want to distribute evenly among your five computer stores. How many computers will be left in your warehouse after you send the same number of systems to each store?

Using the =MOD function, this question can be answered instantly. The =MOD function returns the remainder (modulo) of the division of two numbers. In our example, the function would look like =MOD(183,5).

The result (the remainder) is 3. Each of your stores will receive 36 Macintoshes, and you will have 3 left in your warehouse.

3.16 Trap: *When using Jazz trigonometric functions, if you don't express arguments in radians, results will not be accurate.*

Arguments in trigonometric functions must be given in radians to return accurate results. Unless you deal with numbers that are already expressed in radians, you must convert from degrees to radians. To convert from degrees to radians, use the =PI function: number of degrees * (PI/180). An example of this is =COS(60*PI/180).

Conversely, multiply the number of radians by (180/PI) to get the number of degrees. An example of this is =COS(.5)*180/PI.

3.17 Trap: *If you are not sure which entries =COUNT will count, you may get unexpected results.*

Figure 3-9 shows four different examples of how you might use the =COUNT function (labeled Examples 1-4). The =COUNT function counts the number of

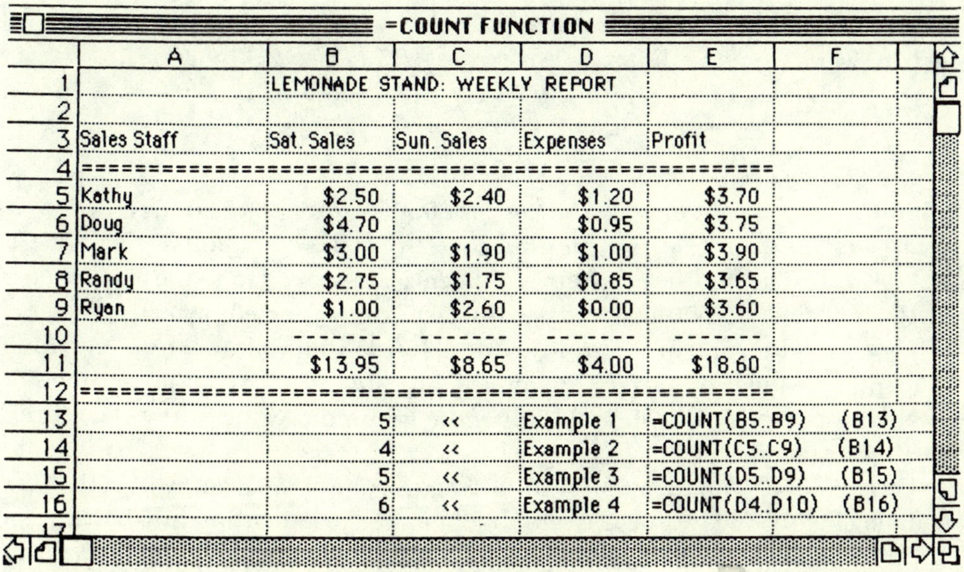

=COUNT FUNCTION

	A	B	C	D	E	F
1		LEMONADE STAND: WEEKLY REPORT				
2						
3	Sales Staff	Sat. Sales	Sun. Sales	Expenses	Profit	
4	================	================	================	================	================	
5	Kathy	$2.50	$2.40	$1.20	$3.70	
6	Doug	$4.70		$0.95	$3.75	
7	Mark	$3.00	$1.90	$1.00	$3.90	
8	Randy	$2.75	$1.75	$0.85	$3.65	
9	Ryan	$1.00	$2.60	$0.00	$3.60	
10		-------	-------	-------	-------	
11		$13.95	$8.65	$4.00	$18.60	
12	================	================	================	================	================	
13		5	<<	Example 1	=COUNT(B5..B9)	(B13)
14		4	<<	Example 2	=COUNT(C5..C9)	(B14)
15		5	<<	Example 3	=COUNT(D5..D9)	(B15)
16		6	<<	Example 4	=COUNT(D4..D10)	(B16)
17						

Figure 3-9. Using the =COUNT function

non-empty cells in a range of cells, accounting for both numeric and text entries.

Example 1 (B13) represents the normal case; cells B5 through B9 each have a numeric entry and the =COUNT function returns a count of 5.

Suppose you want to know how many people are selling lemonade on Sunday. In Example 2 (B14), cell C6 is empty because Doug was absent Sunday and didn't do any selling. The =COUNT function ignores empty cells, so the resulting count is 4. Had a zero entry been entered to denote Doug's absence, =COUNT would have returned a count of 5 because zero is considered to be a valid numeric entry and would be counted. Such a result is misleading; you might conclude that Doug worked Sunday, but didn't sell any lemonade.

In Example 3 (B15) a valid zero entry is entered in D9 to indicate that Ryan did not have any expenses for the weekend. In contrast to Example 2, the count of 5 returned by =COUNT is an accurate and meaningful result.

Example 4 (B16) demonstrates how text entries are counted. The range of cells being counted in Example 4 includes two non-numeric entries. The double dashed lines that appear in E4 are actually part of the label entry in A4; what you see in E4 is an extension of this single entry. The significance of this is that Jazz considers E4 to be a blank cell. On the other hand, cell E10 does in fact contain the single dashed lines you see; this is a text entry and is included in the count. Letters as well as symbols are considered to be text and are counted by the =COUNT function. Tip 3.19 explains the advantage of including text entries in the =SUM function; it can be a very useful convention.

3.18 ***Trap:*** *Empty cells are ignored by =MIN and =AVG functions, which may cause unexpected results to be returned.*

In Figure 3-10 the sales totals are the same for both Saturday and Sunday; however, the entries for the last salesperson are different (B9 contains a zero dollar entry and C9 is a blank cell). The significance of this difference can be seen in Examples 1 and 2, showing how the =MIN function deals with zero entries and empty cells.

The =MIN function in Example 1 returned $0.00, the minimum numeric value for the specified range of cells. In Example 2 the result is $1.25, demonstrating that =MIN ignores the empty cell and returns the minimum value of the remaining entries in the range.

The =AVG function computes the average, or mean, of a range of cells. The calculation involves adding up the values of the entries and then dividing by the total number of entries. Example 3 shows the result of the =AVG function of the range of cells B5 to B9 inclusive. What you don't see taking place is that Jazz is dividing by 5 (total number of entries). Compare this to the calculation in Example 4; Jazz divides

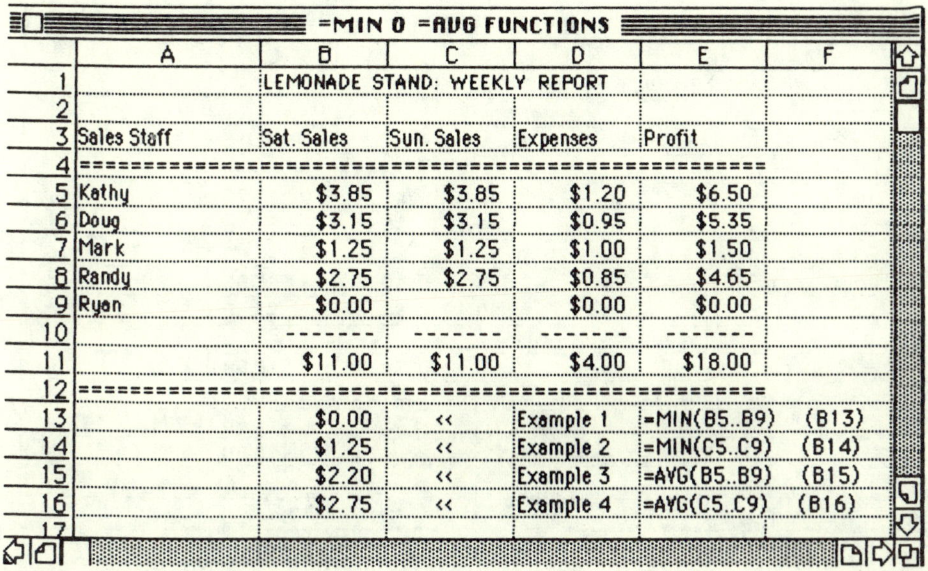

	A	B	C	D	E	F
1		LEMONADE STAND: WEEKLY REPORT				
2						
3	Sales Staff	Sat. Sales	Sun. Sales	Expenses	Profit	
4	==					
5	Kathy	$3.85	$3.85	$1.20	$6.50	
6	Doug	$3.15	$3.15	$0.95	$5.35	
7	Mark	$1.25	$1.25	$1.00	$1.50	
8	Randy	$2.75	$2.75	$0.85	$4.65	
9	Ryan	$0.00		$0.00	$0.00	
10		-------	-------	-------	-------	
11		$11.00	$11.00	$4.00	$18.00	
12	==					
13		$0.00	<<	Example 1	=MIN(B5..B9)	(B13)
14		$1.25	<<	Example 2	=MIN(C5..C9)	(B14)
15		$2.20	<<	Example 3	=AVG(B5..B9)	(B15)
16		$2.75	<<	Example 4	=AVG(C5..C9)	(B16)
17						

Figure 3-10. Using the MIN and AVG functions

by 4 because =AVG ignores the empty cell in C9. Be alert for this difference when you use the =AVG function.

3.19 Tip: *When you specify =SUM ranges, include an extra row or column to allow for insertions and deletions.*

Figure 3-11 shows a weekly sales report that uses the =SUM function to calculate the total sales for each day for five salespeople. The =SUM function in Example 1 specifies a range of E5..E9, and in Example 2 the range is E4..E10 (with two non-numeric entries included). Since the results are identical, it would seem that it doesn't matter which format you use.

But suppose a new salesperson is hired. Now a new line must be inserted in the worksheet. Figure 3-12 shows how the =SUM functions in Examples 1 and 2 are affected by the added entry. The result in Example 2 demonstrates how Jazz will automatically adjust the formula so that it accounts for all the rows, including the new one inserted at line 10. This trick can be extremely useful since you often need to insert or delete rows and columns in your worksheet.

3.20 Tip: *You can use both numeric and text entries in lookup tables.*

=SUM FUNCTION (1)

	A	B	C	D	E	F
1		LEMONADE STAND: WEEKLY REPORT				
2						
3	Sales Staff	Sat. Sales	Sun. Sales	Expenses	Profit	
4	==					
5	Kathy	$2.50	$2.40	$1.20	$3.70	
6	Doug	$4.70		$0.95	$3.75	
7	Mark	$3.00	$1.90	$1.00	$3.90	
8	Randy	$2.75	$1.75	$0.85	$3.65	
9	Ryan	$1.00	$2.60	$0.00	$3.60	
10		-------	-------	---------	-------	
11		$13.95	$8.65	$4.00	$18.60	
12	==					
13			Example 1	>>	$18.60	=SUM(E5..E9)
14			Example 2	>>	$18.60	=SUM(E4..E10)
15						

Figure 3-11. Allowing for insertions and deletions in SUM formula range

The LOOKUP functions allow you to retrieve a number or label from a table in another part of the worksheet. Tables are preconfigured in either vertical or horizontal orientation and can be thought of as mini-databases. The first column or row in

=SUM FUNCTION (2)

	A	B	C	D	E	F
1		LEMONADE STAND: WEEKLY REPORT				
2						
3	Sales Staff	Sat. Sales	Sun. Sales	Expenses	Profit	
4	==					
5	Kathy	$2.50	$2.40	$1.20	$3.70	
6	Doug	$4.70		$0.95	$3.75	
7	Mark	$3.00	$1.90	$1.00	$3.90	
8	Randy	$2.75	$1.75	$0.85	$3.65	
9	Ryan	$1.00	$2.60	$0.00	$3.60	
10	Laurie	$1.50	$1.40	$0.90	$2.00	
11		-------	-------	-------	-------	
12		$15.45	$10.05	$4.90	$20.60	
13	==					
14			Example 1	>>	$18.60	=SUM(E5..E9)
15			Example 2	>>	$20.60	=SUM(E4..E10)
16						

Figure 3-12. SUM formula automatically adjusts to account for inserted row

the specified lookup range (depending on the table's orientation) is the index column or row that Jazz searches for a match with the specified selector. When a match is found, Jazz moves over the number of columns or down the number of rows specified in the formula, and returns the entry found in that corresponding cell.

The format for entering a lookup formula is

=HLOOKUP(sel,table_range,n_rows)
=VLOOKUP(sel,table_range,n_cols)

The first argument (sel), is the selector; it is either a text entry or a number, depending on the type of lookup table (text or numeric). The second argument (table_range) defines the location and size of your lookup table. The last argument (n_rows or n_cols) identifies either the number of columns to the right of the index column or the number of rows below the index row. (Don't forget the rule about starting with 0. See Trap 3.03 in this chapter.)

3.21 Tip: *You can use a lookup table to convert a table of concise codes into corresponding descriptions.*

The worksheet in Figure 3-13 uses lookup formulas in column B to automatically

TEXT LOOKUP (1)

	A	B	C	D	E	F
1	ACCOUNTS RECEIVABLE				CHART OF ACCOUNTS (LOOKUP TABLE)	
2						
3	Account	Name	Amount		Account #	Name
4	--------	-------------	---------		--------	------------------
5	3080	Darling Dolls	$250		1050	Acme Auto Clinic
6	4000	Elegant Etc.	$186		2000	Bookbinders Inc
7	2500	Classic Cars	$207		2500	Classic Cars
8	1050	Acme Auto Clinic	$39		3080	Darling Dolls
9	4000	Elegant Etc.	$458		4000	Elegant Etc.
10	=========	============	=========	====	========	===================
11		Formula				Formula Entered in Cell:
12		=VLOOKUP(A5,$E$5..$G$9,1)				(C5)
13					Formula	
14		=VLOOKUP(A6,$E$5..$G$9,1)			Copied to >	(C6)
15		=VLOOKUP(A7,$E$5..$G$9,1)			"	(C7)
16		=VLOOKUP(A8,$E$5..$G$9,1)			"	(C8)
17		=VLOOKUP(A9,$E$5..$G$9,1)			"	(C9)

Figure 3-13. Text lookup table

extract "Name", using the selector (column A) to locate the corresponding value (column F) in the lookup table. The selector and the result of a lookup formula can be numeric or text.

3.22 Trap: *In creating a lookup formula that you will copy into other cells, you will get the wrong results if you don't reference the lookup table with absolute cell addresses.*

In Figure 3-14 the formula entered in C5 successfully returned the "Name" that matches the "Account" number. When this formula was copied to B6..B9, wrong results were returned. Since lookup tables always occupy a constant range, this range should be specified as an absolute reference whenever it is referenced in a formula that may be copied to another cell. Otherwise, copying the formula will result in a relative adjustment that will return the wrong answer.

3.23 Trap: *Be careful to accurately define the orientation of your lookup table.*

TEXT LOOKUP (2)

	A	B	C	D	E	F
1	ACCOUNTS RECEIVABLE				CHART OF ACCOUNTS (LOOKUP TABLE)	
2						
3	Account	Name	Amount		Account #	Name
4	--------	------------	---------		-------	------------------
5	3080	Darling Dolls	$250		1050	Acme Auto Clinic
6	4000	=	$186		2000	Bookbinders Inc
7	2500	Classic Cars	$207		2500	Classic Cars
8	1050	ERR	$39		3080	Darling Dolls
9	4000	0	$458		4000	Elegant Etc.
10	========	===========	========	====	=======	==================
11		Formula				Formula Entered in Cell:
12		=VLOOKUP(A5,E5..F9,1)				(C5)
13					Formula	
14		=VLOOKUP(A6,E6..F10,1)			Copied to >	(C6)
15		=VLOOKUP(A7,E7..F11,1)			"	(C7)
16		=VLOOKUP(A8,E8..F12,1)			"	(C8)
17		=VLOOKUP(A9,E9..F13,1)			"	(C9)

Figure 3-14. Lookup formulas are inaccurate if lookup tables aren't referenced as absolute

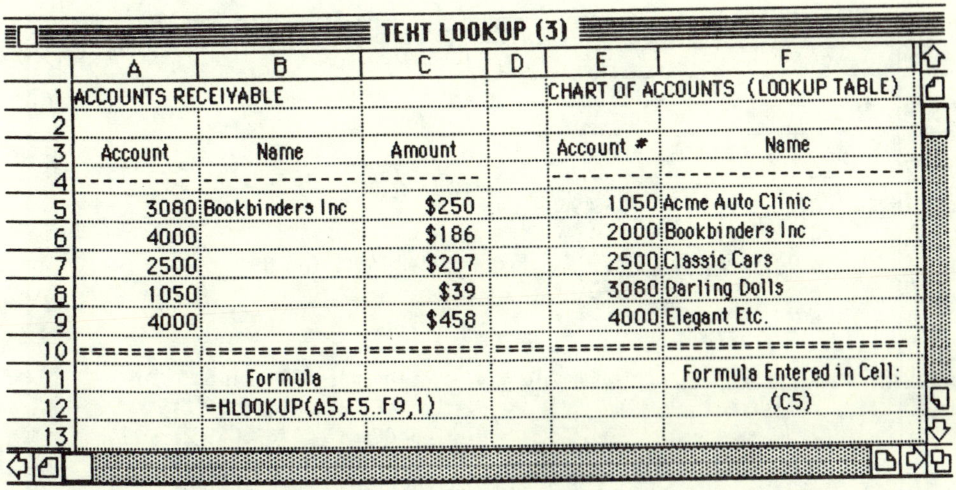

TEXT LOOKUP (3)

	A	B	C	D	E	F
1	ACCOUNTS RECEIVABLE				CHART OF ACCOUNTS (LOOKUP TABLE)	
2						
3	Account	Name	Amount		Account #	Name
4	---------	------------	---------		--------	------------------
5	3080	Bookbinders Inc	$250		1050	Acme Auto Clinic
6	4000		$186		2000	Bookbinders Inc
7	2500		$207		2500	Classic Cars
8	1050		$39		3080	Darling Dolls
9	4000		$458		4000	Elegant Etc.
10	=========	============	=========	====	========	===================
11		Formula				Formula Entered in Cell:
12		=HLOOKUP(A5,E5..F9,1)				(C5)
13						

Figure 3-15. Vertical lookup table incorrectly referenced in lookup formula

The formula in Figure 3-15 returns the wrong name because the lookup formula identifies a horizontally oriented table (HLOOKUP). However, the lookup table in this figure is vertical, and unexpected results are returned in response to this formula. This type of mistake is easy to make and often hard to detect because we usually concentrate on the arguments listed inside the parentheses when looking for the cause of an error.

3.24 **Trap:** *When you construct a numeric lookup table, make sure that the values are unique and in ascending order.*

If this is not the case, the results may be unpredictable. For a numeric lookup to work correctly, you must enter the values in the index column in ascending order. If you have any question at all about the order of entries in a lookup table, use the Sort command on the lookup table.

3.25 **Trap:** *Numbers returned by lookup formulas do not automatically keep the format style set in the lookup table.*

Refer to the lookup table (A5..C9) in Figure 3-16. The numbers in C5..C9 appear in currency format. The results returned by the lookup formulas in C12..C16 are

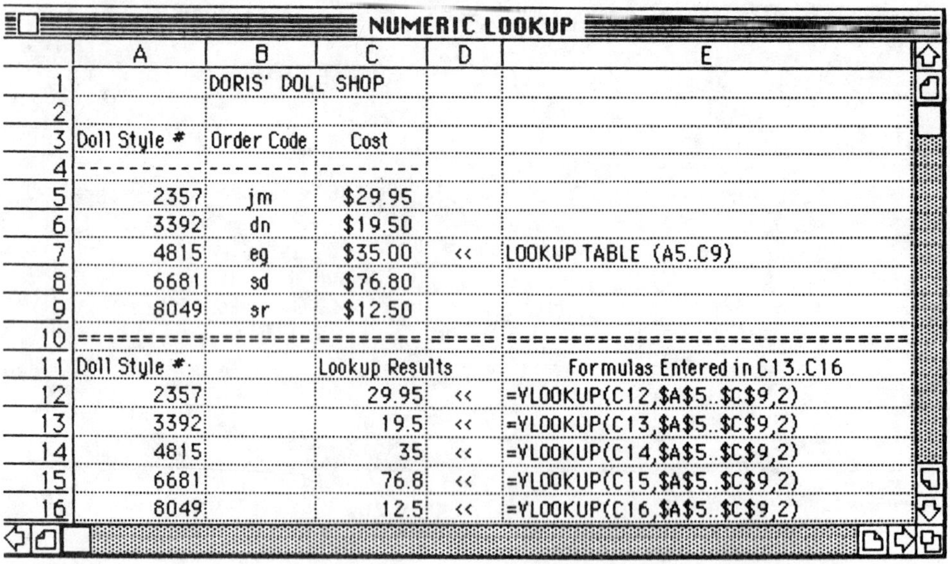

NUMERIC LOOKUP

	A	B	C	D	E
1		DORIS' DOLL SHOP			
2					
3	Doll Style *	Order Code	Cost		
4	---------	--------	--------		
5	2357	jm	$29.95		
6	3392	dn	$19.50		
7	4815	eg	$35.00	<<	LOOKUP TABLE (A5..C9)
8	6681	sd	$76.80		
9	8049	sr	$12.50		
10	=========	========	========	=====	=============================
11	Doll Style *:		Lookup Results		Formulas Entered in C13..C16
12	2357		29.95	<<	=VLOOKUP(C12,$A$5..$C$9,2)
13	3392		19.5	<<	=VLOOKUP(C13,$A$5..$C$9,2)
14	4815		35	<<	=VLOOKUP(C14,$A$5..$C$9,2)
15	6681		76.8	<<	=VLOOKUP(C15,$A$5..$C$9,2)
16	8049		12.5	<<	=VLOOKUP(C16,$A$5..$C$9,2)

Figure 3-16. Lookup formulas return unformatted results

displayed in general format. This is because display style is determined by the format setting of the current cell. Cells C12..C16 are set for general format, the default setting.

3.26 Trap: *If you don't include entries for the lowest and highest possible values when constructing a lookup table, you may get wrong results with lookup formulas that use them.*

In the lookup table in Figure 3-17, the lowest value included is 3 years (A7), and the highest value is 7 years (A11). The lookup formula entered in F6 returns ERR (error) because John has only 2 years of service, and the number 2 isn't included in the lookup table. The lookup formula in F8 returns the highest value; any entry greater than 7 (highest value) will return 20%. These results may or may not be what you want. The solution is to create a lookup table that includes the lowest and highest possible values. On the low end, 0 is a typical entry.

3.27 Tip: *You can use the =CHOOSE function to maintain small databases as single cell entries.*

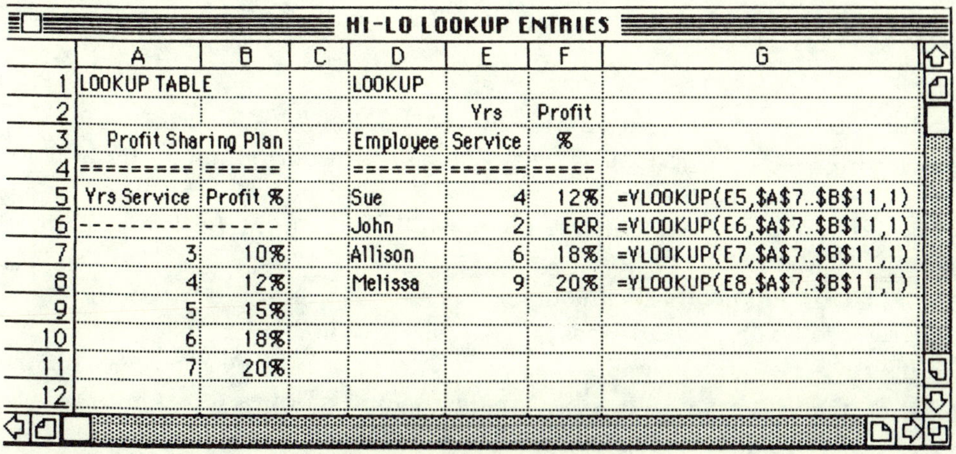

HI-LO LOOKUP ENTRIES

	A	B	C	D	E	F	G
1	LOOKUP TABLE			LOOKUP			
2					Yrs	Profit	
3	Profit Sharing Plan			Employee	Service	%	
4	=========	======		=======	======	=====	
5	Yrs Service	Profit %		Sue	4	12%	=VLOOKUP(E5,$A$7..$B$11,1)
6	---------	------		John	2	ERR	=VLOOKUP(E6,$A$7..$B$11,1)
7	3	10%		Allison	6	18%	=VLOOKUP(E7,$A$7..$B$11,1)
8	4	12%		Melissa	9	20%	=VLOOKUP(E8,$A$7..$B$11,1)
9	5	15%					
10	6	18%					
11	7	20%					
12							

Figure 3-17. Lookup formulas return wrong results when a value is missing from the lookup table

The =CHOOSE function returns a value from an argument list based on its position in the list. This function can deal with labels, numbers, formulas, or cell addresses. The format for this function is

=CHOOSE(1,"Huey","Louie","Dewey")

This example returns "Louie" because it is argument number 1; remember, "Huey" is counted as number 0.

If you need to refer to a table more than once, use =LOOKUP instead of =CHOOSE. A lookup table is entered once in a worksheet range, whereas the =CHOOSE function is entered in individual cells when needed. For a single application of a table, =CHOOSE is appropriate; otherwise, you should set up a lookup table that can be referenced repeatedly.

3.28 Tip: *Use the =CHOOSE function as an alternative to complex nested* =IF formulas.

Suppose you have a "switch" that can have values from 1 to 3, representing three different ways to compute a bonus. You could use a nested IF statement, such as =IF(C3>10000,A3*1.15,IF(C3<10000,A3+1000,IF(C3=25000,A3*1.37,0))).

But complex formulas like this often become unwieldy and very difficult to decipher. An effective alternative to this formula is =CHOOSE(2,A3*1.15,A3+1000, A3*1.37).

3.29 *Tip:* *With Jazz, you can use labels in formulas and functions.*

As with Lotus' Symphony and 1-2-3 version 2.0, Jazz lets you use labels (text strings) in formulas, functions, and logical tests. This is a welcome option for those experienced spreadsheet users who in the past have been frustrated by the fact that most spreadsheet programs do not include the capability to perform text string manipulations.

Jazz has 17 different text functions; there are a multitude of possibilities for using these to perform calculations with and to manipulate text.

Figure 3-18 is a worksheet that compares sales figures for 1984 and 1985. Figure 3-19 contains 13 examples that illustrate the usefulness of text functions. In some cases, more than one text function is used in the same entry. We'll look at each of the examples in Figure 3-19, which shows the actual cell entry displayed as well as the result of the calculation.

Example 1: With the EXACT function you can test whether two text entries are identical. If it is true that they are exactly the same, then Jazz displays the number 1. In the false case, when they are different, you will see a zero (0). In this example, the text entry "West" is entered in both cells D5 and D9, and so Jazz returns a 1.

Example 2: FIXED converts a number to text and displays it in fixed format,

TEXT FUNCTIONS

	A	B	C	D	E	F
1			SALES BY DIVISION			
2						
3	First Name	Last Name	Department	Division	1984 Sales	1985 Sales
4	---------	---------	---------	---------	---------	---------
5	Laurie	Einstein	Alpha	West	$145,000	$167,000
6	Victor	Pasteur	Beta	East	$187,000	$173,000
7	Mary	Curie	Gamma	North East	$128,000	$149,000
8	Daniel	Bell	Delta	South	$109,000	$117,000
9	Michael	Edison	Epsilon	West	$152,000	$162,000
10	---------	---------	---------	---------	---------	---------
11			Company Totals:		$721,000	$768,000
12			Percent Increase in 1985:			6.12%
13						

Figure 3-18. *Worksheet comparing sales figures for 1984 and 1985*

TEXT FUNCTIONS

	A	B	C	D	E	F	G
16		EXAMPLE #	TEXT FUNCTION			RESULT	
17							
18		1	=EXACT(D5,D9)			1	
19		2	=FIXED(E11,0)			721000	
20		3	=LEFT(C11,4)			Comp	
21		4	=LENGTH(C3)			10	
22		5	=REPEAT("Hi ",4)			Hi Hi Hi Hi	
23		6	=REPLACE("I Like Jazz",3,3,"ove")			I Love Jazz	
24		7	=TRIM(D7)			North East	
25		8	=TRIM(LOWER(C16))			text function	
26		9	=VALUE(F12)			0.0611979	
27		10	=A6			Victor	
28		11	=A5&" "&B5			Laurie Einstein	
29		12	=SUBSTR(F23,7,4)&" is No.1"			Jazz is No.1	
30		13	=B5&REPLACE(F23,0,6," Loves")			Laurie Loves Jazz	
31							

Figure 3-19. Examples of text functions applied to worksheet in Figure 3-18

rounded to the number of digits to the right of the decimal point specified. The first argument is the cell address of the numeric value you wish to convert to text (E11), and the second argument specifies the number of decimal digits (0). The entry "$721,000" is now the label "721000" entered in cell F19 in left-justified format, the default alignment for labels. Decimals are rounded off by specifying a zero (0) in the second argument.

Example 3: If you wish to extract the left or right part of a text entry, the LEFT or RIGHT functions are useful. The format is to identify the cell (C9) and the number of characters you want returned (4). In this example we are extracting the four leftmost characters of the entry in cell C11, "Company Totals." "Comp" is the result of this operation.

Example 4: You can determine the length of a text entry by employing the LENGTH function and specifying the cell address (C3). An error (ERR) will be indicated if you apply this function to a numeric entry. If your text entry includes spaces, the resulting number will take into account the number of space characters. If needed, the TRIM function can be used to eliminate the trailing blanks before the LENGTH function evaluates the entry. (See the explanation of =TRIM below.)

Example 5: REPEAT duplicates the specified text ("Hi ") the number of times indicated (4). The text entry must be enclosed by double quotes, and you are free to use letters, numbers, symbols, or any combination of these. Even spaces and punctuation can be included; in this example, a space is used after the word "Hi" to space out the repeated text pattern.

Example 6: You can replace a segment of a text entry with new text. This involves using the REPLACE function and specifying three arguments in this order: the original text entry or cell reference, the position in the original text to begin removing characters, the total number of characters to be removed, and the replacement text. Both the original text and the replacement text must be enclosed in double quotes. When you specify the starting position, keep in mind that the first character position is 0, not 1.

Example 7: You can trim extra spaces from a text entry. Cell D7 contains the entry "North   East". Notice the extra spaces between the two words. The TRIM function gets rid of all spaces before the first non-space character and all spaces following the last non-space character as well as all but one space between words.

Example 8: The function LOWER is used to convert all letters to lowercase. The text in cell C16 was originally entered as uppercase letters with some leading spaces. By nesting the TRIM and LOWER functions, we are able to eliminate embedded spaces and convert the text to lowercase. You can nest any combination of text functions as long as you specify all required arguments and have the same number of open and closed parentheses.

Example 9: The =VALUE function converts a cell entry into its actual numeric value. For example, cell F12 contains the formula "=(F9−E9)/F9" and is formatted to display the result of the calculation as a percent with two decimal places. By using the VALUE function, cell F26 displays the result of the formula as an unformatted value, "0.0611979". You can also use the =VALUE function to convert numbers that were originally entered as text.

Example 10: The simple "=A6" transfers the label "Victor" from cell A6. Text—as well as numbers and formulas—can be transferred in this way. Be careful to include the equal sign as a prefix; this indicates a formula. Without it, cell F27 would instead display the label "A6".

3.30 Tip: *Jazz makes it possible for you to connect two or more labels.*

Examples 11 through 13 demonstrate the usefulness of merging cell entries into one cell and, if desired, adding additional text. This procedure is known as concatenation. The ampersand (&) is used as the concatenation operator and double quotes serve to bracket a literal label string.

Example 11: In this example, we have concatenated two separate cell entries

(Laurie; cell A5) and (Einstein; cell B5) into one entry (Laurie Einstein; cell F28) with a space inserted between the two names. Without the space, cell F28 would read "LaurieEinstein," and the notation would be =A5&B5. Only the ampersand can be used to concatenate text entries. If you mistakenly use a plus, for example, Jazz returns ERR. You will also get ERR if you try to concatenate a text entry with a numeric entry or with the value of an empty cell.

Example 12: SUBSTR returns the characters in a text entry, starting at the specified position and for the number of characters you specify. In this example, we have extracted the substring "Jazz" from cell F23 by starting at the seventh character (remember, the first character is zero) and continuing for a length of four characters. We then concatenated this substring ("Jazz") with a literal label string (" is No.1"). The result of this procedure is displayed in F29 ("Jazz is No.1").

Example 13: This last example uses three previously defined text functions to modify and concatenate text strings from two cells, with the results displayed in F30. It is very easy to nest functions, and doing so offers flexibility and increased capability in dealing with text functions.

3.31 Tip: *Use text formulas to replicate label entries from an input area to an output report area.*

It is often advantageous to set aside separate work areas for data entry and reporting. Let's say that two of the entries in the entry area are for State and Region, and you have assigned them corresponding range names. The formula =STATE&"−"&REGION can be entered to merge these two entry fields together in one output field.

If you were to enter California in the STATE field and West Coast for REGION, the result of this formula would be the string "California-West Coast."

3.32 Tip: *Use the =NA function as a placeholder in your worksheet when you are unable to enter a value that a formula is dependent on.*

This function is used to place the notation "NA" in a cell when you have formulas that reference that cell, but the cell isn't ready to provide the needed data. Without this convention, ERR would appear in all dependent cells. When appropriate, the NA can be replaced with a real value and all dependent formulas will recalculate. Figure 3-20 demonstrates the usefulness of this function in the context of an inventory-tracking application. Rows 1 through 7 track current inventory levels. A code is

LOGICAL FUNCTIONS

	A	B	C	D	E
1		LILL'S DRESS SHOP INVENTORY			
2	Style #	Reorder Qty	# in Stock	Reorder Code	$ Per Item
3	--------------	--------------	--------	--------------	--------
4	254	3	2	1	$39.95
5	601	5	5	1	$72.50
6	788	8	12	0	$25.89
7				=IF(C8<=B8,1,0)	
8	==============	==============	========	==============	========
9		ORDER SHEET			
10	Style #	$ Per Item	# Ordered	Total Cost	
11	--------------	--------------	--------	--------------	
12	254	$39.95	4	$159.80	
13	601	$72.50	2	$145.00	
14	NA	NA		$0.00	
15					
16	Formula (A12-A14)	Formula(B12-B14)		Formula(D12-D14)	
17	=IF(D8=1,A8,NA)	=IF(A17>0,E8,NA)		=MAX(0,C17*B17)	

Figure 3-20. Using the NA function as a placeholder

displayed in column D: 1=need to reorder because current stock quantity is not sufficient, 0=sufficient quantity. Rows 11 through 16 represent an actual order sheet with formulas keyed to the inventory list according to the reorder code (0 or 1) entered in column D. If the logical functions in A16 and B16 result in the false case, "NA" is returned instead of a number value. This convention is often used because 0 can be a valid numeric entry.

If you aren't careful, the "NA" option will propogate itself through a string of formulas. Consider the formula entered in D16: =MAX(0,C16∗B16). Without the =MAX function, the formula =C16∗B16 would return a result of ERR (error) because multiplying a number by NA always results in ERR. The =MAX function ignores blank cells and assigns a value of 0 to all text cells. A number multiplied by a 0 equals 0, and the ERR result is avoided.

3.33 Tip: *You can create a generic error-checking formula to check for errors anywhere in a worksheet.*

A single formula can assess whether there are errors anywhere in your worksheet. Assign one range name to account for all active cells in a particular worksheet (such as "BONUS"). Then enter the formula =IF(ISERR(SUM(BONUS)),"ERROR", "NO ERROR").

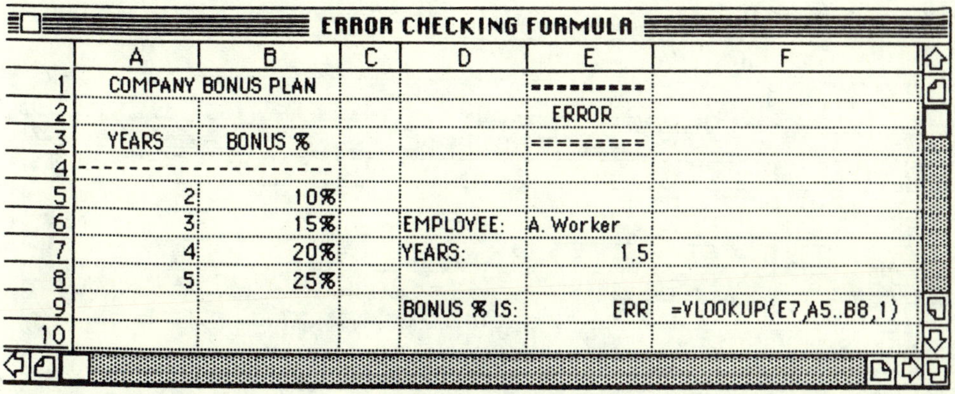

Figure 3-21. Generic error-checking formula for detecting errors anywhere in the worksheet

This formula is entered in cell E2 of the worksheet in Figure 3-21. Notice the "ERROR" message displayed, referring to the result in F9. In this case the formula entered in F9 returned an ERR because the lookup wasn't successful: the lowest possible value is not accounted for in the lookup table (1.5 years referenced in E7 and the lowest value in the table is 2 years).

Using an error-flagging formula like this can be particularly important when developing large worksheets that contain several formulas.

Calendar Functions

3.34 **Tip:** *If you enter dates and times correctly, Jazz will store them as special kinds of numbers. You can then do arithmetic with them or use them in conditional tests.*

Figure 3-22 shows a project-planning worksheet. You can see the length of time allocated for each task (column D, the DAYS column) and the slack time available between any pair of tasks, where the following one is dependent on the previous one (column E). As the Contents box shows, the =DATE function has been used to enter dates in columns C and E. (See the *Jazz Handbook* for the detailed rules on using this function.) When you enter dates in this way, Jazz actually stores each one as a serial number that represents the number of days elapsed since December 31, 1899. (Jazz returns an ERR, however, if you attempt to enter a date earlier than December 31, 1903.)

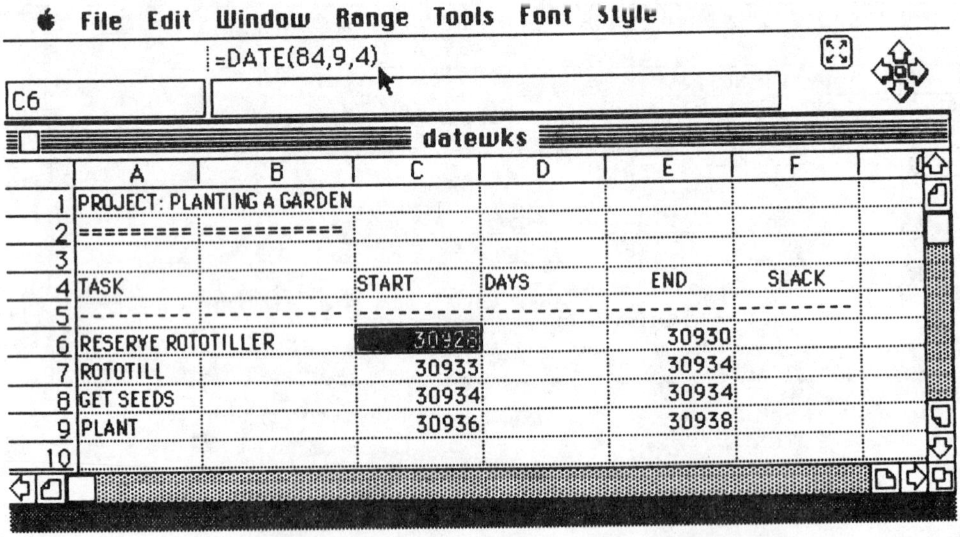

File Edit Window Range Tools Font Style

C6 =DATE(84,9,4)

datewks

	A	B	C	D	E	F
1	PROJECT: PLANTING A GARDEN					
2	=========	===========				
3						
4	TASK		START	DAYS	END	SLACK
5	---------	-----------	---------	---------	---------	---------
6	RESERVE ROTOTILLER		30928		30930	
7	ROTOTILL		30933		30934	
8	GET SEEDS		30934		30934	
9	PLANT		30936		30938	
10						

Figure 3-22. Project planning worksheet showing serial numbers returned by Jazz calendar functions

You can see from Figure 3-22 that Jazz has stored the =DATE(84,9,4) we entered into C6 as the serial number 30928. Storing dates in this way makes it possible to use them in formulas. However, we certainly don't want these dates to display as serial

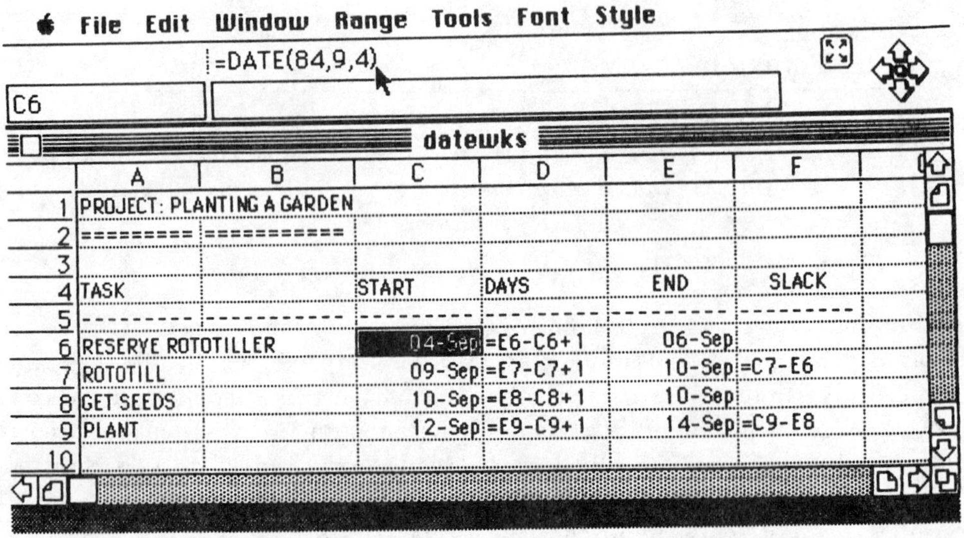

File Edit Window Range Tools Font Style

C6 =DATE(84,9,4)

datewks

	A	B	C	D	E	F
1	PROJECT: PLANTING A GARDEN					
2	=========	===========				
3						
4	TASK		START	DAYS	END	SLACK
5	---------	-----------	---------	---------	---------	---------
6	RESERVE ROTOTILLER		04-Sep	=E6-C6+1	06-Sep	
7	ROTOTILL		09-Sep	=E7-C7+1	10-Sep	=C7-E6
8	GET SEEDS		10-Sep	=E8-C8+1	10-Sep	
9	PLANT		12-Sep	=E9-C9+1	14-Sep	=C9-E8
10						

Figure 3-23. Formulas to compute number of days for each task and slack time (Formula Text display option)

numbers, since numbers like 30928 don't usually mean much to anybody. Therefore, as soon as we completed these entries, we used Range Format to format both column C and column E with the DD-MMM date format. Figure 3-23 shows the result; now we have a display format that lets us see what dates we're dealing with.

Figure 3-23 also shows the formulas we've now entered into columns D and F to compute the number of days we have for each task and the slack time available between tasks where a dependency exists. We've temporarily formatted columns D and F with the Formula Text option so we can see what all the formulas in these columns look like. Note that the formulas in column D subtract the start date for a particular task from the corresponding end date and then add 1 to get the total inclusive days from the beginning of the task to the end. The formulas in column F subtract the end date of the controlling task from the start date of the dependent task to determine the number of slack days available between these two tasks. In Figure 3-24 we've set the format on columns D and F back to General to show the results of the calendar formulas.

You can express not only days, but also the time of day, using the Jazz serial date number scheme. Suppose you were to add 0.5 to the serial date number in C6 in Figure 3-24, resulting in the entry 30928.5. Jazz would interpret this as noon on September 4, 1984, resulting in a value of 2.5 instead of 3 for the total days for that task

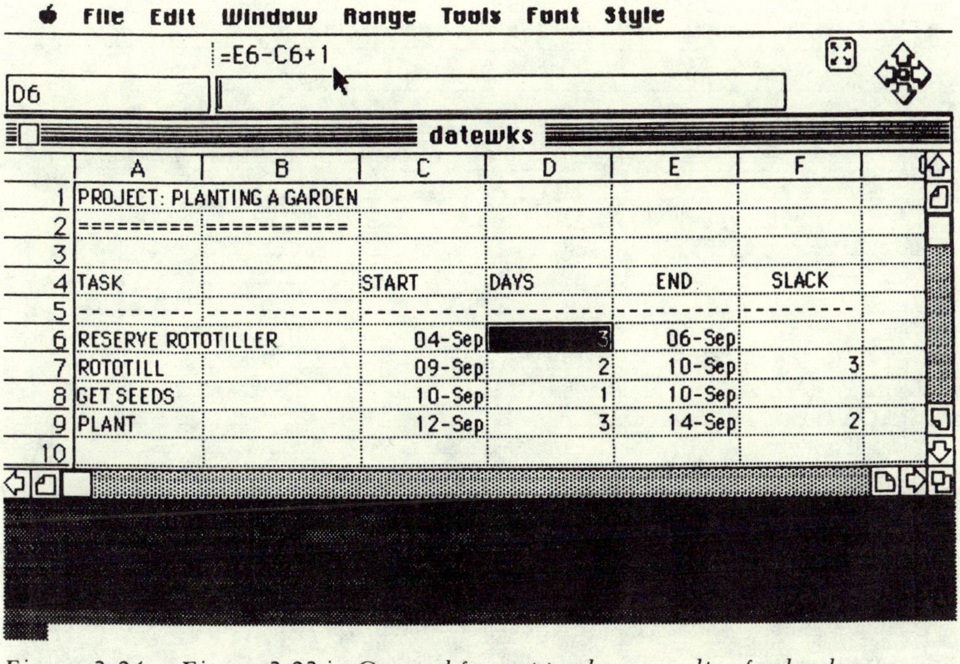

Figure 3-24: Figure 3-23 in General format to show results of calendar functions

(cell D6). You could format this cell to show the time of day in any one of four time formats that Jazz allows. (See the *Jazz Handbook* for details. But see also the following Trap.)

You can also use Jazz serial date numbers in conditional tests. Suppose you want to construct a formula that compares the two dates in C6 and E1 in Figure 3-25. You could use this to create a kind of "tickler" formula to signal when it's time to start a particular task. The formula might look like =IF(C6=E1,"RESERVE ROTOTILLER!","RELAX").

When the two dates become equal, the text "RESERVE ROTOTILLER" will display in the cell; otherwise, the text "RELAX" will display. You must be careful in such comparisons, however. In order for two serial date numbers to compare as exactly equal, they must be the same in their fractional portion as well as in their whole number portion. For instance, 31227.337 (7:22 A.M. on June 30, 1985) will not compare as equal with 31227 (0:00 A.M. on June 30, 1985).

3.35 Trap: *Don't expect to be able to format a particular cell for both date and time at once.*

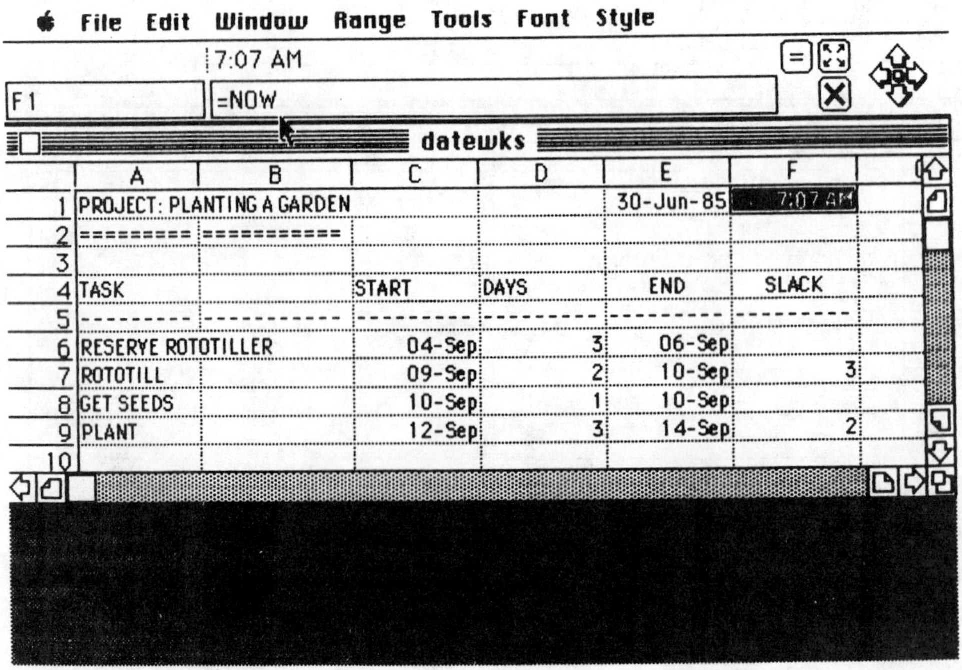

Figure 3-25. "Tickler" formula to signal when to start a particular task

As you saw in the previous Tip, Jazz lets you format a cell containing a serial date number in one of four date formats or one of four time formats. But what if you want to show both the date and the time? You can't do both in one cell. There is, however, a simple technique that will get you what you want in most cases. Usually you want to show both the date and time only when you're trying to show exactly when you created a particular document. In fact, it's a good idea to form this habit for every document that you create; that way you can always tell from the printed copy which version you're dealing with. As the Contents box in Figure 3-26 shows, cell E1 contains the =NOW function, which results in a serial number giving the current date and time. Cell F1 also contains the same =NOW function. However, we've formatted E1 using a date format and F1 using a time format. This gives us both the current date and time, even though it took us two different cells to get them. But see Trap 3.37 for more related to the =NOW function.

3.36 Tip: *If you enter dates and times as text in one of the allowable Jazz date or time formats, Jazz will both enter the proper serial date number and format the cell with the format you've used on entry.*

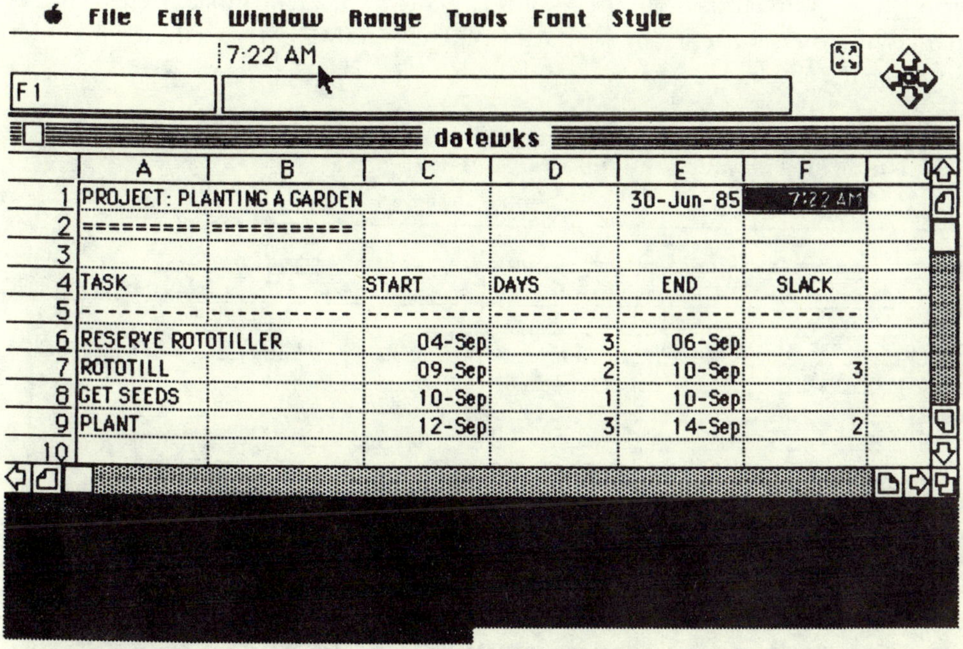

Figure 3-26. *Time entry in cell F1 taken as text entry because it was not entered using the TIME function*

The first Tip in this section describes the use of the =DATE function for the entry of dates as serial numbers. You can also use the =TIME function to enter a particular time of day. However, it's usually quicker and easier to simply enter the date or time in one of the allowable Jazz formats. This relieves you of having to format the cell (or range of cells) in a separate step. Suppose, for instance, that you want to enter the date September 4th this way. You could enter it as 4-Sep, and Jazz would treat it as a serial date number and format the cell with the DD-MMM date format.

Be careful when using this date and time entry method, however. If you enter just the day and month, as in our example (4-Sep), Jazz will assume the current year; make sure that this is what you want. If you enter a time without specifying AM or PM, Jazz will assume you're using the 24-hour format. (For example, if you enter 11:00, Jazz will assume 11:00 A.M.) This method has its drawbacks when you wish to edit a date or time entry later and turn the entry into an arithmetic expression. Why? Consider cell F1 in Figure 3-26. The time has been entered here as 7:22 AM (one of the Jazz allowable time formats); Jazz converts this into a serial date number and formats the cell accordingly. But then suppose you want to edit the cell and add 0.5 to it to change the entry from 7:22 AM to 7:22 PM. If you had entered this time originally, using the =TIME function (=TIME(7,22,0)) or simply as a "raw" serial date number (.3069444), you could edit it in this way without any problem. But if you try that here, Jazz converts the entry into a text entry instead of performing the calendar arithmetic we wanted, as in Figure 3-27. As a general rule, remember, if you want to edit date and time entries later, use the =DATE or =TIME entry method when you first make the entry.

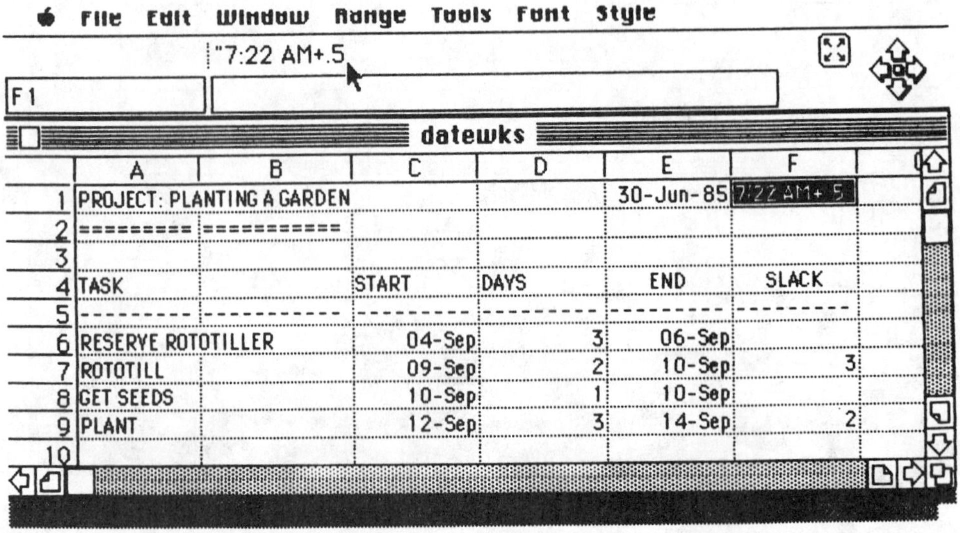

Figure 3-27. Time entry in cell F1 is text and can't be successfully edited

Finally, the shortcut method we're discussing has one more drawback: If you mistakenly enter the wrong format, Jazz accepts the entry as text instead of as a serial date number. For instance, entering 7:22AM without a space between the 7:22 and the AM results in a text entry, not a serial date number.

3.37 Trap: *If your Macintosh clock is not set correctly, the =NOW function will not return the correct result.*

The Jazz =NOW function gets the current date and time from the Macintosh clock. This clock can become inaccurate because of a low battery and time changes to and from daylight savings time. See your Macintosh manual for instructions on how to reset the clock and replace its battery. You should also be aware that if you are in Manual recalculation mode, cells containing the =NOW function will not be brought up to date unless you recalculate.

3.38 Tip: *You can easily convert a serial date number into years, hours, minutes, or seconds.*

A serial date number represents a certain number of days and a fraction thereof. Suppose you have the serial date number 31227 in cell E1 of a worksheet. (This is the serial date number for June 30, 1985, and represents the number of days from December 31, 1899, until that date.) You could convert this number of days into other time units as follows:

- From days to years by dividing by 365.25
- From days to hours by multiplying by 24
- From days to minutes by multiplying by 24*60
- From days to seconds by multiplying by 24*60*60.

3.39 Tip: *You can easily extract the year, month, day, hour, or minute by using the Jazz =YEAR, =MONTH, =DAY, =HOUR, or =MINUTE functions to reference a cell containing a serial date number.*

Cells C12 through C16 in Figure 3-28 contain formulas that show examples of the

datewks

	A	B	C	D	E	F
1	PROJECT: PLANTING A GARDEN				30-Jun-85	7:22 AM
2	=========	===========				
3						
4	TASK		START	DAYS	END	SLACK
5	---------	-----------	---------	---------	---------	---------
6	RESERVE ROTOTILLER		04-Sep	3	06-Sep	
7	ROTOTILL		09-Sep	2	10-Sep	3
8	GET SEEDS		10-Sep	1	10-Sep	
9	PLANT		12-Sep	3	14-Sep	2
10						
11						
12		=YEAR(E1)	85			
13		=MONTH(E1)	6			
14		=DAY(E1)	30			
15		=HOUR(E1)	8			
16		=MINUTE(E1)	52			

Figure 3-28. Examples of date functions

use of these functions; they all refer to the serial date number in E1. (Column B contains text labels that identify the corresponding formulas in column C.) This ability to extract any component of the date or time from a serial date number can be useful in a number of different circumstances. See the following Tip for an example.

Note that the point here is to pick out the particular time unit (year, month, day, hour, minute, or second) that forms a component of the serial date number in question. The method described in the previous Tip has a different purpose: to compute the *total count* of a particular time unit represented by the serial date number in question.

3.40 Tip: *You can use =DATE, =YEAR, =MONTH, and =DAY to construct columns of dates in MMM-YY format that cross yearly boundaries.*

It's common to want to construct a table like the one shown in Figure 3-29, where the formula entered in row 48 of the Date column and copied down to all subsequent rows makes an automatic transition from one year to another. The Entry box at the top of the figure shows what that formula looks like. (Where the arrow at the top of the figure is pointing, there is actually a + sign following the MONTH(B47) at the end of the first line in the Entry box. For some reason, Jazz doesn't make the Entry

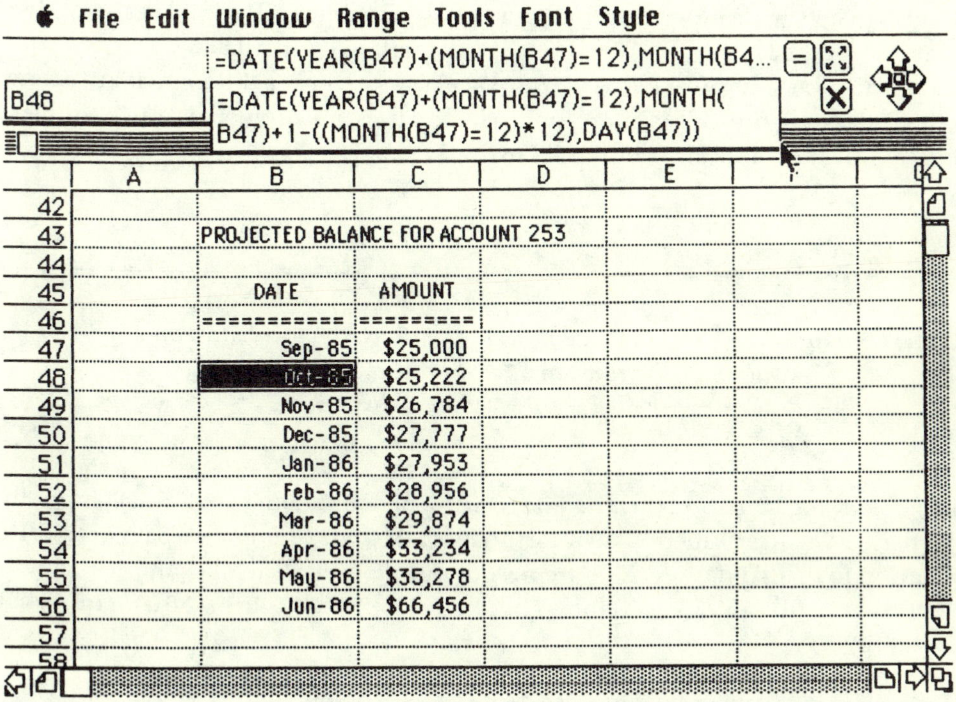

Figure 3-29. *Column of dates constructed using dates that cross yearly boundaries*

box large enough to display this, though it is there in the cell.) The encompassing function here is the =DATE function; this function takes three arguments: the year, the month, and the day. In this case, we're using the =YEAR, =MONTH, and =DAY extraction functions to extract those components of the date in the previous row.

For the first argument of =DATE (the year portion), we supply the expression YEAR(B47)+(MONTH(B47)=12). When the previous row's month is anything other than December, the (MONTH(B47)=12) part of this expression is false and therefore zero, resulting in a year argument the same as that of the previous row. But when the previous row's month is December (month 12), (MONTH(B47)=12) is true and therefore equal to 1, resulting in a year argument 1 greater than that of the previous row. The MONTH(B47)+1−((MONTH(B47)=12)*12) expression uses similar logic to make sure that the month argument for the current row is always one greater than the previous row's month, except when the previous row's month is December. Finally, the last argument of the =DATE function is DAY(B47), supplying a day exactly equal to that of the previous row.

If the day of the first row is less than 29, this formula will always work. But if that day is 29 or greater, you may generate some incorrect dates. The best solution in a case like this (where we really don't care about the day portion at all) would be to supply a 1 in place of the DAY (B47). Then the formula will work in all cases.

If you need to have each row of your Date column show a different day in a long series of days crossing one or more month boundaries, the problem is much simpler. Simply construct a formula of this form: B47+1.

Data Range Functions

3.41 Tip: *Using Data Range functions, you can get statistics on a subset of the rows in a worksheet table without having to transfer the data into a Database document.*

The Data Range functions are the Jazz equivalent of the Lotus 1-2-3 and Symphony Database Statistical functions. Unfortunately, the *Jazz Handbook* pays very little attention to them, but they are extremely useful. Let's look at an example that will show some of the options available. The range A3. . F8 in Figure 3-30 contains what

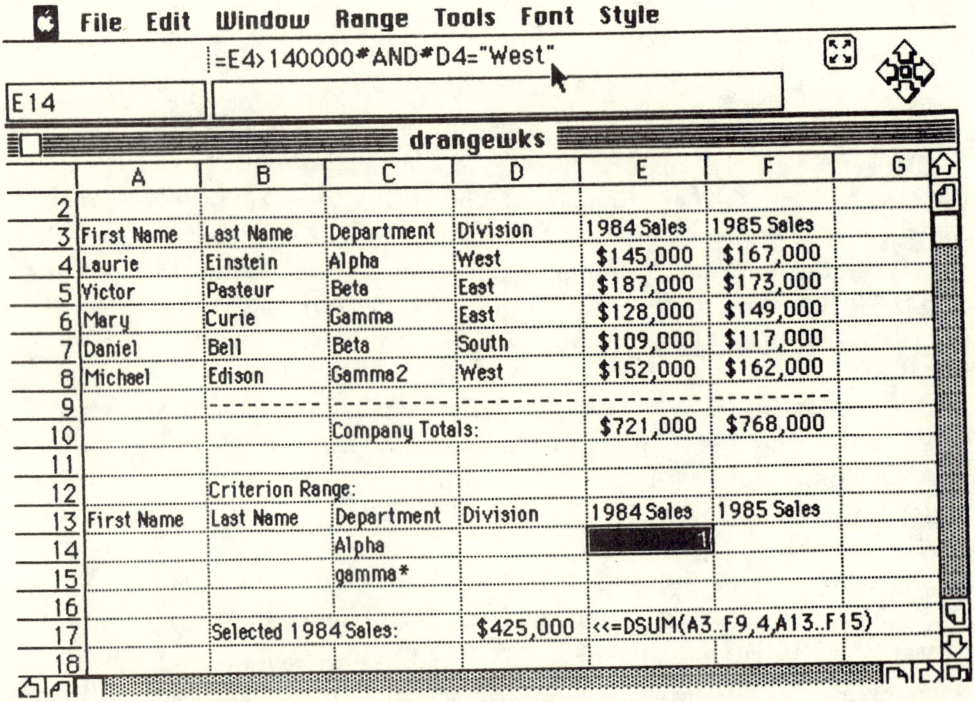

Figure 3-30. Using data range functions

is really a small database, though it resides in a Worksheet document; Jazz calls this area an Input Range for Data Range function purposes. If you set up what's called a Criterion Range that matches one or more fields in the Input Range, you'll have all the elements you need to construct Data Range formulas.

We created the Criterion Range shown in A13..F15 in Figure 3-30 by copying the row of field names from the top of the Input Range (A3..F3) to A13. (Though in this example we've included every field in the Criterion Range that existed in the original Input Range, you're free to include any combination of fields in the Criterion Range in any order, so long as you use exactly the same column titles as in the Input Range. The simplest Criterion Range would contain only one field.)

We left room for three criterion records below row 13, though in this example we'll use only two. In each criterion record, you can place a criterion in one or more cells. As Figure 3-30 shows, here we've placed three different criteria in two different records. Each of these criteria limits in some way the records from the Input Range that will be used in the computations performed by whatever Data Range functions we construct that refer to this Input Range and this Criterion Range. Cell D17 contains an =DSUM Data Range function that's designed to show the total sales produced by salespersons that satisfy the criteria specified in the Criterion Range. These three criteria are intended to select the records that satisfy the following rule: select all records for Department Alpha for which 1984 Sales were greater than $140,000 and the salesperson was in the West Division; also select all records for Departments beginning with "gamma".

The text label in E17 shows the formula that we've placed in cell D17 to get the total 1984 Sales for all records that are selected by the criteria in the Criterion Range. Let's look at the effect of each of the criteria in turn and then try to see why we get a result of $425,000 in D17:

1. The criterion in C14 is a simple value criterion. The value you enter as a value criterion may be either numeric or text, but must refer to the value of the field whose title in the Input Range agrees with the title of the cell in the Criterion Range in which you place it. The result of this criterion is that so far you're looking for all records with Alpha in the Department field; this includes only the record on row 4.

2. The criterion in E14 is a formula criterion. A formula criterion must begin with an = sign or a number, and it can be a complex expression, as in our example. Formula criterion can refer to cells in the Input Range with titles other than the criterion cell in which it resides. Note also that a formula criterion refers to a column in the Input Range by addressing the cell in that column immediately below the title. The formula criterion in E14 thus addresses columns D and E by referring to cells D4 and E4. The result of this criterion is that we're looking for all records for which 1984 Sales are greater than 140000 for those salespersons in the West Division. By placing this criterion on the same row as that in C14, we're telling Jazz that they both have to

be satisfied at once. In other words, so far we're looking only for those salespersons from Alpha Department in the West Division whose 1984 Sales exceeded 140000. If you look closely at the original Input Range, you'll see that Laurie Einstein is the only one who satisfies all these conditions. But we're not done yet.

3. The second criterion record in the Criterion Range (row 15) introduces a new concept. Jazz Data Range functions select the records for each criterion record independently of all others and then put them all together to get the total set of records selected. This last criterion results in the selection of all records in the Input Range that begin with "gamma" and end with any string of characters. This includes the records in rows 6 and 8 of the Input Range. Note that Jazz ignores case in comparing criteria against the values in the Input Range, so that "gamma" is equivalent to "Gamma". (The asterisk at the end of the entry in C15 is called a *wildcard character* and means "any string of characters." Jazz also allows you to use the question mark (?) wildcard character to specify that you're willing to accept any character in a given position. See the Database chapter for more information on wildcard characters.) When you add the two records from Departments Gamma and Gamma2 to Laurie Einstein's record selected by the first two criteria in combination, you have the total set selected by the Data Range formula in D17. If you add up the 1984 Sales for these three records, you'll get the $425,000 shown in D17 in Figure 3-30.

3.42 Trap: *If you're not careful, there are a number of ways that you can go wrong in using Data Range functions.*

Here are some of the things to watch for:

1. You will probably get incorrect results if any of the column titles in the Criterion Range are not spelled exactly the same as the corresponding column titles in the Input Range. The safest procedure is to copy the titles from the Input Range rather than re-enter them at the top of the Criterion Range.

2. The Data Range functions may not work correctly if the Input Range column titles aren't in the row immediately above the first data row in the Input Range. For the database in Figure 3-30, for example, a row of underlines or dashes between the titles in row 3 and the first data row in row 4 would confuse the Data Range functions and yield incorrect results.

3. Make sure that you include the Input Range titles row in the Input Range you specify and the Criterion Range titles row in the Criterion Range you specify; only then do the Data Range functions know where these title rows are.

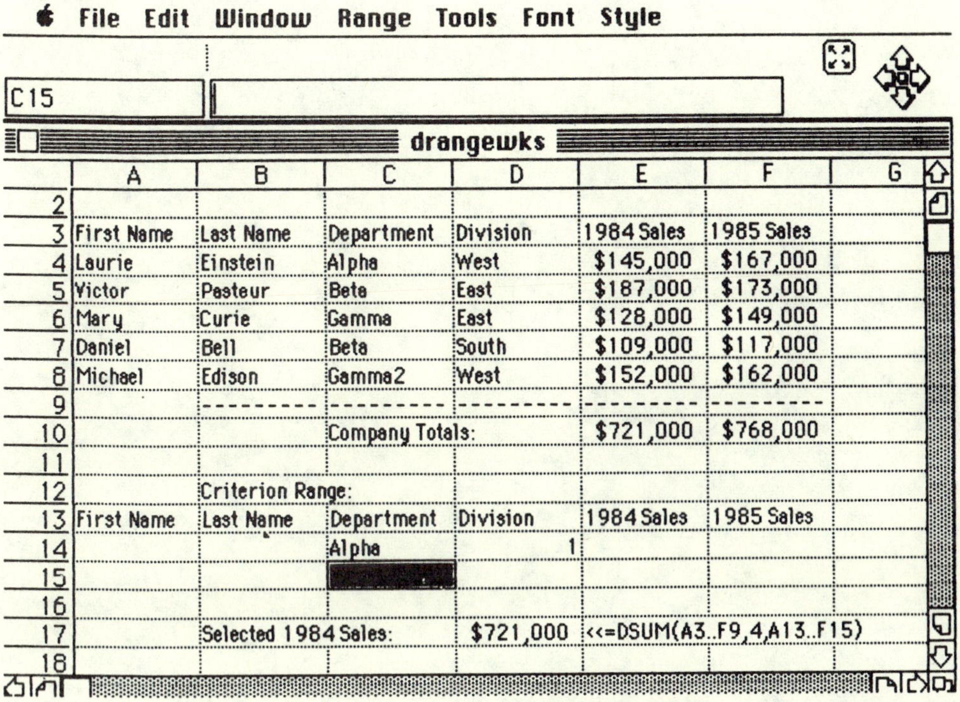

Figure 3-31. Totally empty row in Criterion Range causes all records to be selected

4. Make sure that the data rows included in the Input Range and the data rows included in the Criterion Range cover all the ones you want.

5. Be aware of the fact that a totally empty row in a Criterion Range will cause all records to be selected, regardless of what criteria appear in the other rows. This means, for instance, that you shouldn't specify your Criterion Range as having more than one row unless you intend to place criteria in those other rows. (If we make row 15 in the Criterion Range in our example empty, as in Figure 3-31, the result is that all records are selected, as a comparison between D17 and E10 shows.) This could be called the "universal criterion trap."

6. Don't forget that the Input Range column offset number you supply as the second argument to all Data Range functions must be counted from the first column in the Input Range as column 0.

7. If you don't begin a formula criterion with an = sign or a number, you'll enter a text label instead of a formula.

8. When you refer to literal text in a formula criterion, as in E14 of Figure 3-30, don't forget to bracket it with double quotes; otherwise, Jazz will inform you, quite rightly, that the formula is invalid.

4

Database

We are all familiar with databases. A database is simply an organized collection of information, so the phone book, a box of recipes, and your checkbook all qualify as databases. Because the information in each collection is specific and organized in a particular way, the database becomes a valuable tool for keeping information.

Jazz lets you create electronic databases that not only store information but also retrieve it and organize it in different ways.

In this chapter, the earlier Tips and Traps focus specifically on techniques you use to set up your database. Subsequent sections introduce advanced features, including those that allow you to extract specific information by using Jazz's Query, Sort, and Report functions, and control data entry through the Form function.

See Chapter 2, The Worksheet Environment, for Tips relating to entering and editing data. Chapter 3 contains information on the formulas and functions that can be used in the database.

Getting Started

4.01 Tip: *In planning a database, the clearer you are on what you want to get from it, the easier it is to set up.*

A handy way to begin thinking about a database is to envision what you want to get from it. The Jazz database can store large amounts of different kinds of data. It can selectively report on that data and also perform computations on it. By thinking carefully about what you may want to know, you can begin to define the fields of your database.

Figure 4-1 shows a sample database that records and reports sales. Each column, called a *field,* contains information of only one kind. The ten fields here were chosen to contain the kind of information helpful in running a sales organization. Notice that the Order field contains only the numbers of the sales orders, the Date field only contains dates, and so forth. Strictly adhering to this principle is what makes a database useful.

Each row in the database is called a *record.* In our example, each record represents the details of one sale. Once the fields are defined, the appropriate data is simply typed into each cell to complete a record for every sale.

It is important to note that some fields are used simply to store information, while others, such as the Total and Margin fields in our example, contain formulas that compute the contents of other fields.

	Order	Date	Company	Cnslt	Product	Price	Cost	Quan	Total	Margin
1	1006	6/22/85	Net 1	SK	Jazz	$415.00	$365.00	6	$2,490.00	12.05%
2	1007	6/23/85	Merrill Lynch	JR	Sideways	$49.00	$26.00	2	$98.00	46.94%
3	1007	6/23/85	Merrill Lynch	JR	1-2-3	$290.00	$265.00	1	$290.00	8.62%
4	1008	6/24/85	New Wave Corp.	DK	Jazz	$415.00	$365.00	1	$415.00	12.05%
5	1009	6/25/85	G.E.	GM	1-2-3	$290.00	$265.00	10	$2,900.00	8.62%
6	1010	6/24/85	Net 1	SK	1-2-3	$290.00	$265.00	8	$2,320.00	8.62%
7	1011	6/25/85	G.E.	GM	Sideways	$49.00	$26.00	2	$98.00	46.94%
8	1012	6/24/85	Net 1	SK	dBase III	$400.00	$325.00	10	$4,000.00	18.75%
9	1013	6/26/85	Burroughs	MCK	dBase III	$400.00	$325.00	4	$1,600.00	18.75%
10	1014	6/26/85	Campbell Soup	MCK	Jazz	$415.00	$365.00	5	$2,075.00	12.05%
11	1015	6/26/85	G.E.	GM	dBase III	$400.00	$325.00	2	$800.00	18.75%
12	1016	6/27/85	New Wave Corp.	DK	dBase III	$400.00	$325.00	4	$1,600.00	18.75%
13	1017	6/27/85	Campbell Soup	MCK	Sideways	$49.00	$26.00	6	$294.00	46.94%
14	1018	6/21/85	Merrill Lynch	JR	1-2-3	$290.00	$265.00	3	$870.00	8.62%

Figure 4-1. Sales Order database

4.02 Tip: *Make a paper mock-up of the database you want to create before actually creating a Jazz Database document.*

Before creating a database on the computer, it may be helpful to write out the fields on a piece of paper. Write down every category of information that is important, including fields containing computations that involve other categories, such as those that calculate profit by subtracting price from cost, as in Figure 4-2.

It's also helpful to note the format in which the data should appear: currency, number of decimal points, and percent. Figure 4-1 shows that the Order field has been formatted to center text; the Price, Cost, and Total fields to show numbers as currency with two decimal places; and the Margin field to show decimal numbers as percents.

Notice that the fields Total and Margin are *computed fields.* For example, the Total field multiplies the data in the Quantity field by the data in the Price field. The Margin field computes the profit margin on each sale using Price and Cost information.

You can have up to 100 fields in each record, but because each field takes up memory and thus limits the potential size of the database, you should be careful to only create fields that serve a purpose.

4.03 Tip: *Make the first field of your database a sequence number field.*

Creating the first field in a database to hold numbers in sequence can prove useful in several situations.

When a database is sorted, the original order is altered. In some cases it is important to recover the original order. If you enter a sequence number in the first field at the same time as you enter the rest of the data, you will be able to sort on that sequence to recover the original order.

Another use for a sequence number field is to tip you off to accidentally deleted records as well as duplicates. It can also be useful in referring to the record in formulas if you copy database information to a worksheet for calculations. Refer to Chapter 8 for more information.

In case it isn't convenient to use a numeric sequence field, an alternative method to preserve the original order is to save the database every time you add new records and do any tasks involving sorting afterward. If the sorted version needs to be kept, it can be saved under a new name. Be careful to use the Save As option to rename the sorted version if you want to save it. Using Save replaces the original file with the sorted one.

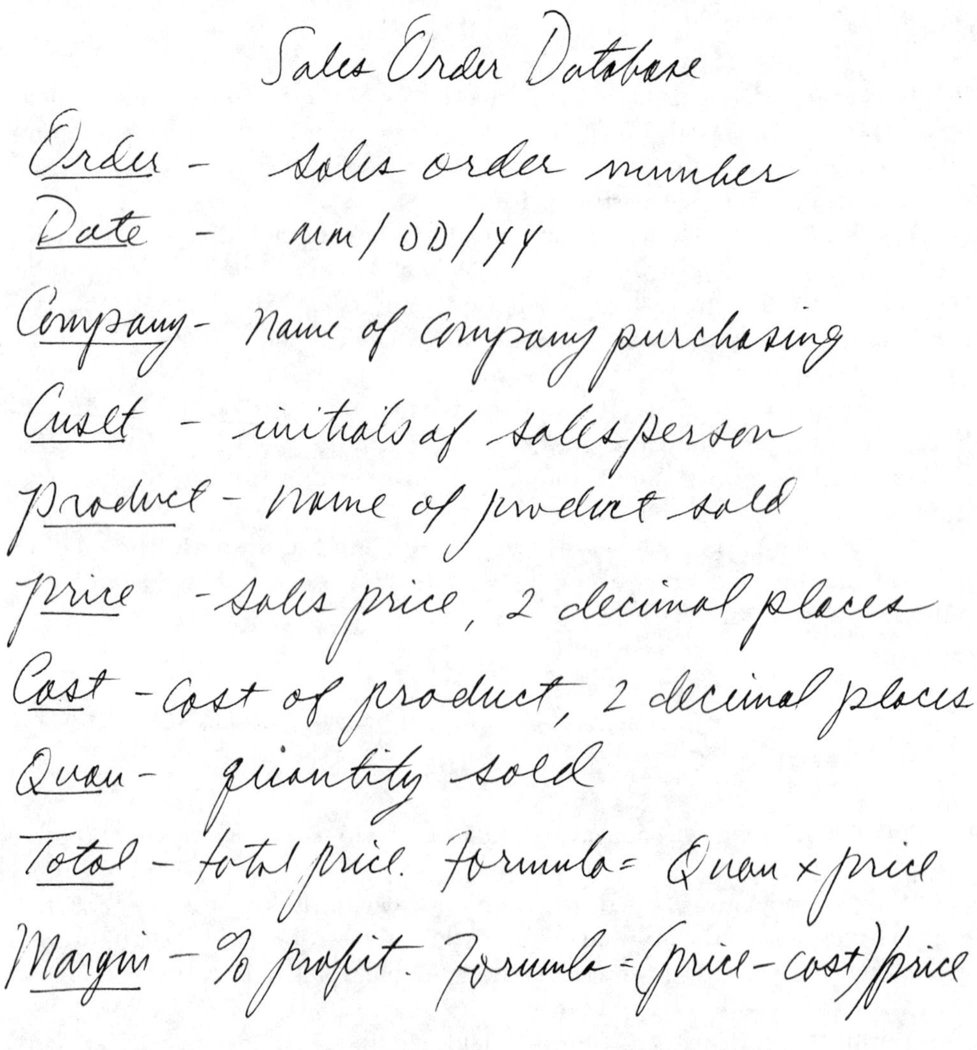
Sales Order Database
Order - sales order number
Date - MM/DD/YY
Company - Name of company purchasing
Cust - initials of salesperson
Product - name of product sold
Price - sales price, 2 decimal places
Cost - cost of product, 2 decimal places
Quan - quantity sold
Total - total price. Formula = Quan x price
Margin - % profit. Formula = (price - cost)/price

Figure 4-2. Beginning to create a database

4.04 Tip: *To get a quick picture of what a database looks like, assign descriptive field names before worrying about assigning any of the other field attributes.*

Sometimes you haven't planned your database completely but want to get a quick view of what it might look like. When you open a new database document, you are immediately presented with the Field Attribute box, which lets you give each field a name, as well as assign other attributes. You can type in the name of the first field, click on Add Another Field, type in the name of the next field, and so on. In this way you can create a database very quickly.

It's helpful to use names that represent clearly the contents of the field. Leaving the first field named Field 1, for example, would probably not help to remind you of its contents.

If you type a character that Jazz isn't able to use in a field name, you will hear a beep.

To go to the next field, select Add Another Field. Thus you can quickly create your database fields without having to worry about all the details.

After entering the last field name, selecting Done takes you to the first record of your new database for data entry.

When you have named the fields and viewed the database, go back and use the Edit menu to select the other attributes and formats. See the following Tip:

4.05 Tip: *Change the attributes of your fields after you have created them by selecting the field name and choosing Field Attributes from the Edit menu.*

In the Field Attributes dialog box (Figure 4-3), Check Entry Format allows data to be entered in a field only in the chosen format. Selecting Use Formula allows you to type a formula to perform computations in the field. Locked prevents any new entry or change to existing data in the field. Typing in the Initial Value box places the same value in every record; the Display Width box sets the width of the field. See individual Tips for more details.

To go from one selection to another in the Field Attributes box without causing Jazz to accept the box as Done, use the mouse to select the next portion or use the TAB key. If you press the RETURN or ENTER key, you may move to the next field or return to the database before you are ready.

4.06 Tip: *Help maintain the accuracy of your data by using the Check Entry Format option.*

When entering data, it's easy to make errors, and it's often not so easy to catch them. For instance, you might confuse which field you're in and put a text entry in a field

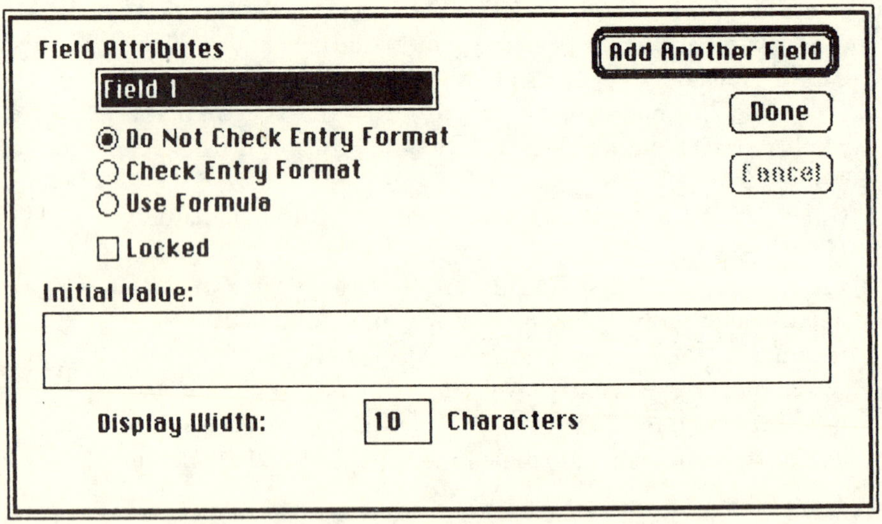

Figure 4-3. Using the Field Attributes dialog box

for numbers, or use an incorrect date or time format. If Check Entry Format has been selected, you will be unable to enter information in a different format from the one you have assigned to the field. Instead, you will get a beep and a message.

Jazz can't prevent you from entering inaccurate information, but at least it can help you be sure it is the right type.

4.07 Tip: *Protect valuable data from being changed by using the Locked option.*

When you select Locked in the Field Attributes box, you are prevented from changing any data already in the specific field or from entering data in that field in new records. If you try, Jazz alerts you with a beep and a message. By clicking again on Locked, you can release the protection.

4.08 Tip: *If the same value is repeated in many records, enter it as an initial value in the Field Attributes box to place it in each record automatically.*

Sometimes a field in many records may contain the same information. For example, every person in a name and address database for mailing might be in the same state, or all employees might work in the same department. To avoid having to retype the information every time a new record is created, you can place the information in the Initial Value box when entering Field Attributes. Then whenever a record is created, the field is filled in automatically.

Be careful to type over the automatically entered data when there are exceptions. You can stop having the initial value added whenever you want by opening the Field Attributes box for that field and deleting the value. Records added after deleting the initial value will not contain the information, but previous records will retain it.

4.09 Tip: *You can use formulas and functions to create computed fields.*

You can assign a formula to a field by using the Field Attributes box. The database in Figure 4-1 contains formulas in the Total and the Margin fields. Below is the Field Attributes box for the Total field. The results of the computations appear in each record:

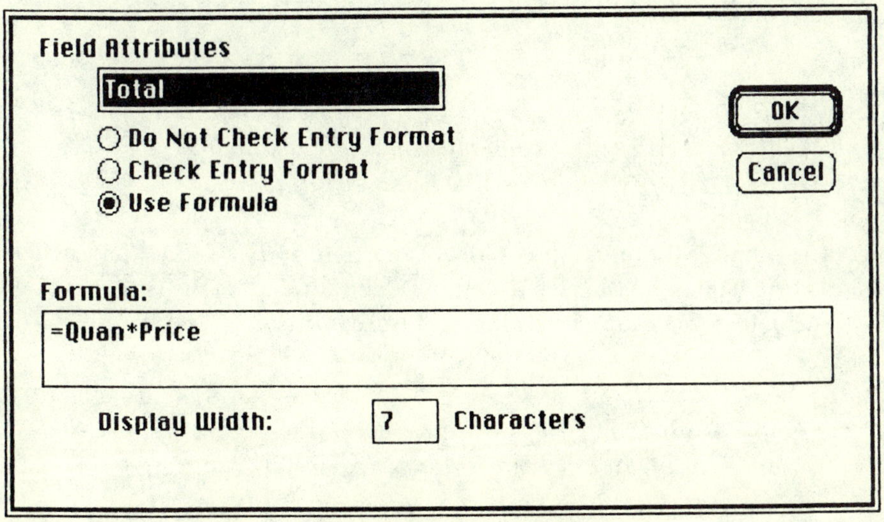

You can see that as in the worksheet, formulas begin with =. When Use Formula is selected, Jazz will not accept information in the formula box unless it is preceded by the equal sign. Jazz will also beep if the syntax of your formula is wrong. However, Jazz won't tell you if your formula is ill conceived or if you have included the wrong fields to compute. Those formulas that require a multicolumn or multi-row range as an argument (e.g. =VLOOKUP) cannot be used in a database because there's no way of specifying such a range. Refer to Chapter 3, Formulas and Functions, and the Report section of this chapter for more information on using formulas.

4.10 Tip: *You can change the appearance of your data to suit the needs of your application with Field Format options.*

You want to have numbers representing currency look like dollars and cents, text to be neatly aligned, and the data and time in the format you are accustomed to. After creating each field, you can control the format in which the data will appear by using Field Format in the Edit menu. The name of the field to be formatted must be selected (by clicking on the field name in the top margin) before Field Format is available in the Edit menu.

For many fields, the default text and number formats will probably be sufficient. However, centering text, making numbers appear as dollars and cents, or formatting for percent signs instead of just decimal numbers can make your database easier to use.

Pages 242 and 243 of the *Jazz Handbook* show all the format options.

4.11 Trap: *If you can't access Field Attributes or Field Format, it may be because you have not clicked on the field name.*

If you need to change the attributes or format of a field and find that Field Attributes and Field Format are not available to you in the Edit menu, make sure that you first click on the field name in the top margin of the database.

4.12 Trap: *If you don't create all your fields at the beginning, use the Edit menu to Insert or Add fields one at a time.*

It often is necessary to create new fields in a database, either inserting them between current fields or at the end. However, you can only do this one field at a time, which means you have to reselect Add Field or Insert Field from the Edit menu each time.

To add a new field at the end of a database, select Add Field from the edit menu. Jazz then presents you with the Field Attributes dialog box and when you are done, places the new field at the end of the database.

To insert a new field between existing database fields, first select the field heading *before* (to the right of) where you want the new field to go. Then select Insert Field from the Edit menu. Jazz presents the Field Attributes box and when you are done, inserts the new field before the selected field.

***4.13* Tip:** *When you want to see the full field name and contents displayed, assign a field display width that's at least as long as each.*

Field names can be up to 15 characters long. The contents of a field, however, can be up to 254 characters, and by changing the Field Display Width in the Field Attributes box you can see up to a full screen, about 65 characters.

Usually, you'd like to see both the full field name and the full field contents displayed on the screen. If, for instance, your order number only takes three characters, you probably want to make the field five characters wide so you can display the full field name. The default display width is 10 characters. Even at this width, you can still type up to 254 characters; though only 10 characters will display, the remainder are still being stored.

On the other hand, you might prefer to see as many fields as possible on the screen at once. In such a case, you might want to keep the display width at a minimum, even though your data has more characters. Narrow fields can be easier to work with because you can see more of your data, so you might not always want to set the display width as wide as the data.

The following Tip gives you a shortcut for widening or shrinking your field width.

***4.14* Tip:** *You can adjust the field width to optimum size without using the Field Attributes box.*

You can quickly widen or shrink field width directly from the database by placing the pointer on the field headings line at the top margin, exactly on the right border of the field heading box. The pointer changes to a horizontal double arrow crossed with a vertical bar. Dragging it in the desired direction changes the width. The width shown in the Field Attributes box is automatically adjusted.

There are several instances when you may want to widen or shrink field width. If the field name or contents won't display fully, you can widen them. Shrinking the field width to the smallest useful size also allows more fields to be displayed on the screen at one time.

4.15 Tip: *To add one or more empty records to a database, press COMMAND-N one or more times.*

When you have entered data in the last field in a record, you can't go on to the next new record until you add an empty one. Do this by choosing Add Record from the Edit menu or using COMMAND-N. Each time you do this, one new record is added.

4.16 Trap: *Creating too many empty records unnecessarily uses up valuable memory.*

Every record added, whether full or empty, uses up a little memory. It is best to add records only when you are placing information in them. See Chapter 1 for hints on memory management techniques useful throughout Jazz.

4.17 Tip: *You can enter data into database records by row or column by using the TAB and RETURN keys.*

The database structure is very similar to that of the worksheet; it is composed of columns and rows. The columns are the fields and the rows are the records. Filling in every cell in a row means one record has been completed.

As with the worksheet, what you type appears first in the entry box; then, when you press ENTER, RETURN, or TAB, or select another cell, the information appears in the active cell. However, your choice of entry method depends on which cell (field) you wish to be made active next.

To enter data in a record from left to right, use the TAB key. To enter data in a column, use the RETURN key. The SHIFT key used with TAB or RETURN reverses their direction. The ENTER key leaves the current cell active.

4.18 Tip: *You can edit cell contents by using the edit techniques that are common to every application.*

To replace the contents of a cell, just select it to make it active and type the new entry. Pressing ENTER, TAB, or RETURN, or clicking on another cell enters the cell's contents.

Double-clicking on a cell places its contents in the Entry box. There you can click to locate the insertion bar to insert new characters or use the BACKSPACE key to delete one character at a time. You can also point and drag to select characters to be replaced and then replace them simply by typing new ones or completely delete them by pressing the BACKSPACE key.

You can review in detail the different editing techniques by referring to Chapter 2, "The Worksheet Environment."

Changing Fields and Records

4.19 Tip: *To delete an existing field, select the field name at the top of the column and select Clear Field from the Edit menu.*

Jazz allows you to cut, copy or clear only one entire field — one column at a time — in your database. When you want to remove an entire field, selecting the field name and selecting Clear removes it from the database, including all the data in it. The fields to the right (if any) move in to take its place. If you mistakenly do this and haven't chosen another command or entered new information, you can select Undo Clear to bring the material back.

4.20 Tip: *To delete an entire record, click on the record number in the left margin and select Clear Record from the Edit menu.*

You can remove an entire record by clicking on its number in the left margin. The entire record will be selected; by choosing Clear, it will be removed, including all the data in it. By dragging across the record numbers, you can select many adjacent records and then clear them all at once. (You can't cut or clear all records or fields.)

Undo Clear can bring the data back if you haven't chosen another command or entered new information.

4.21 Tip: *You can select non-adjacent specific records for deletion by using the OPTION key and selecting the record numbers.*

You can select several records for deletion by pressing the OPTION key while clicking on the record number in the left margin. First select one record number; then press the OPTION key to select the others you wish to delete. The Clear Record command deletes all selected records from the database.

4.22 Trap: *Don't confuse Clear Record or Clear Field with Clear Value, or you may remove entire fields or records.*

To clear one value or a whole range of values, you can select them by dragging the pointer across the range containing them. Then you can use Clear Value to remove them. If you mistakenly select the field name or the row number, Clear Field or Clear Record will be presented in the Edit menu and you may mistakenly remove the entire field or record. If you make a mistake, the Undo command can reverse the Clear command if no other command has been chosen or data entered.

Before you use the Clear command, check to see if the Edit menu reads Clear Record to clear a record, Clear Field to clear a field, or Clear Value to clear cell contents.

4.23 Trap: *Jazz won't allow you to Cut or Clear all records in a database.*

Suppose you wanted to Cut or Clear an entire database. Choosing Select All and Cut or Clear would not work. In order to get around this,

1. Select the first record by clicking on its number.
2. Select Insert Record.
3. Choose Select All.

4. Press the OPTION key and click on the number of the new record. This deselects only that record.

5. Select Cut or Copy.

4.24 Trap: *When you cut or copy a portion of a record, make sure that the area you paste it in is large enough to receive it, or the operation will fail.*

When you cut or copy selected values, you need to select just the right size range. Unlike the worksheet, where you need only select the first cell in the range, if the new range is not at least as large as the cut material you will get the message "The selection is too small for pasting."

If you select a range larger than the material you are cutting or copying, the material will duplicate itself as many times as it can within the extra space. (See Tip 4.27.)

4.25 Tip: *You can select more than one adjacent record for cutting, copying, or clearing by dragging along the row numbers. To select non-adjacent records, use the OPTION key while clicking.*

This technique allows you to select several adjacent records quickly. Holding the OPTION key down and clicking on row numbers allows you to select several non-adjacent records.

4.26 Tip: *You can select more than one non-adjacent value for cutting, copying, or clearing by using the OPTION key.*

When you want to perform editing operations on common fields in non-adjacent records, using the OPTION key can let you select them.

The need for this might occur, for example, when transferring selected sections of a database to a worksheet or word processing document.

1. Select the number of the record containing the first value, Merrill Lynch, here in record 2:

Sales Orders

	Order	Date	Company	Cnslt	Product	Price	Cost
1	1006	6/22/85	Net 1	SK	Jazz	$415.00	$365.00
2	1007	6/23/85	Merrill Lynch	JR	Sideways	$49.00	$26.00
3	1007	6/23/85	Merrill Lynch	JR	1-2-3	$290.00	$265.00
4	1008	6/24/85	New Wave Corp.	DK	Jazz	$415.00	$365.00
5	1009	6/25/85	G.E.	GM	1-2-3	$290.00	$265.00
6	1010	6/24/85	Net 1	SK	1-2-3	$290.00	$265.00

2. Hold the OPTION key down and click on the field name containing the value. In our example, this is Company. The cell at the intersection of the selected field and record will be selected.

Sales Orders

	Order	Date	Company	Cnslt	Product	Price	Cost
1	1006	6/22/85	Net 1	SK	Jazz	$415.00	$365.00
2	1007	6/23/85	Merrill Lynch	JR	Sideways	$49.00	$26.00
3	1007	6/23/85	Merrill Lynch	JR	1-2-3	$290.00	$265.00
4	1008	6/24/85	New Wave Corp.	DK	Jazz	$415.00	$365.00
5	1009	6/25/85	G.E.	GM	1-2-3	$290.00	$265.00
6	1010	6/24/85	Net 1	SK	1-2-3	$290.00	$265.00

3. To select each additional value in the Company field, hold the OPTION key down and click on the record number of the record that contains it, here record 4 and record 6:

Sales Orders

	Order	Date	Company	Cnslt	Product	Price	Cost
1	1006	6/22/85	Net 1	SK	Jazz	$415.00	$365.00
2	1007	6/23/85	Merrill Lynch	JR	Sideways	$49.00	$26.00
3	1007	6/23/85	Merrill Lynch	JR	1-2-3	$290.00	$265.00
4	1008	6/24/85	New Wave Corp.	DK	Jazz	$415.00	$365.00
5	1009	6/25/85	G.E.	GM	1-2-3	$290.00	$265.00
6	1010	6/24/85	Net 1	SK	1-2-3	$290.00	$265.00

4.27 Tip: *When you copy entire records, you don't need to select a target range as large as the selection.*

In copying entire records, the database functions similarly to the worksheet. When you select the records by clicking on their numbers in the margin, you can use the Copy command to duplicate them in another area by clicking on the record number where you want them to be placed. No matter how many records have been copied, they will all be inserted just before the selected record.

To place the records at the end of a database, add a blank record and select it as the target; otherwise, selecting the last completed record causes the copied records to be inserted before it.

Using the Query Command

4.28 Tip: *You can find specific information in your database by using the Query command.*

A valuable quality of a database is being able to find particular information without looking at every record. The Query command allows you to do that.

Assume you want to select all the sales for the consultant SK in the database shown in Figure 4-1. When you select Show Definition from the Query menu, you are presented with the Query window. Here SK has been entered in the Cnslt field:

After choosing Select With Criteria from the Query menu, Figure 4-4 shows that all the records fulfilling the conditions of the query have been selected. The ability of Query to select specified records also has other applications.

4.29 Tip: *Keep from having to redefine queries by saving ones frequently used under separate names.*

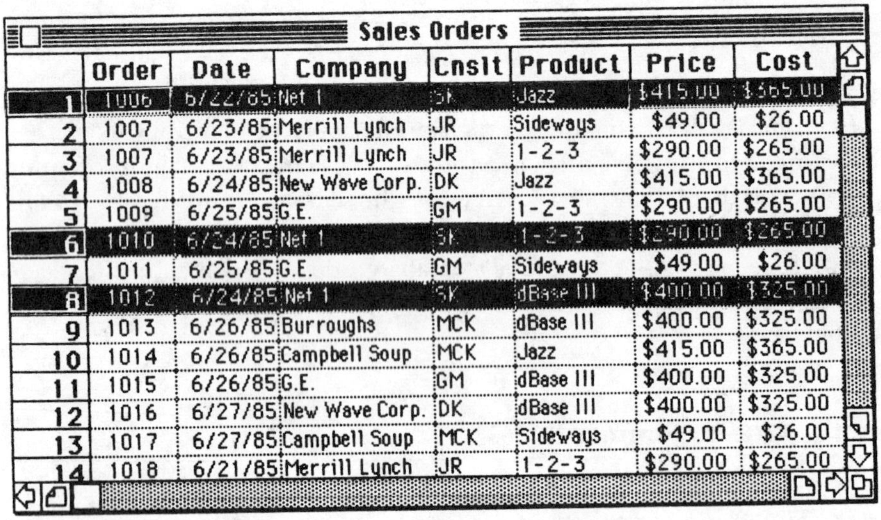

Sales Orders

	Order	Date	Company	Cnslt	Product	Price	Cost
1	1006	6/22/85	Net 1	SK	Jazz	$415.00	$365.00
2	1007	6/23/85	Merrill Lynch	JR	Sideways	$49.00	$26.00
3	1007	6/23/85	Merrill Lynch	JR	1-2-3	$290.00	$265.00
4	1008	6/24/85	New Wave Corp.	DK	Jazz	$415.00	$365.00
5	1009	6/25/85	G.E.	GM	1-2-3	$290.00	$265.00
6	1010	6/24/85	Net 1	SK	1-2-3	$290.00	$265.00
7	1011	6/25/85	G.E.	GM	Sideways	$49.00	$26.00
8	1012	6/24/85	Net 1	SK	dBase III	$400.00	$325.00
9	1013	6/26/85	Burroughs	MCK	dBase III	$400.00	$325.00
10	1014	6/26/85	Campbell Soup	MCK	Jazz	$415.00	$365.00
11	1015	6/26/85	G.E.	GM	dBase III	$400.00	$325.00
12	1016	6/27/85	New Wave Corp.	DK	dBase III	$400.00	$325.00
13	1017	6/27/85	Campbell Soup	MCK	Sideways	$49.00	$26.00
14	1018	6/21/85	Merrill Lynch	JR	1-2-3	$290.00	$265.00

Figure 4-4. Database after using Select With Criteria

When you define a query, it is automatically saved with the file under a default name. You can create several queries and save them with a file, but you should give each a descriptive name before defining the criteria. Here's how to create a new query:

1. Select Names from the Query menu.
2. Select New.
3. Type a name that reflects the use of the query.
4. Select Done.
5. Choose Show Definition from the Query menu.
6. Enter the query criteria in the appropriate fields.

To activate an existing query, select Names and then select the query name you wish to use. Choosing Select With Criteria highlights the records meeting the criteria.

4.30 Tip: *To select broad categories of records in a query, use the wild-card characters ? and *.*

In a query the * means "everything". For instance, using the asterisk in the query definition by itself selects all the records, as long as the asterisk is placed in a text field. Placing the asterisk after other characters, such as Sm*, selects every record in which the field begins with Sm. The asterisk won't work unless it's the last character in a definition.

The question mark replaces one character only. Placing the question mark with other characters, such as Sm?th, selects records with "Sm" as the first two characters, "th" as the fourth and fifth, and any letter in the position of the ?.

4.31 Tip: *You can select all records in a database by using an * in a text field of a query.*

One way to universally select all records in a database is to use the asterisk in a query text field. The result is the selection of every record.

4.32 Trap: *Don't use #and# when you mean #or#.*

In the database shown in Figure 4-4, if you wanted to select all the records for SK and GM, you might think you should enter the query in the Cnslt field as SK#and#GM. However, if you did this you would get a message that no records matched the criteria. This is because none of the records have SK and GM in the same field. What should have been entered is SK#or#GM.

4.33 Tip: *You can delete selected records by using the Query command.*

You can easily delete records selected by a query with the Clear Record command. Be careful to check the results and use Undo Clear, if necessary, to bring the cleared records back.

4.34 Tip: *To copy selected records into another document, define the set of criteria; then use the Select With Criteria and Copy commands.*

A very convenient way of copying selected records into another document is to use

Query to select all the records you wish to copy. All it takes is figuring out what criteria will fulfill the required selection.

4.35 Tip: *Drop duplicates from a Query selection by using Query Drop Duplicates after Select With Criteria.*

It's easy to make sure that there are no duplicate records in a selection by choosing Drop Duplicates after Select With Criteria. The query will not display duplicates as selected, though they will remain in the database.

General Database Tips

4.36 Tip: *You can duplicate your database structure by saving it under another name, adding a blank record, and clearing the contents of all other records.*

It's often helpful to duplicate a database structure. For example, disk space or RAM limitations may not allow you to create as large a file as you might need. Separated files could be identical in structure but might be distinguished by each covering a different time period, ZIP code, or other subject. To prevent having to recreate the structure, here's how to duplicate it.

1. Open the database.
2. Select Save As to rename the file and save it under a new name.
3. Insert a new record at the beginning or end of the database.
4. Select all records except the blank one.
5. Select Clear Record.

All records except the blank one will be deleted, but the structure will remain. If you want, you can now cut or copy selected records from the old database.

4.37 Tip: *Create a duplicate-free database by using Drop Duplicates after selecting all other records with a universal criteria and then copying them into another database.*

It's easy to enter a record twice without noticing it. This extra record may cause inaccuracies in any report run from the database. It's easy to remove duplicate records that have identical fields.

Select all records by using Query with an * in a text field. Then choose Drop Duplicates. Duplicates will not be highlighted. If you have prepared a duplicate database, you can use the Cut or Copy commands and paste the "non-duplicate" version in the new document. Close the original version; then save the new version under the original name.

4.38 Tip: *Get added meaning from your data by using the Sort feature.*

Changing the order of records can prove useful in getting more information from a database. Looking at the records in your database in the order in which they were entered may not be very helpful. You can arrange the records in useful ways by choosing Set Fields from the Sort menu. Type the name of the field you wish the database sorted on; then select Sort. The records in your database will be arranged in the order you specify.

In sorting a database, Ascending ranks text records in alphabetical order and numbers from smallest to largest. Descending does the opposite.

By sorting under additional sort keys, you can order records even more selectively. For example, in Figure 4-5 the records have been sorted by consultant (Cnslt). If Total was the second sort key, the records would be ranked first by consultant and then within the records for each consultant, with the biggest sale ranked first. You can sort on a total of three sort keys.

4.39 Trap: *Always enter data that is identical from one record to the next in an identical way, or queries and sorts may separate data improperly.*

Sorting a database rearranges the records according to the fields you choose to sort on. If you enter the same item of information in different ways, common records may not appear together in a sort. This is especially important when you create reports.

For example, if one of your customers is General Electric and you enter the name as G.E., General Electric, and General Elec. in different records, a sort by company will not group them together. Because you may want to create a report to show total sales by company, each version of the company name would have its own total. To avoid this, enter data shared by multiple records in an identical way.

Sales Orders

	Order	Date	Company	Cnslt	Product	Price	Cost
1	1008	6/24/85	New Wave Corp.	DK	Jazz	$415.00	$365.00
2	1016	6/27/85	New Wave Corp.	DK	dBase III	$400.00	$325.00
3	1015	6/26/85	G.E.	GM	dBase III	$400.00	$325.00
4	1009	6/25/85	G.E.	GM	1-2-3	$290.00	$265.00
5	1011	6/25/85	G.E.	GM	Sideways	$49.00	$26.00
6	1007	6/23/85	Merrill Lynch	JR	Sideways	$49.00	$26.00
7	1007	6/23/85	Merrill Lynch	JR	1-2-3	$290.00	$265.00
8	1018	6/21/85	Merrill Lynch	JR	1-2-3	$290.00	$265.00
9	1017	6/27/85	Campbell Soup	MCK	Sideways	$49.00	$26.00
10	1014	6/26/85	Campbell Soup	MCK	Jazz	$415.00	$365.00
11	1013	6/26/85	Burroughs	MCK	dBase III	$400.00	$325.00
12	1010	6/24/85	Net 1	SK	1-2-3	$290.00	$265.00
13	1012	6/24/85	Net 1	SK	dBase III	$400.00	$325.00
14	1006	6/22/85	Net 1	SK	Jazz	$415.00	$365.00

Figure 4-5. Database sorted on the Cnslt field

4.40 Tip: *You can print selected records or individual values by using the Print Selection command.*

The Print Selection command is very handy for printing just the records or individual values you have selected. The settings in Page Set up are observed, but only what is highlighted will print. If you wish, you can use the Style menu to hide the database grid or the record numbers before you print. See the following section on Database Reporting for more powerful printing options.

Database Reporting

You can produce printed reports based on all or just selected records in your database. These reports can be simple lists, or you can break a report into sections and include summary statistics at each break. The following Tips and Traps assume that you know the basics of database reporting, including preparing the database, defining the Report Definition, and previewing and printing the report. Refer to your *Jazz*

SALES REPORT

	Name	Customer	Factory	Sales	Percent	Comm	Code
1	Laura	1100	40	$3,850	4.50%	$173.25	1
2	Michael	700	30	$3,285	3.50%	$114.97	1
3	Victor	1020	30	$3,170	3.00%	$95.10	1
4	Laura	340	60	$3,095	5.00%	$154.75	1
5	Michael	250	10	$3,020	4.00%	$120.80	1
6	Daniel	800	10	$3,005	3.00%	$90.15	1
7	Laura	240	10	$2,860	4.50%	$128.70	0
8	Merry	880	20	$2,800	3.00%	$84.00	0
9	Michael	400	50	$2,650	4.50%	$119.25	0
10	Laura	610	40	$2,550	4.50%	$114.75	0
11	Victor	670	10	$2,285	3.00%	$68.55	0
12	Daniel	1000	50	$2,075	2.50%	$51.87	0
13	Merry	990	30	$1,975	2.50%	$49.37	0
14	Victor	1020	30	$1,500	2.00%	$30.00	0
15	Daniel	900	20	$1,195	2.50%	$29.87	0
16	Merry	950	10	$1,165	5.00%	$58.25	0

Figure 4-6. Sample Sales Report database

Handbook if you are unfamiliar with any aspect of the process. Examples in this section are based on the database shown in Figure 4-6.

4.41 Trap: *If you don't first select the records you want to report, Jazz won't preview or print a report.*

Before Jazz can preview or print your report, you must specify the records to be included. If you don't select any database records, you will get a message telling you that no records match the specified criteria. As few as two records can be specified. If you want to specify the entire database, use the Select All command.

There are two ways to select a subset of your database. One is to first sort your database and then manually select records by highlighting them. A second, and much more reliable, procedure is to set up a Query with the selection criteria you want and then choose Select With Criteria (COMMAND-Q) from the Query menu. The point is you must select records first, before previewing or printing a report.

4.42 Trap: *If you don't sort first, set the Break Field, and make sure that the Break Field and the First Sort Field refer to the same field, you'll probably get strange report results.*

Jazz breaks a report into sections according to the Break Field you specify. For example, if you want a report that lists sales figures by salesperson, sort the database using the Name field (Salesperson Name) as the First Sort Field. You also need to specify the Name field as the Break Field in the Report Definition. This lets Jazz know to break for a new section at each new set of names. The report in Figure 4-7 shows a sales analysis of the entire database by salesperson. The corresponding Report Definition is shown in Figure 4-8, and the selected sort fields are indicated in Figure 4-9. Notice that the Break Field in Figure 4-8 matches the First Sort Field in Figure 4-9.

Figure 4-10 shows part of a report based on a database that was sorted using the Sales field as the First Sort Field. There is a problem here, however. Though the First Sort Field was changed to Sales, we neglected to match the Break Field to it in the Report Definition (Figure 4-11). The result was that Jazz first sorted the data records according to Sales but broke up the sections according to individual salesperson.

4.43 Tip: *You can produce a report that includes only records that meet a specific criteria by choosing Select With Criteria before printing.*

The analytical value of your database reports can be increased by using Select With Criteria when selecting records. Using this querying option makes it possible to select for reporting data records that are related by a specified criteria setting. Suppose that you want to summarize sales figures by salesperson for only those accounts with more than $3000 in sales. The first step is to sort the database by salesperson name: Specify the Name field as the First Sort Field and select the Sort command from the Sort menu. Then specify the same field name on which you sorted as the Break field in the Report Definition. (Trap 4.42 discusses the potential hazard if you don't specify the same field for both the Break Field and the First Sort Field.)

The final step is to select the records to be included in your report. Start by typing in the criteria in a Query chosen with the Query Names command, and then use the Select With Criteria command in the Query menu to select the records that meet the criteria. Those records with sales greater than $3000 will be selected and included in the report shown in Figure 4-12.

4.44 Trap: *When you're working on a report definition, Jazz won't allow you to cut, copy, or clear more than one cell entry at a time.*

SALES ANALYSIS
COMMISSION REPORT

Salesperson Name	Customer Acct Number	Sales Amount	Sales Commission
Daniel	900	$1,195	$29.87
Daniel	1000	$2,075	$51.87
Daniel	800	$3,005	$90.15
		==========	==========
Total	Daniel	$6,275	$171.90

Salesperson Name	Customer Acct Number	Sales Amount	Sales Commission
Laura	610	$2,550	$114.75
Laura	240	$2,860	$128.70
Laura	340	$3,095	$154.75
Laura	1100	$3,850	$173.25
		==========	==========
Total	Laura	$12,355	$571.45

Salesperson Name	Customer Acct Number	Sales Amount	Sales Commission
Merry	950	$1,165	$58.25
Merry	990	$1,975	$49.37
Merry	880	$2,800	$84.00
		==========	==========
Total	Merry	$5,940	$191.62

1986 Sales Figures 1

Figure 4-7. Sales analysis by salesperson

Page Header				
		SALES ANALYSIS		
		COMMISSION REPORT		
Section Header				
	Salesperson	Customer	Sales	Sales
	Name	Acct Number	Amount	Commission
	-----------	-----------	-----------	-----------
Record Detail Line				
	=Name	=Customer	=Sales	=Comm
Section Summary				
Page Footer				
	1986 Sales Figures			=FPAGE
Report Summary				
			===========	===========
		Total Sales	=FSUM(Sales)	=FSUM(Comm)
		Average Sale	=FAVG(Sales)	=FAVG(Comm)
		Largest Single Sale	=FMAX(Sales)	=FMAX(Comm)
Break Field:	=Name	**Page Size:**	48	

SALES REPORT - Page 1

Figure 4-8. Report Definition

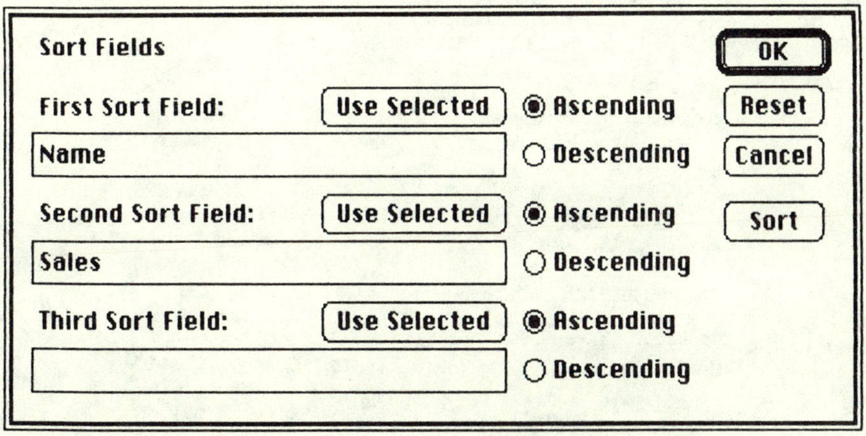

Figure 4-9. Selected sort fields

The standard Jazz commands from the Edit menu are used to edit and change cell entries in the report definition. Unfortunately, you can only operate on one cell at a time, which makes cut and paste procedures rather tedious and time-consuming. You're better off getting both text and formulas in the right position to begin with.

4.45 Tip: *You can cut or copy and paste single cells from another document into a Report Definition document.*

Suppose you have a worksheet heading that you want to use as the Page Header in a database report. Using the copy and paste procedure, you could duplicate the heading. Keep in mind, however, that this operation will have to be executed by copying and pasting one cell at a time. See Trap 4.44.

If you cut or copy multiple cells from another document, Jazz pastes only the first cell of the specified range into your Report Definition document.

4.46 Trap: *If you don't insert Report Definition lines in the right order to begin with, you may find it difficult later to insert lines where you want.*

SALES ANALYSIS
COMMISSION REPORT

Salesperson Name	Customer Acct Number	Sales Amount	Sales Commission
Laura	1100	$3,850	$173.25
Total	Laura	$3,850	$173.25

Salesperson Name	Customer Acct Number	Sales Amount	Sales Commission
Michael	700	$3,285	$114.97
Total	Michael	$3,285	$114.97

Salesperson Name	Customer Acct Number	Sales Amount	Sales Commission
Victor	1020	$3,170	$95.10
Total	Victor	$3,170	$95.10

Salesperson Name	Customer Acct Number	Sales Amount	Sales Commission
Laura	340	$3,095	$154.75
Total	Laura	$3,095	$154.75

1986 Sales Figures 1

Figure 4-10. Partial report on sorted database

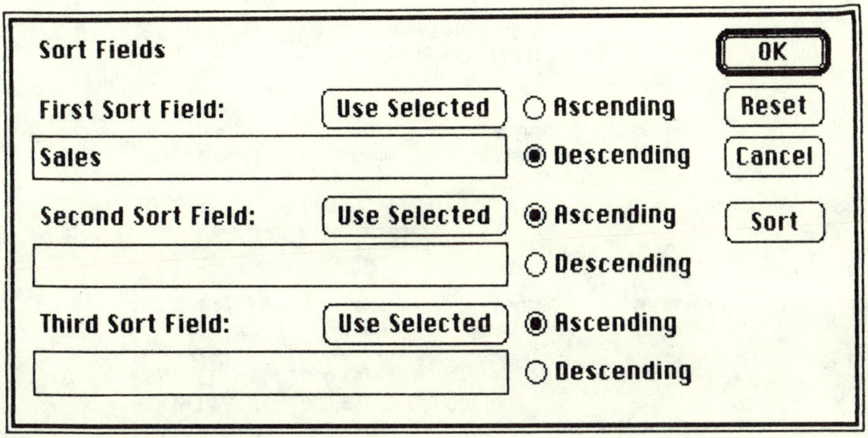

Figure 4-11. Corresponding Report Definition

Inserting lines in a Report Definition is easy enough; however, where you can insert them is restricted by which cells can be selected. (Refer to Figure 4-8 for a sample Report Definition.) Suppose you want to insert a blank line between the two text entries in the Page Header. You would select a cell on the line containing the entry COMMISSION REPORT and select Insert Report Line from the Edit menu. Jazz will insert a new row above the row that contains a highlighted cell.

You encounter problems when you want to insert lines at the end of a section because you can't select a Report Definition heading row. For example, if you try to insert a line just above the Report Definition heading, Jazz beeps. The way around this is to insert lines where you can, and then cut and paste to rearrange your cell entries. In the Report Definition shown in Figure 4-8, the only place where a line could be inserted in the Record Detail Line section is directly below the header Record Detail Line. To insert a line just above the Section Summary line in Figure 4-8, you can follow this roundabout procedure: highlight one cell in the line containing the field name formulas (such as =Name), and then select the Insert Report Line command in the Edit menu. Then cut and paste the field name formulas one at a time into the newly inserted line. You will have to check the format of each cell involved in the cutting and pasting process. See the next Trap (4.47) for an explanation of why this is so important.

SALES ANALYSIS
COMMISSION REPORT

Salesperson Name	Customer Acct Number	Sales Amount	Sales Commission
-----------	-----------	-----------	-----------
Daniel	800	$3,005	$90.15
		===========	===========
Total	Daniel	$3,005	$90.15
Salesperson Name	Customer Acct Number	Sales Amount	Sales Commission
-----------	-----------	-----------	-----------
Laura	340	$3,095	$154.75
Laura	1100	$3,850	$173.25
		===========	===========
Total	Laura	$6,945	$328.00
Salesperson Name	Customer Acct Number	Sales Amount	Sales Commission
-----------	-----------	-----------	-----------
Michael	250	$3,020	$120.80
Michael	700	$3,285	$114.97
		===========	===========
Total	Michael	$6,305	$235.77
Salesperson Name	Customer Acct Number	Sales Amount	Sales Commission
-----------	-----------	-----------	-----------
Victor	1020	$3,170	$95.10
		===========	===========
Total	Victor	$3,170	$95.10

1986 Sales Figures 1

Figure 4-12. Report showing selected records

The best approach, however, is to plan your report layout in advance to minimize having to use this tedious and potentially hazardous procedure.

4.47 Trap: *If you format a cell in the Report Definition, the assigned format remains in effect for that specific cell unless a new format is specified.*

Suppose you assign currency format to a cell in the Section Summary that contains a formula to calculate total sales. In the process of refining your report format, you cut this formula and paste it into another cell in the Report Definition. The cell in the Section Summary where you had originally entered the formula still has a currency format assigned to it. Any subsequent entries made in this same cell will be displayed in currency format unless you specify a new format attribute. However, if you cut a cell that has already been formatted in the Report Definition, the format is pasted along with the cell when the cell is pasted to a new location.

4.48 Tip: *For all sections of a Report Definition, you should use labels to identify the formula fields. Otherwise, you may have difficulty identifying what's printed out.*

The report in Figure 4-13 includes summary statistics. However, it is virtually impossible to decipher the meaning of this report in its current format. Figure 4-14 shows the same report, but with labels added. This facilitates identifying the different statistical operations and makes the report more readable. The Report Definitions for these two reports are shown in Figure 4-15.

4.49 Tip: *Positioning the Report Definition window so you can see the field names in the Database window can be very helpful while entering formulas.*

When you work in a window it becomes active and is placed on top of all other windows on the Desktop. While defining a Report Definition, you can't view the field names in your database unless you position both the Report Definition window and the Database window so they can be viewed simultaneously (see Figure 4-16). It

SALES ANALYSIS
COMMISSION REPORT

Salesperson Name	Customer Acct Number	Sales Amount	Sales Commission
-----------	-----------	-----------	-----------
Laura	1100	$3,850	$173.25
Michael	700	$3,285	$114.97
Victor	1020	$3,170	$95.10
Laura	340	$3,095	$154.75
Michael	250	$3,020	$120.80
Daniel	800	$3,005	$90.15
		===========	===========
		$19,425	$749.02
		$3,238	$124.84
		$3,850	$173.25

1986 Sales Figures 1

Figure 4-13. Summary statistics

SALES ANALYSIS
COMMISSION REPORT

Salesperson Name	Customer Acct Number	Sales Amount	Sales Commission
-----------	-----------	-----------	-----------
Laura	1100	$3,850	$173.25
Michael	700	$3,285	$114.97
Victor	1020	$3,170	$95.10
Laura	340	$3,095	$154.75
Michael	250	$3,020	$120.80
Daniel	800	$3,005	$90.15
		===========	===========
	Total Sales	$19,425	$749.02
	Average Sale	$3,238	$124.84
	Largest Single Sale	$3,850	$173.25

1986 Sales Figures 1

Figure 4-14. Adding labels

Page Header				
		SALES ANALYSIS		
		COMMISSION REPORT		
Section Header				
	Salesperson	Customer	Sales	Sales
	Name	Acct Number	Amount	Commission
	-----------	-----------	-----------	-----------
Record Detail Line				
	=Name	=Customer	=Sales	=Comm
Section Summary				
Page Footer				
	1986 Sales Figures			=FPAGE
Report Summary				
			===========	===========
			=FSUM(Sales)	=FSUM(Comm)
			=FAVG(Sales)	=FAVG(Comm)
			=FMAX(Sales)	=FMAX(Comm)
Break Field:	=Name	**Page Size:**	48	

a. SALES REPORT - Page 1

Figure 4-15. Report Definitions

Page Header				
		SALES ANALYSIS		
		COMMISSION REPORT		
Section Header				
	Salesperson	Customer	Sales	Sales
	Name	Acct Number	Amount	Commission
	-----------	-----------	-----------	-----------
Record Detail Line				
	=Name	=Customer	=Sales	=Comm
Section Summary				
			===========	===========
	Total	=Name	=FSUM(Sales)	=FSUM(Comm)
Page Footer				
	1986 Sales Figures			=FPAGE
Report Summary				
Break Field:	=Name	**Page Size:**	48	

b. SALES REPORT – Page 1

Figure 4-15. Report Definitions (continued)

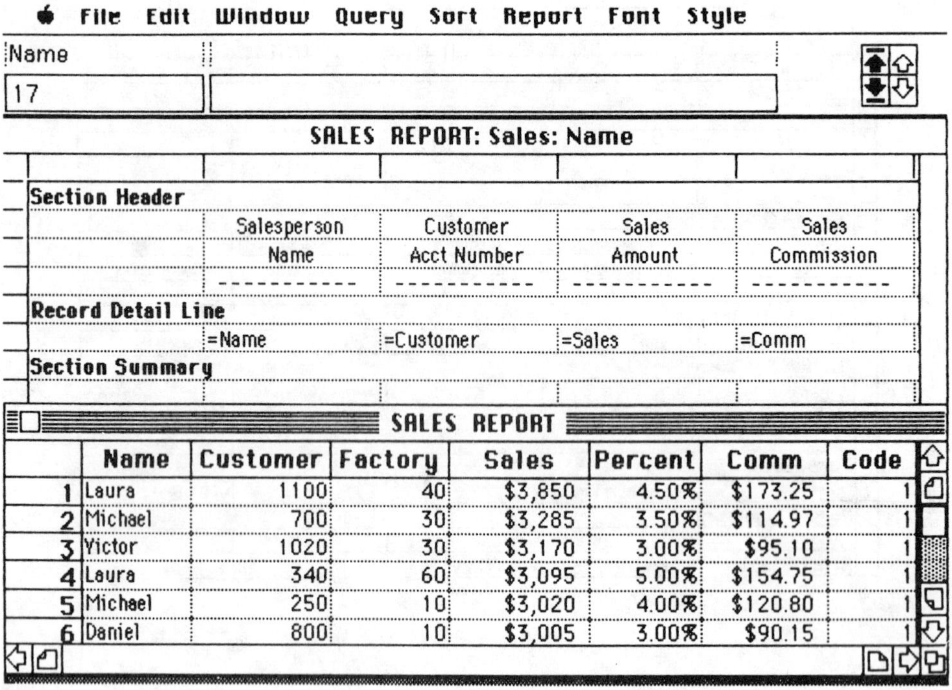

Figure 4-16. Viewing the Report Definition window and the database

can be particularly useful to see both windows at once when defining the Record Detail line of the Report Definition, since you are indicating the fields whose values you want to include in your report, and exact spelling is critical. Jazz won't accept a field name if you don't type it exactly the way you did in the database.

For example, entering a formula like =FSUM(Comm) could be problematic since an abbreviation was used for the word *commission*. Suppose you couldn't recall the exact notation used in your database. You would have to activate and display the Database window to check the notation and then return to the Report Definition window to complete the formula entry. It is much more effective to position the Database and Report Definition windows so that you don't have to switch back and forth between the two environments.

4.50 Tip: *You don't have to worry about saving a Report Definition separately from the database.*

A database can exist without a Report Definition; however, you can't define a Report

Definition unless you first create a new or activate an existing database. When you save a database, Jazz automatically saves all Report Definitions associated with it. You can't save Report Definitions as independent files.

Jazz automatically assigns default names for Report Definitions (Report 1, Report 2, and so on). However, you will probably want to choose names that are more meaningful.

4.51 Tip: *You can have several Report Definitions for a single database.*

Suppose you are responsible for weekly reports like those in Figures 4-17 and 4-18. The report in Figure 4-17 is a sales analysis by factory, while Figure 4-18 summarizes sales activity by individual salespeople. These two database reports are linked to the same database; however, their report definitions have different Break fields specified (see Figures 4-19 and 4-20). (You would of course have to sort the database before reporting on the Break field corresponding to the current Report Definition.) It would be quite time-consuming if you had to make the changes in your Report Definition before printing each report.

Jazz simplifies this task because it allows you to use the Names command in the Report menu to create multiple report definitions with unique names. Since report definitions are automatically saved when you save your database, you can use them again to produce additional reports with the same database, even if the database has been modified.

4.52 Trap: *If you don't type a field name in a Report Definition formula exactly as it appears in the database, Jazz won't accept it and you get a beep.*

When creating Report Definitions, you must be careful when typing a field name; it must be an exact match with entries in your database. The one exception is that uppercase and lowercase differences are ignored. (See Tip. 4.51 above.)

4.53 Trap: *Until you correct or cancel an invalid formula entry in your Report Definition, Jazz won't let you do anything else.*

You encounter a minor and yet very frustrating Trap when you enter an invalid

SALES ANALYSIS
COMMISSION REPORT

Factory 10

Salesperson Name	Customer Acct Number	Sales Amount	Sales Commission
Michael	250	$3,020	$120.80
Daniel	800	$3,005	$90.15
Laura	240	$2,860	$128.70
Victor	670	$2,285	$68.55
Merry	950	$1,165	$58.25
		============	============
Total for Factory	10	$12,335	$466.45

Factory 20

Salesperson Name	Customer Acct Number	Sales Amount	Sales Commission
Merry	880	$2,800	$84.00
Daniel	900	$1,195	$29.87
		============	============
Total for Factory	20	$3,995	$113.87

Factory 30

Salesperson Name	Customer Acct Number	Sales Amount	Sales Commission
Michael	700	$3,285	$114.97
Victor	1020	$3,170	$95.10
Merry	990	$1,975	$49.37
Victor	1020	$1,500	$30.00
		============	============
Total for Factory	30	$9,930	$289.45

Figure 4-17. Sales analysis by factory

SALES ANALYSIS
COMMISSION REPORT

Salesperson Name	Customer Acct Number	Sales Amount	Sales Commission
Daniel	800	$3,005	$90.15
Daniel	900	$1,195	$29.87
		$4,200	$120.02

Salesperson Name	Customer Acct Number	Sales Amount	Sales Commission
Laura	240	$2,860	$128.70
		$2,860	$128.70

Salesperson Name	Customer Acct Number	Sales Amount	Sales Commission
Merry	990	$1,975	$49.37
Merry	880	$2,800	$84.00
Merry	950	$1,165	$58.25
		$5,940	$191.62

Salesperson Name	Customer Acct Number	Sales Amount	Sales Commission
Michael	700	$3,285	$114.97
Michael	250	$3,020	$120.80
		$6,305	$235.77

Salesperson Name	Customer Acct Number	Sales Amount	Sales Commission
Victor	1020	$1,500	$30.00
Victor	670	$2,285	$68.55
Victor	1020	$3,170	$95.10
		$6,955	$193.65

Figure 4-18. Sales activity by salesperson

Page Header				
		SALES ANALYSIS		
		COMMISSION REPORT		
Section Header				
		Factory	=Factory	
	Salesperson	Customer	Sales	Sales
	Name	Acct Number	Amount	Commission
	-----------	-----------	-----------	-----------
Record Detail Line				
	=Name	=Customer	=Sales	=Comm
Section Summary				
			============	============
	Total for Factory	=Factory	=FSUM(Sales)	=FSUM(Comm)
Page Footer				
Report Summary				
Break Field:	=Factory	**Page Size:**	48	

SALES REPORT - Page 1

Figure 4-19. Corresponding Report Definition for sales analysis report

Page Header				
		SALES ANALYSIS		
		COMMISSION REPORT		
Section Header				
	Salesperson	Customer	Sales	Sales
	Name	Acct Number	Amount	Commission
	-----------	-----------	-----------	-----------
Record Detail Line				
	=Name	=Customer	=Sales	=Comm
Section Summary				
			============	============
			=FSUM(Sales)	=FSUM(Comm)
Page Footer				
Report Summary				
Break Field:	=Name	**Page Size:**	48	

SALES REPORT – Page 1

Figure 4-20. Corresponding Report Definition for sales activity formula. Jazz displays an error message and you hear a beep; then you can't make additional entries until you correct or cancel the invalid entry. Click on the Cancel icon to cancel and continue.

4.54 Tip: *Use the Field Format command in the Edit menu to format cells in the Report Definition.*

You can format cells on an individual basis: select the cell and then use the Field Format command to access a dialog box. The format options are the same as those in the worksheet and the database.

4.55 Trap: *Don't expect formatting a cell to affect the appearance of data in the Report Definition; a cell's format only affects how values appear in the report.*

When you assign a format attribute to a cell in a Report Definition, the cell itself is not directly affected. The contents of formatted cells will be displayed in the specified format when you preview or print a database report. You can identify a cell's format in the Report Definition by highlighting it and selecting the Field Format option; the assigned format appears in the dialog box.

4.56 Trap: *Don't expect to use statistical functions in Database Reports just as you would in worksheet documents.*

When defining the Record Detail Line, you can enter either a field name or a formula that refers to a field name. Formulas will be calculated in the same way as those entered in a worksheet. You can use most Jazz functions in this way by using field names as the arguments. For example, to round the values of each sales commission to the nearest dollar, type =ROUND(Comm,0). A function like =INDEX(range,col, row) can't be used since the first argument must be a multicolumn or multirow range and there's no way of specifying such a range in a database formula.

There are nine database report functions, and they can only be used in database Report Definitions. Seven of these functions, FAVG, FCOUNT, FMAX, FMIN, FSTD, FSUM, and FVAR, are virtually identical to the statistical functions used in worksheets, the only difference being that the names are preceded by the letter F.

These functions can be entered in either the Section Summary or the Report Summary areas of the Report Definition to get summary statistics by section or for the entire report.

You use the Record Detail Line to specify which field values you want to include in your report. Fields are defined by typing either a field name preceded by an equal sign or a formula that references a field name. Be sure that these entries are aligned with the corresponding column heading in the Page Header.

The FPREV function keeps a cumulative total of field values by record or by section, depending on whether the function is entered in the Record Detail Line or the Section Summary. The format for the FPREV function is =FPREV+Field Name. Suppose you want your report to print cumulative sales figures for each record. Instead of entering =Sales in the Record Detail Line, you would use =FPREV+Sales.

The FPAGE function is included in the Page Header or Page Footer to number report pages automatically and consecutively.

4.57 Trap: *Don't forget to start a formula with an equal sign (=) or you'll get a text entry.*

If you don't preface formulas with an equal sign, they will become text entries and the calculation won't occur. For example, if you enter SUM(Sales), the total sales amount won't be calculated; the text entry SUM(sales) will appear in your report.

4.58 Trap: *If you assign an inappropriate format to a field, it may be printed as a question mark (?) in a report.*

The report in Figure 4-21 shows a question mark (?) in the last line. The FPAGE function was entered in the page footer to number the report pages. However, the cell containing this function was formatted as a date. Jazz is confused and returns the questioning response. You can easily correct the problem by reformatting the cell.

Let's consider another formatting problem in this same report. The total sales amount is not displayed in currency format, as you would expect. This cell has been formatted to display contents as left-aligned text. This is obviously not the intended setting, but it's an easy mistake to make since a cell's format is not visible in the Report Definition. Not until you preview or print a report will you see how the data is formatted.

SALES ANALYSIS
COMMISSION REPORT

Factory 10

Salesperson Name	Customer Acct Number	Sales Amount	Sales Commission
-----------	-----------	-----------	-----------
Michael	250	$3,020	$120.80
Daniel	800	$3,005	$90.15
Laura	240	$2,860	$128.70
Victor	670	$2,285	$68.55
Merry	950	$1,165	$58.25
		============	============
Total for Factory		12335	$466.45

1986 Sales Figures ?

Figure 4-21. Result of using inappropriate format

4.59 Tip: *Use Report Preview to check your reports before printing, because reports rarely print out as expected.*

After your database has been sorted and you have selected the records to be included in your report, you might think you are ready to print your report. But you may be wasting time and paper and find out that your printed report doesn't look the way you expected. If you select Preview from the Report menu, a screen version of the printed report will be displayed, from which you can quickly detect and correct any possible problems.

The screen preview in Figure 4-22 reveals two formatting errors: truncated numbers and numbers displayed without expected format. Some of the figures in the Sales Comm column have been truncated because the Report Definition column is not wide enough to display all digits. Since the total Sales Amt for Factory 10 is displayed in currency format, you would expect that the column entries would also be shown as dollar amounts, but this won't happen unless you've formatted the corresponding field in the database accordingly. These are minor formatting errors, and yet they produce an unreadable report. You can't edit a report while it is being

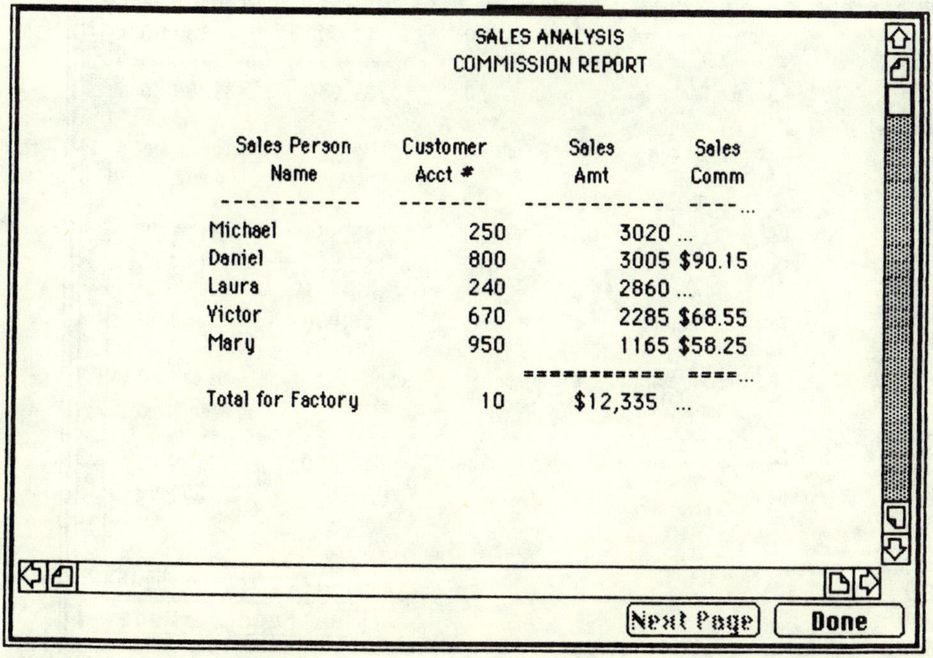

Figure 4-22. Previewing a report

previewed, so you'll have to select Done and make changes in the Report Definition or the database itself.

If you use the Preview option with multiple-page reports, you will be alerted to possible pagination problems. Suppose your report exceeds a single page, and you are concerned with where page breaks will occur. The screen preview in Figure 4-23 shows the second page of a three-page report. The vertical scroll box is down as far as it can go, indicating that the last line of the current page is visible. There is a page break in the middle of this section summary, resulting in the totals being printed out on the next page. It is easy to find out if your report will be printed on additional pages: the words Next Page will appear as they are in Figure 4-23. In contrast, notice the muted Next Page in Figure 4-22, which is a screen preview of a single-page report.

You might also decide that there should be more spaces between the sections. These and other aesthetic issues can be addressed while previewing a report, and necessary changes can be made to the Report Definition before printing is attempted.

4.60 Trap: *When previewing a report, once you choose Next Page you can't see the first page again without selecting Done and choosing Preview again.*

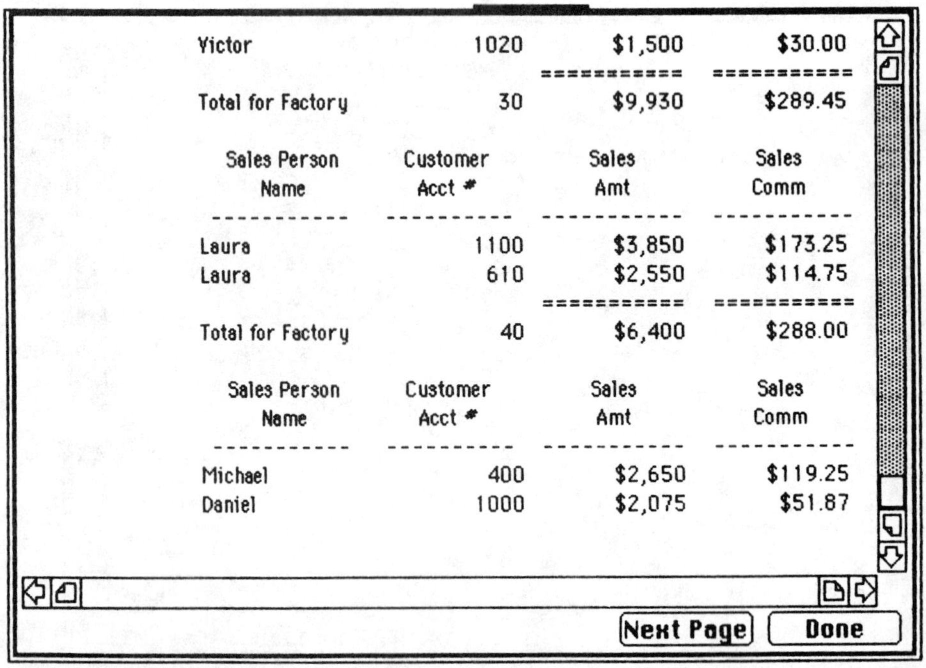

Figure 4-23. Previewing the second page

If you want to view subsequent report pages, click on Next Page. The Trap is that once you go on to the next page, you can't return to previous pages. You will have to click on Done and select Preview again. Also, while previewing a report, don't confuse the printed page with the screen page. If you want to scan a printed page from top to bottom, use the vertical scroll box. You can scan one printed page at a time; this may include several screen pages.

4.61 Tip: *Document all your reports by printing the Report Definition.*

A printed copy of the Report Definition serves as good documentation for your reports. Your memory may fail you if a substantial period of time passes since you last worked on a particular report. Disk failure might require recreating a report format. These and other situations can arise, making documentation a requirement rather than a choice. To print a Report Definition, select Print Document from the File menu while the Report Definition is open and respond to the dialog box that appears.

4.62 Trap: *If you don't widen the formula cells before printing a Report Definition, you won't be able to decipher your formula entries.*

The Report Definition shown in Figure 4-24 is not good documentation because the formulas in the Sales Amount column have been truncated. This happens when a cell isn't wide enough to display the entire entry. The solution is to widen the entire column by moving the right-hand top border line for the column and then printing the report. (When you place the mouse arrow over the right-hand vertical border line for the column you want, it turns into a horizontal double arrow crossed with a vertical bar. You can then point and drag to the right to widen the column.)

4.63 Trap: *If you set the Page Size (number of lines per printed page) too small, your report will have strange page breaks.*

The number entered in the Page Size area of the Report Definition specifies the number of printed lines per page. Variables affecting this setting are type style and size, margin settings, number of detail lines, header and footer lines, summary lines,

Page Header				
		SALES ANALYSIS		
		COMMISSION REPORT		
Section Header				
	Salesperson	Customer	Sales	Sales
	Name	Acct Number	Amount	Commission
	-----------	-----------	------...	-----------
Record Detail Line				
	=Name	=Customer	=Sales	=Comm
Section Summary				
			=======...	============
	Total for Factory	=Factory	=FSUM(Sa...	=FSUM(Comm)
Page Footer				
Report Summary				
	Total all Factories		=FSUM(Sa...	=FSUM(Comm)
Break Field:	=Factory	**Page Size:**	48	

SALES REPORT - Page 1

Figure 4-24. Report Definition with truncated formulas

and size of paper. If the number you specify for Page Size isn't appropriate in terms of the combined effects of these variables, your report will have page breaks in unexpected places. The default is 48 and there are no restrictions as to a minimum or maximum value. Figure 4-25 is an example of a report whose Page Size was set to 15.

4.64 Trap: *You can't selectively change fonts and styles in the report document; changes will be global in effect.*

The result of this Trap is that you can't do things like print report headings in a print style different from the rest of the report. To increase styling flexibility, you can transfer your report document to the Jazz word processing environment (Tip 4.65).

4.65 Tip: *You can save a report in text format that can be transported to other Jazz applications.*

Using the Generate Document command in the Report menu produces a report on disk that can be accessed by the Jazz word processor. You can then use all the available font and style options to enhance your reports. The text-only version created by the Generate Document command can also be used with other Macintosh programs.

SALES ANALYSIS
COMMISSION REPORT

Salesperson Name	Customer Acct Number	Sales Amount	Sales Commission
-----------	-----------	-----------	-----------
Michael	250	3020	$120.80
Victor	670	2285	$68.55
Laura	240	2860	$128.70
Merry	950	1165	$58.25
1986 Sales figures			1

Figure 4-25. Report with Page Size of 15

Database Form

Whenever you create a database, you can create one or more forms that can be used for data entry and editing on that database. Figure 4-26 shows a form we created for the Sales Report database shown earlier in Figure 4-6. A form has two different screen views associated with it: you use the Use Form screen for working with existing records or to add new ones and the Modify Form screen to create customized forms for specialized applications. Jazz saves forms as separate files, and they should be located on the same disk as the database to which they are linked. The following Tips and Traps outline the important issues you should be aware of when creating and using database forms.

4.66 Tip: *Using a form for data entry and editing allows you to present a customized user interface.*

The following is a list of some of the reasons why you might prefer to interact with a database in the Form mode:

- You have the option of including on-screen explanatory information. Explaining the rationale behind a particular data field often elicits a more

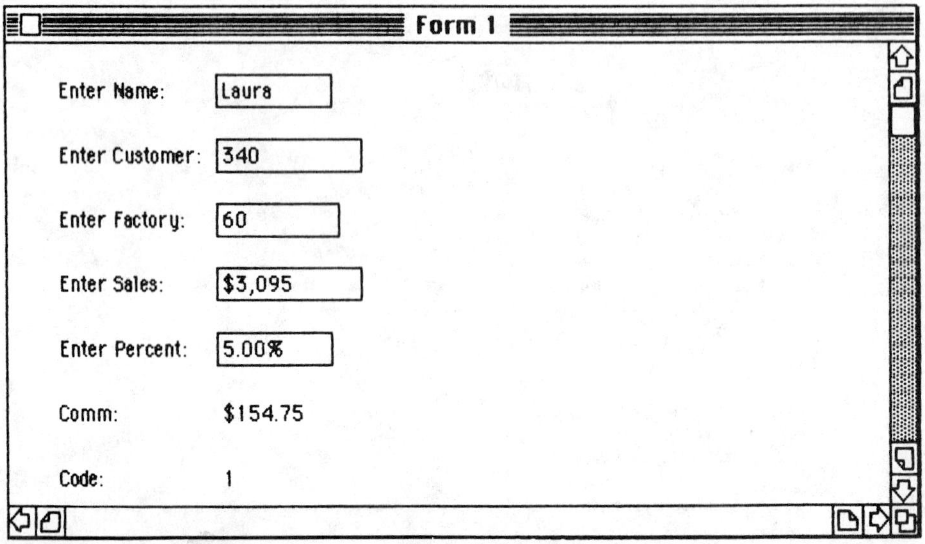

Figure 4-26. Form for Sales Report database

meaningful response. The matrix design of a database doesn't allow this.

- Form style relates to the psychology of collecting data. How you ask a question is sometimes more important than the question itself. Flexible styling gives you the opportunity to phrase data entry prompts and organize them in terms of your audience.
- You have a lot of flexibility in customizing the design of a form, such as changing the position of fields, print style and fonts, and so on. Refer to the Jazz manual for suggestions and instructions on form design.

4.67 Tip: *You can create more than one form for each database.*

The fact that you can have multiple forms associated with a single database raises the question, When would you need more than one form?

There are times when selective presentation or locking of fields is necessary. This is generally a security issue. Suppose you have an employee database that includes demographic as well as salary information. You can create a form that displays only demographic data and locks those fields related to salary. A data entry clerk would be able to maintain an updated list of employee addresses and phone numbers, but would be prevented from making changes to confidential salary data.

In a given office environment, you might find it advantageous to have different forms to present to different employees. For example, one database may need to be maintained by more than one employee. If you create different entry forms, a database can be divided into several groups of fields for purposes of data entry, with a different form associated with each group. In such a case, you'd probably repeat a key field, such as name, on each form. The *Jazz Handbook* describes how you can use Modify Form in the Edit menu to add and delete fields on a form.

4.68 Trap: *If you try to open a new form without having a database active, you'll get an error message and won't be able to do anything.*

Because of the direct link between a database and a form, Jazz requires that a database be active before you can create forms for it. If you don't activate a database first, you get an error message. After you select OK to close the box, you will see a blank Form window that appears to be functional. However, most of its menu options are not operational, making it impossible to create a form. Should you find yourself in this situation, simply close the Form window and either create a new database or activate an existing one.

4.69 Tip: *You don't need to open an existing database to use the form linked to it.*

Jazz automatically links a new form to the currently active database. Once you save a form as a separate entity, you then can open it independent of the database it is linked to. In this case, Jazz automatically makes the link to the underlying database. When you close the form, Jazz gives you the opportunity to save any changes you made to the database. However, if your form is saved on a different disk from your database, you will be prompted to switch disks. This becomes a hassle, so we strongly recommend you avoid this by saving your database and all related forms on the same disk.

4.70 Trap: *If the database linked to your form is in memory and you don't save the database, entries made to the form won't be saved.*

Jazz maintains a link between a database and its associated forms by automatically updating the database in memory when additions, deletions, or editing changes are made to the underlying database through the form. However, if you don't re-save your database after such changes are made, these changes will not be recorded on disk.

4.71 Tip: *You can add, insert, cut, or modify records in a database from its linked forms.*

Editing records in the Form window automatically updates corresponding fields in your database. Jazz transfers all entries made in the form to the database. You can add, insert, or cut records from the Edit menu while you're in a Form window.

4.72 Tip: *To view selected records through a form, use Define Criteria and the View Matching Records command.*

Searching for information is one of the most common uses of a database. You can use the Form window to specify search criteria and then view matching records one at a time. The Define Criteria command displays your form with empty boxes that allow you to specify the criteria. When you're doing this, most of the same rules apply in the Form window as for the Query Definition window used in the Database environment. (See Trap 4.73 for the exceptions). Valid entries include text, numbers, logical and mathematical operators, and formulas. If you want to specify several criteria, enter values for more than one field.

When you select the View Matching Records command, the first record in the database that matches your criteria is displayed. Use the Record Navigator to view the other records selected. The number of matching records can be determined by looking at the numeric entry in the Console after you have scanned the last selection.

4.73 Trap: *Don't expect a Form query to be identical to a database query.*

There are several differences:

- You can't have more than one Form query in existence at once. To define an additional query, you must first clear the original entry and then enter a new set of criteria.
- You can't have more than one criterion per field.
- You can't save criteria entries in a Form query.
- You view matching records one at a time.

Because of these differences, Form queries are not as powerful as database queries, but are easier to use.

4.74 Trap: *If a box is not wide enough for you to type the criterion, you'll have to widen it.*

If you find that you can't complete a criterion entry, choose Modify Form from the Edit menu and enlarge the box as needed. You can then return to Use Form mode and finish typing.

4.75 Trap: *Don't click on the Close box of the Modify Form window or you'll close the Form window itself.*

If you close a Modify Form window, you will close the Form window as well. To get back to the form, select Use Form from the Edit menu.

4.76 Trap: *Don't confuse locking a field in the database with locking a field in a form; they have different effects.*

If you lock a field in a form, information in that field can be viewed but not changed from the form. Locking a field in the form does not lock the same field in the database, so field values can still be added to the field in the database through a database window. A field locked in the database is also locked in the form.

By locking a field in an existing database, you can prevent unintentional changes to the data. You may also want to lock a field in a newly created database to prevent data from being entered. The locking option offers some measure of security to guard against data loss or entry error.

4.77 Tip: *You can specify criteria for locked fields.*

Even though a field is locked, you can still specify search criteria. Suppose you have a database of employee records, and the Salary field is locked for security reasons. You might need to access the records for those employees making over $50,000. The only way to search for these records is to specify the criterion >50000 in the Salary field. This is possible even if this field is locked, since all fields are made available when defining search criteria.

4.78 Trap: *Don't expect the No Duplicates option in the Query menu to delete duplicate records from your database.*

No Duplicates is a viewing option and does affect the database itself. You can't delete records with this command. Duplicate records are removed from the selection of records being viewed but not from the database. This command is accessible only after you have defined the criteria to be used and selected the View Matching Records command.

4.79 Trap: *When you add a new field to a form, make sure you select the correct underlying database field, or you'll get surprising results.*

If you've added a field to your database, you may want to add a corresponding field on a linked form. To do so, first select Modify Form from the Edit menu in the Form window, make the underlying database active (by opening it first, if necessary), and then click on the field name to select the field. Next, make the form active, click the anchor well in the Console, select the location where you want to place the field, and select Place from the Field menu. If the field name selected in the database was the wrong one, you'll create the wrong new field on the form.

4.80 Tip: *By printing a blank form, you can create a paper form that corresponds to the screen form.*

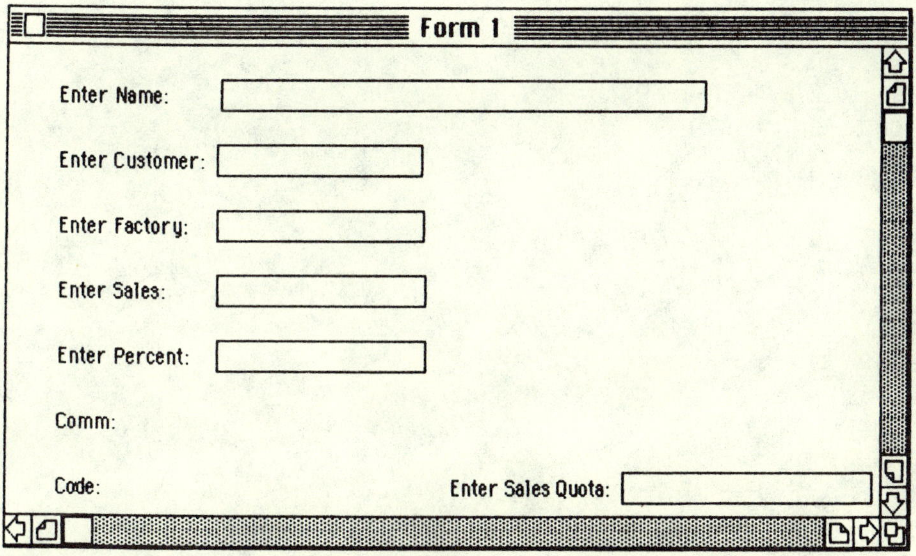

Figure 4-27. Sample form for tracking sales transactions

A printout of a blank form can be used for data collection. The form shown in Figure 4-27, for example, could be used by salespeople to track individual sales transactions without having to use a computer or when they are on the road. You would probably want to enlarge the field boxes to accommodate handwriting. You can print the blank form from the screen by holding down the COMMAND, SHIFT, and 4 keys simultaneously.

5
Word Processing

With Jazz word processing you can write, edit, format, and print multipage documents. Those familiar with MacWrite will find Jazz word processing very similar — but with some powerful additional features.

This chapter is divided into several sections and contains information useful to both beginner and expert. The "Getting Started" section incorporates those Tips and Traps that can assist you with the basic tasks encountered in creating a document and that are particularly useful for beginners. Other sections are "Cutting, Copying, and Pasting"; "Using Headers and Footers"; "Finding and Replacing Text"; and "Printing."

Jazz offers many features for exchanging information between functions, so many, in fact, that we have devoted a chapter to the subject of data transfer (Chapter 8). There you can find Tips and Traps on bringing information from other Jazz functions into your word processing documents and learn about the HotView feature.

Getting Started

5.01 *Trap:* *Don't mistake the mouse pointer for the Insertion bar.*

In Jazz word processing your typing appears at the flashing Insertion bar. The I-beam pointer belongs to the mouse. It's easy to mistake the I-beam for the Insertion bar: if you do, you'll be surprised to see your typing appearing at an entirely unexpected place.

5.02 *Tip:* *Insert text anywhere in a document by using the mouse to point and click.*

Move the Insertion bar to any point you want in a document and anchor it there by pointing and clicking. Any typing will appear at that point. If you can't get the insertion point to stick, see if Trap 5.20 can help.

5.03 *Tip:* *Correct typing mistakes as you work by using the BACKSPACE key.*

The BACKSPACE key removes text as it moves. Keep holding it down and it will erase everything on the page. This feature makes it easy to fix small mistakes as they occur.

5.04 *Tip:* *You can select large areas quickly by using the SHIFT-click method.*

Selecting large areas by dragging can be laborious, especially if the area spans more than one screen. A shortcut is to select the beginning of the section and then move the pointer to the end of the section, hold the SHIFT key down, and click.

5.05 *Tip:* *To unselect a selection, simply click anywhere else on the page.*

It's easy to make mistakes when selecting. To remove the highlighting, point anywhere else on your page and click.

5.06 Tip: *Replace text quickly by selecting and retyping.*

To replace text of any size, you don't need to delete it first. Just select the section to be replaced and type the new material. The old text will disappear and the new text will be inserted in its place.

5.07 Tip: *When you make a mistake typing, cutting, or copying, the Undo command might be able to help.*

The Edit menu's first command is Undo (you can also use the key combination COMMAND-Z). It can erase typing or reverse cutting and copying. For instance, if you cut some text and realize before you move the insertion point that you want it back, choosing Undo Cut from the Edit menu brings the text back to the original spot. Similarly, if you have entered some text that you don't like, you can select Undo Typing from the Edit menu. But see the following Trap.

5.08 Trap: *Don't count on Undo to remedy cutting or clearing errors if you have moved the Insertion bar.*

The Undo command is most helpful when you have accidentally cut or cleared text and want it back, but it won't work if you have moved the insertion point. (The Undo choice will read Can't Undo.)

5.09 Tip: *To insert blank lines, use the RETURN key.*

You can insert blank lines whenever you need to by pressing the RETURN key. This makes it easy to add lines between paragraphs or create space for an illustration.

5.10 Tip: *You can remove blank lines with the BACKSPACE key.*

If you want to bring text separated by blank lines closer together, simply place the Insertion bar at the left margin of the blank line and press the BACKSPACE key once for each blank line to be deleted.

5.11 Tip: *You can quickly remove extra spaces with the BACKSPACE key and the SHIFT-click method.*

To bring text separated by extra spaces or lines closer together, select the space you want to delete with the SHIFT-click method. Place the Insertion bar at the beginning of the space to be deleted, press the SHIFT key, and click at the end of the space. It will be selected as shown:

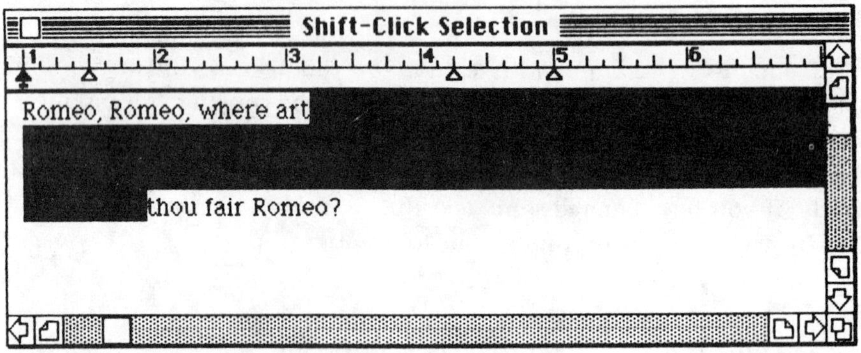

When you press the BACKSPACE key, the space is deleted.

5.12 Tip: *You can quickly look at offscreen sections of your document by using the Scroll box, Page box, and Scroll arrows.*

Figure 5-1 shows where these features are on your word processing window. By dragging the Scroll box in the direction you wish to move, you can view other parts of a long document. The amount of text scrolled by using the box depends on how long the document is: dragging the box from the top to the bottom will take you to the end of the last page of your document. Clicking above or below the Scroll box will move you forward or backward in a document one screen at a time.

Clicking on the Page box also moves you one screen at a time. Clicking on the Scroll arrows takes you one line at a time. All three features can also be used in a similar fashion to scroll horizontally.

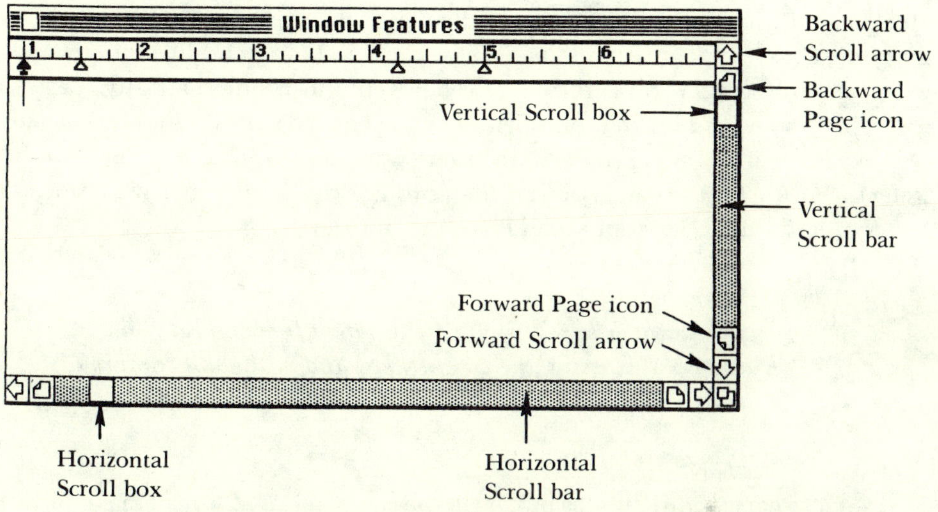

Figure 5-1. The word processing window

5.13 Tip: *Let Jazz automatically number your pages.*

Jazz can insert page numbers for you automatically if you create a header or a footer and use the Page command in the HotView menu. A header places the page number at the top of the page and a footer at the bottom.

First, select Header or Footer from the Format menu. A header (or footer) window will open:

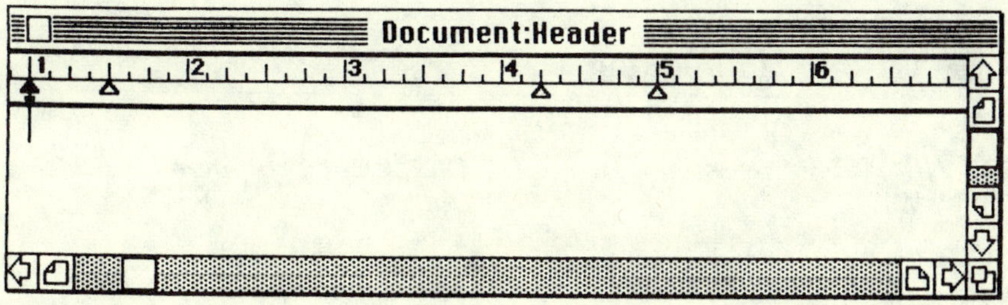

The Ruler line, Console settings, and any menu selections can be changed and will affect only the header or footer. You can edit material in headers and footers as you would edit regular text.

To insert page numbers, position the Insertion bar at the point where you wish the page number to appear on the page; then select Page from the HotView menu. HotView will insert a page number at that spot when you click on the Close box. Every page (except page 1 in the case of a header) will have its number inserted. Even when you are doing a lot of editing, HotView renumbers automatically.

There are other HotView options. They can be used to insert the current date or time, keeping it always current, in the same way that you inserted page numbers. Refer to "Using Headers and Footers" for more Tips and Traps on using headers and footers and Chapter 8 for Tips and Traps on HotView.

5.14 Tip: *Prevent wordwrap from splitting text that should run together by using the OPTION key and SPACEBAR combination.*

Text such as dates should not be broken at the end of a line. You can make Jazz treat any phrase as a unit by creating "hard spaces" between words in the phrase by holding down the OPTION key and pressing the SPACEBAR when the cursor is on the space.

5.15 Tip: *You can enhance your text with special symbols by using OPTION key combinations.*

When you select Key Caps from the Apple menu, you are presented with an image of the Mac keyboard. By pressing the OPTION key you can see the special symbols available. You can use the OPTION key in combination with the letter key on which the special symbol appears to insert that symbol into your text.

Copying, Cutting, and Pasting

5.16 Tip: *Avoid retyping by using the Cut or Copy command.*

The Cut command removes text from its original location and puts it in the Clipboard. You can then paste it into its new location. The Copy command places a duplicate in the Clipboard, leaving the original text in place. You can then paste the copy at a new spot.

If you cut text, the surrounding text will move to fill in the empty space. Remember that if you are trying to cut or copy to an area below your last current line, you may have to expand your active area by pressing RETURN several times to get the Insertion bar to the appropriate line and column.

You can use the COMMAND key in combination with other keys to cut, copy, and paste: Cut is COMMAND-X, Copy is COMMAND-C, and Paste is COMMAND-V.

5.17 Tip: *You don't need to reselect text to copy it more than once.*

When you cut or copy text, it stays in the Clipboard until something else is cut or copied. If you want to copy something several times, just move the insertion point each time to the new location and select Paste (or COMMAND-V). The text will stay in the Clipboard until the next cut or copy replaces the previous one.

5.18 Trap: *If you try to cut or copy and find the Edit menu choices dimmed, it is probably because there is no text selected.*

Text cannot be cut, copied, or cleared unless it has first been selected.

5.19 Trap: *If you try to paste and find the menu choice dimmed, it is probably because you have not placed anything in the Clipboard by cutting or copying.*

Text can only be pasted when it is in the Clipboard, and it can only get there if you have cut it or copied it.

5.20 Trap: *If you have trouble cutting or copying to an area below your last line, you need to expand the active area.*

The last line you type defines the end of the active area. If you want to insert new material below your last line, use the RETURN key to expand your active area.

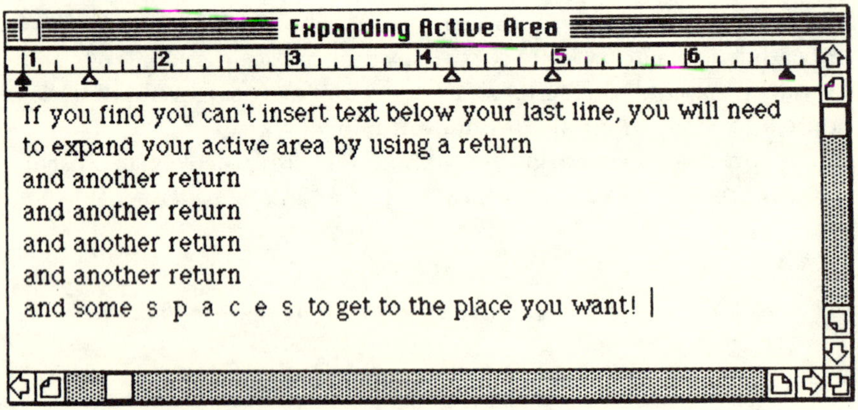

5.21 Tip: *Keep a library of frequently used text (boilerplate) in a separate word processing document for copying when needed.*

The same or similar text is often used in many documents. For example, a law office compiles many documents, like wills, which differ only in a few particulars. If you keep standard text in a separate document, you can copy and edit it for specific needs more quickly than if you type a new document from scratch.

When using the library, you can use the Search command to locate the needed text and then copy it in the new document.

Changing Spacing, Typefaces, and Formats

5.22 Trap: *When you enter Jazz word processing, the margins will be too narrow to look good on 8 1/2 × 11-inch paper.*

Jazz sets its margins by default so that all of a line will appear on the screen. This is handy when editing, but the document may look better when printed if you expand the margins. As a guide, we assume that one-inch margins on both the left and the right are standard. We also assume you have aligned the left tear line of computer paper, or the left edge of cut sheet paper, with the red line on the Imagewriter's paper bail when inserting paper in the printer.

To create a one-inch left margin, move both the indentation marker and the left margin marker to the 1 3/8 setting. The text will realign itself whenever margin settings are changed.

To expand the right margin, drag the right margin marker to 8 3/4.

5.23 Tip: ***Temporarily use the narrow default margins until you are ready to print in order to see all your work.***

Jazz default margins are set so that all of a line can appear on the screen at one time. It can be distracting to have the screen jump back and forth when you read your text as it is typed.

As you saw in the previous Tip, you can widen your margin settings for printing. Because this wider margin will change the position of paragraphs, headings, and illustrations, scroll through your document after setting the margins, but before printing, to see that the new page breaks don't split material inappropriately. You can add or delete blank lines to improve positioning.

5.24 Tip: ***You can control the line spacing and justification of your document by changing the Console settings.***

Icons in the Console control line spacing, the way text is related to the margins on the page (justification), and tabs. If you don't change them, Jazz gives you single-spaced lines and text justified on the left. However, the Console allows you to set 1, 1.5, or 2 spaces between lines and also to align your text with the left or right (or both) margins justified. You can also center the text on the page.

When you change one of these settings, remember that the entire document is changed. See Tip 5.31 on using Ruler lines to change the settings for sections of text.

5.25 Tip: ***You can change the typeface used, the size of the letters, and the style of type for all of your document or for selected portions of it.***

Jazz provides several different typefaces and sizes of type, as well as bold, italic, underline, outline, and shadow styles. If you don't make any changes, Jazz uses 12-point New York font and plain text. You can change any of these by simply selecting the text to be changed and choosing the appropriate font, point, or style from the menus. The selected text will appear in the new format. The current font, point, and style (which control all text you enter from now on) remain what they were before. You can use COMMAND key combinations to implement style options quickly.

If you simply select a new font, point, or style from the menus (or with COMMAND-key combinations) without first selecting a portion of the text, all text you enter after the change will appear in the new format, since this actually resets the current settings.

If you want to change the format for all the text you've entered, open the Edit menu and choose Select All (you can also use the key combination COMMAND-A).

5.26 Tip: *To indent the beginnings of paragraphs or single lines, use the TAB key.*

Jazz lets you indent text in several different ways: you can simply space to the desired spot with the SPACEBAR, set a tab stop and use the TAB key, or use the indentation marker. Figure 5-2 shows the different features of the Ruler line and Console that are involved with using tabs.

The TAB key method is best suited for indenting the first line of a paragraph or indenting single lines. Jazz has preset the first tab stop at five spaces, and several other tabs are also preset in the Ruler line. Just press the TAB key to move the insertion point to the tab stop and start typing.

To move a tab marker, simply drag it to its new location. To add a tab marker, select the tab icon (tab well) in the Console: then select the desired spot on the Ruler line.

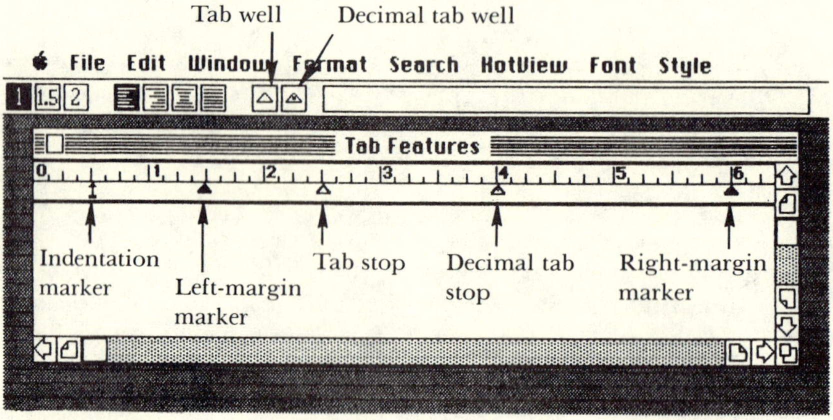

Figure 5-2. Tab features

While the tab well is selected, every time you click on the Ruler line a new tab marker is added. If you click on an existing tab marker, it is removed. Be careful not to try to move a current tab marker when the tab well is selected: you will erase the tab. (See the next Trap.)

If you need to indent several lines of text, see the next Tip.

5.27 Tip: *Use hanging indentation when you want to indent all but the first line of each paragraph.*

Using Jazz's indentation marker is helpful when you need to indent paragraphs after the first line. When you are indenting only part of your document, use a Ruler line. See the series of Tips and Traps on using Ruler lines, beginning at Tip 5.31.

When you drag the indentation marker to the left of the margin marker, it will function as your true left margin. You'll start each new paragraph at the indentation marker, but when you come to the end of a line of text and the line wraps, the insertion point will return to the margin marker. After you start a new paragraph, pressing RETURN begins your typing at the indentation marker. The following illustration shows an example of hanging indentation:

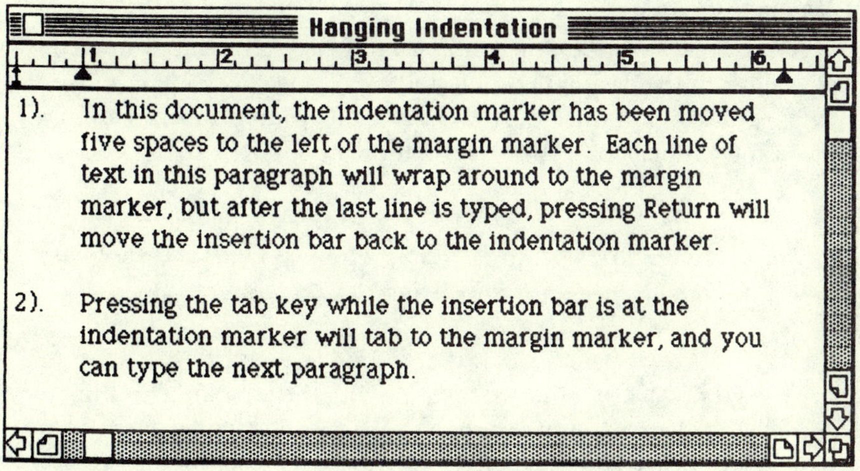

5.28 Trap: *You cannot move your margin or indentation markers until the tab well has been deselected.*

To move your margin markers, click on the tab well to deselect it. If you don't, clicking anywhere on the Ruler line will only add another tab. Clicking on a tab marker will remove the tab.

5.29 Tip: *Use decimal tabs when entering columns of numbers to align them at the decimal point automatically.*

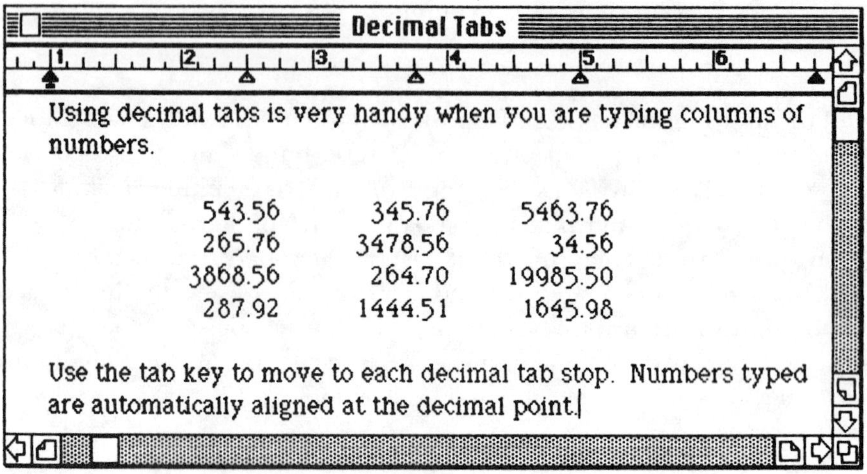

To set a decimal tab, select the decimal tab well and then select the point on the Ruler line where you want the decimal point to fall.

As with regular tabs, if you remove a decimal tab, your numbers realign with the next tab or at the left margin if there are no more tabs.

5.30 Trap: *Moving or deleting a tab stop also moves all text that has been aligned with it by using the* TAB *key.*

If you have used the TAB key to indent text, moving the tab marker will realign the text. This can be a help in realigning text or a nuisance if you inadvertently move the tab to a new spot for use with later text. (Don't forget that you can insert a new Ruler line to control later text differently. See the following Tip.)

If you delete a tab stop, all the text originally aligned with it shifts to the next tab stop. If there are no more tab stops, the text aligns with the left margin marker.

5.31 Tip: *You can control the formatting and appearance of sections of text by using Ruler lines.*

When you open a new word processing document, its formats are set in the Ruler line at the top of the document and highlighted on the Console. Because at this point there is only one Ruler line, changing Console settings affects the entire document. If you want to change the line spacing, justification, tabs, or indentation for only one section of text, you need to insert a new Ruler line.

Figure 5-3 shows how using several different Ruler lines can change a document's appearance.

When you insert a new Ruler line (by selecting Insert Ruler from the Format menu), it appears at the insertion point with the settings of the previous Ruler line. Changing its margin and tab settings affects all the text you enter below it until you insert another Ruler line.

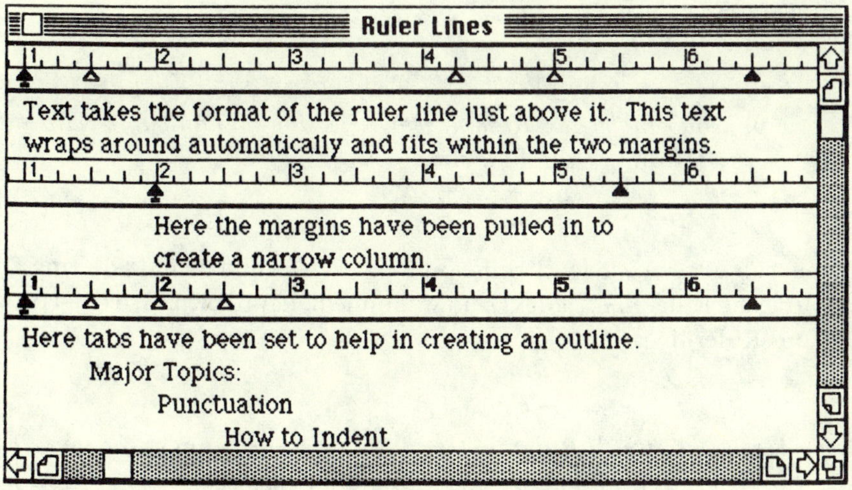

Figure 5-3. Ruler lines

5.32 Tip: *You can quickly duplicate a Ruler line used more than once by copying it.*

If you want to use a Ruler line that's already in your document, just copy it and paste it where you need it, rather than inserting and resetting a new one.

5.33 Trap: *If you have more than one Ruler line in your document, changing Console settings only changes the section of text where the Insertion bar is.*

If you want to change settings for your entire document, you'll have to go into each section with a Ruler line and change the settings there.

5.34 Tip: *You can see more of your text if you hide the Ruler lines.*

Ruler lines take up space on screen. Select Hide Rulers from the Format menu and they will disappear.

5.35 Tip: *You can delete a Ruler line by selecting it and then selecting Clear from the Edit menu.*

Ruler lines can be removed by clicking on them to select them and selecting Clear. When you clear a Ruler line, the text below it immediately reformats to the settings of the previous Ruler line.

5.36 Trap: *Inserting a Ruler line with the insertion point at the margin will create a blank line that you may not want.*

To avoid this, insert the Ruler line at the end of the last line of old text, not in the next blank line's margin.

5.37 Tip: *Save commonly used Ruler lines in a separate file so you can copy them when you need them.*

Create Ruler lines with margin settings that you frequently need and save them in one file. Copy them as needed.

Figure 5-4 shows how such a library of Ruler lines might look. Descriptive text has been inserted below each Ruler line as a reminder of its function. You can cut and paste these Ruler lines into any other word processing document when both documents are open.

5.38 Tip: *Save a frequently used format, including margin settings, line spacing, font, point, and style.*

If you have a group of settings that you use frequently, save them as a document with no text. When you want to use the format, open the document and write your text, saving it under a new name. This way your format file will still be on disk ready for use again.

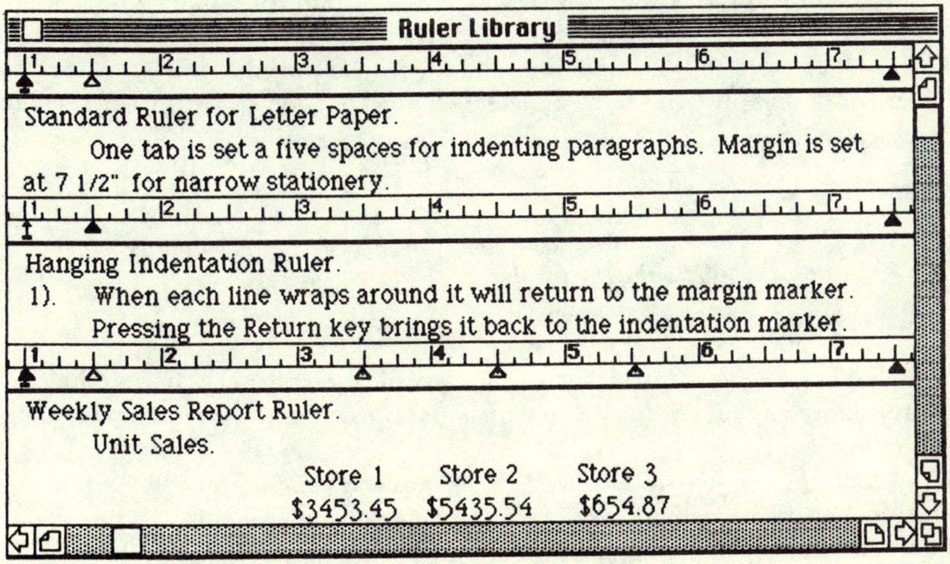

Figure 5-4. Ruler library

5.39 Tip: *You can have printing stop at any point and be continued on the next page by selecting Insert Page Break from the Format menu.*

Jazz prints a certain number of lines on each page based on the paper size you choose. (See the section on printing.) If you want to leave space on a page for an illustration or at the end of a chapter, select Insert Page Break to tell the printer to continue the text on the next page. To remove a page break, just backspace over it. The space between the last word and the first will close up. You may need to insert a space to separate the joined text properly.

Using Headers and Footers

5.40 Tip: *You can automatically print text or graphics at the top or bottom of every page.*

Jazz will print any text or graphics you wish at the top of every page but the first (a header) or at the bottom of every page (a footer).

You can include illustrations from MacPaint in a header by placing them in the Scrapbook or Clipboard and copying them into the header or footer window. This would be very handy, for instance, if you wanted to have a logo printed on every page.

You may want the date, the time, and the page number printed in a header or footer. You accomplish this by first selecting Header or Footer from the Format menu and then the appropriate options from the HotView menu.

5.41 Trap: *The formatting of headers and footers doesn't change when you change the formatting of your text.*

This may be good news and bad news. Headers and footers can be changed independently of the word processing document. This allows you to format them separately from the text.

It can cause problems, however. For example, if you are working with narrow margins, in order to see all your work and expand your margins, the headers and footers will not move. If you have carefully aligned a header with the right margin, it will not be aligned with the new formatting. Changing any other formatting, such as font, style, or point size, does not affect the font, style, or point size of the headers.

5.42 Trap: *Headers and footers cannot be edited from within your text.*

Headers and footers can be edited only by reselecting Header or Footer from the Format menu and making changes there.

5.43 Trap: *Unless you include a return under the text in headers or above the text in footers, the regular text will crowd up against them on the page.*

Headers and footers look best when set slightly apart from the regular text. Inserting a return at the end of the header or at the beginning of a footer creates a nice separation.

You can also put a return in a footer by itself to keep text from getting too close to the page break.

5.44 Tip: *You can number sections of text separately from each other, but you will need to keep them as separate documents.*

In creating a document you may want to have sections numbered separately, such as page 1.1, 1.2, 2.3, 2.4, and so on. Because you can have only one header or footer in a document, you can have only one numbering scheme, but you can get around this by placing the section number in the header or footer and saving each section as a separate document.

For example, the following illustration shows a header containing the word "Page" followed by the section number and a period.

Selecting Page from the Hotview menu inserts the actual page number at the Insertion bar. The document will then be numbered Page 1.1, Page 1.2, and so on.

When you need to create another section (section 2, for example) you must do so in a new document. If you try to cut or copy one section to another, the source document will be renumbered according to the header or footer of the target document and the section numbering will be spoiled.

Finding and Replacing Text

5.45 Tip: *You can easily locate specific text in a document by using the Find command.*

First select Find from the Search menu; then in the Entry box type the word or phrase you want to find.

Forward means the search will begin at the top of the document. Backward means it will begin searching from the end of the document. If you select Partial Word, Jazz will search for the combination of letters, even within a longer word.

When you click on Find First, Jazz finds the first occurrence of the word or phrase in the document. Click on Find Next to locate the next occurrence. Then you can simply press the RETURN key to find the next occurrences.

5.46 Tip: *You can use seldom used symbols to indicate places you want to come back to.*

If you want to mark a place in a document for adding more text or filling in missing information, you can type an unusual symbol or word at the spot. When you're ready to continue working, the Find command can locate the symbol for you. For instance, the word EdEd may mark a spot where you know future editing is needed.

If the Find command cannot locate your marking symbol or word, try searching for it as a partial word and as a whole word.

5.47 Tip: *You can easily replace misspellings throughout your entire document by using the Replace command.*

If you realized that you have misspelled or incorrectly punctuated a word or phrase consistently in a document or simply want to replace certain words or phrases, you can use the Replace command in the Search menu:

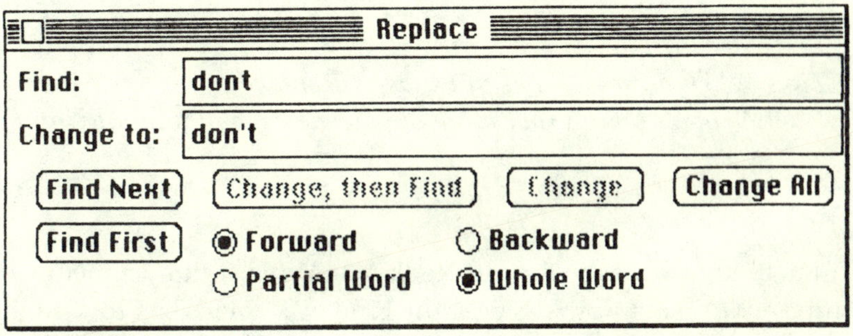

When you select Find First, Jazz finds the first instance of the text to be replaced.

- If you want to replace only the first example found, select Change.
- If you want to replace it and see if there is another instance needing to be changed, select Change and then Find.
- If you want to replace all instances of the text, select Change All.

5.48 ***Tip:*** *Avoid repetitious typing by using an abbreviation in your text and later replace it with the full spelling by using Find and Replace.*

You can use an abbreviation for phrases or words of up to 40 characters and later use Find and Replace to substitute the full spelling. This could prove useful when using complex legal, medical, or scientific terms or mathematical formulas.

For example, you might need to type a long name, such as Aloysious J. Pillowpounder, or a medical term, such as coccidioidomycosis, several times in your document. Using an abbreviation lets you type the words only once.

Because the abbreviation you specify in the Find box will be the only one replaced by the full spellings, make sure you always use the same abbreviation. Any variations will be ignored by the Replace command.

5.49 ***Tip:*** *Use Copy and Paste to enter text from your document into the Find and Change To boxes.*

When you are entering text in any of the search function boxes, you can edit it by clicking to insert text, clicking and backspacing to delete text, or selecting and backspacing to erase it. You can even use the Copy and Paste commands to bring text from the word processing document into the boxes.

5.50 *Tip:* *When doing a series of Finds or Replaces, drag the Find or Replace box so that more of your document window can be seen.*

It is helpful to be able to see the Find or Replace box and your document window at the same time. The easiest way is to drag the Find or Replace box toward the top of your screen. It will go almost to the Menu bar. You can also drag the document window downward.

5.51 *Tip:* *Don't inadvertently enter extra spaces within a phrase or before or after text you want to find.*

Jazz regards spaces as characters and in searching will look for exactly what you have typed, spaces and all. If you search and can't find what you are pretty sure is really there, check to see how you have entered the text to be found. You may have some extra spaces.

5.52 *Tip:* *You can easily delete all occurrences of specific text by leaving the Change To box empty.*

The Replace function allows you to replace a string of characters, a word, or a phrase with nothing if you want to. Just leave the Change To box empty.

Printing

5.53 *Tip:* *You can print selected pages of a document by using the From: and To: boxes in the Print Document dialog box.*

If you leave this box blank, printing will begin at page 1. Enter another page number if you want printing to begin on other than page 1. If, for example, you just want to print page 2, enter 2 in both From: and To:.

Unfortunately, Jazz will not let you print a partial page. You can simulate this, however, by inserting temporary page breaks around the text you wish to print. You then print the page and delete the page breaks.

5.54 Tip: *Speed printing time by choosing Draft quality from the Print Document menu.*

Jazz gives you three options for print quality. Selecting High results in dark but slow printing. Standard is adequate for most needs. Draft gives the fastest printing time, but it prints only in one typeface, with only plain style. If you are just printing to review your writing, Draft is a good choice.

5.55 Trap: *If you don't use the Monaco font when printing in Draft mode, your text will be unevenly spaced.*

Using Draft mode with fonts other than Monaco causes irregular spacing to appear in the text when printed. Formatting your text in Monaco font before printing will cause it to appear with normal spacing.

With all fonts, Draft mode will only print text in the plain style, ignoring the other style enhancements of bold, italic, underline, outline, and shadow.

5.56 Tip: *You can use letterhead or other single-sheet paper by selecting Cut Sheet from the Print Document dialog box.*

When you choose Cut Sheet from the Print Document dialog box, Jazz prompts you to insert your next sheet of paper after each page is printed. See your printer's manual for setting the printer to feed cut sheets. Select Continuous for continuous-roll printer paper.

5.57 Tip: *You can print wider than normally possible by choosing Wide from the Page Setup dialog box.*

Choosing Wide in the Page Setup box causes the text to be printed sideways. If you select US Legal as well as Wide, using legal paper in the printer will give you a 14-inch-wide document.

The printer will observe the length of the paper as its new width and the old width as its new length. The type quality in Wide looks best when your document is set at 12 point, the Jazz default setting. However, when you print in Wide mode, a 14-point type is used. Changing your document point size to 10 to compensate reduces the type size when printed, but the quality suffers. Draft mode is not available with the Wide choice.

6

Graphics

A graph organizes a set of data in graphics form so it is easier to understand and analyze. Jazz's graphics application can produce most of the common forms of business graphs, and all can be embellished in various ways.

To create a graph in Jazz, the data must reside in a worksheet or database. When a range of data is selected in the worksheet or database, you can plot it on the graph. You can create as many plots as you wish on a graph. For instance, you may want to create a sales projection graph with a line for each sales office. Each line would be a separate plot with its own selected range of data.

Once a range is plotted, a link is formed in two ways. The range is linked to the plot: any changes made to the data are automatically reflected in the plot. The graph document is linked to the supporting document: whenever the graph document is opened, it automatically looks for the supporting document and redraws the plot from the range.

This link affects how you work with ranges and plots as well as with graphs and supporting documents as a whole. Reading the first few Tips and Traps in this chapter should help in clarifying this. The first Tip outlines the steps in creating a graph, and the following three Traps isolate the difficulties you might encounter if you don't follow the first Tip carefully.

In this chapter, the "Getting Started" section focuses on how you create a graph, add basic enhancements, and print a graph. Later sections deal with topics involving the link between ranges and plots. The section "Enhancing Graphs" expands on ways you can embellish graphs. The concluding section, "Using Graphs Effectively," focuses on choosing a graph that best reflects the meaning you want the data to convey.

Getting Started

6.01 Tip: *To create a graph, open a worksheet or database, select a range of data, open a graphics document, and select a plot.*

First, open a worksheet or database and select the range of data that you wish to graph. For example, you might select a series of monthly sales totals.

Next, leaving the worksheet or database open and the range selected, open a graphics document. From the Type menu select the type of plot you wish to make. For example, a line plot might be a good choice for representing the change in the selected sales totals over time. Select Plot to actually plot the graph.

You can enhance your graph by adding a title, labeling the values, changing its size, and so on. You can also print it. If you want to save the graph, you must first save the supporting worksheet or database and then the graph. The following Tips and Traps will give you the details.

6.02 Trap: *Don't expect to create a graph before first creating or opening a Worksheet or Database document containing the data you wish to view graphically.*

Some graphics programs allow you to directly enter the data to be graphed, but Jazz Graphics does not. Each Jazz Graphics document expects to get its source data from either a Worksheet document or a Database document. When you first create a graphics document, its source document must be the last one that was active before you activated the current graphics document.

Data is not transferred through cutting, copying, or pasting, as you might think. It is transferred by opening a worksheet or database, making a range active by selecting it, making a graphics document active, and using the Plot command to graph that data.

If you open a graphics document for the first time without first making a Database or Worksheet document active and selecting a range of data as source data, you'll have nothing to graph.

***6.03* Trap:** *Don't expect to see anything on your graph until you've selected a source data range in a Worksheet or Database document and selected a plot type from the Plot menu.*

You must select a range in a Source worksheet or Database document before you can plot any data on the graph. Once you've done this, the Plot menu lets you take the data in the selected range and graph it in several different ways. With the area selected in the worksheet shown in Figure 6-1, the graph that results from choosing Area from the Plot menu is shown in Figure 6-2.

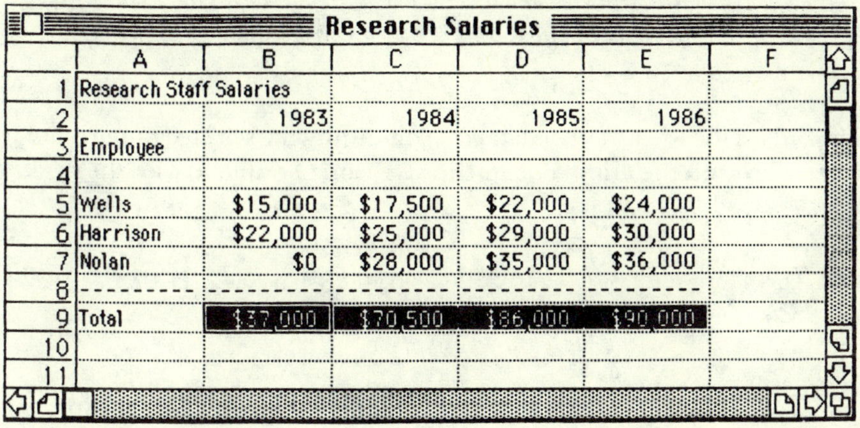
Research Salaries

	A	B	C	D	E	F
1	Research Staff Salaries					
2		1983	1984	1985	1986	
3	Employee					
4						
5	Wells	$15,000	$17,500	$22,000	$24,000	
6	Harrison	$22,000	$25,000	$29,000	$30,000	
7	Nolan	$0	$28,000	$35,000	$36,000	
8	---------	---------	---------	---------	---------	
9	Total	$37,000	$70,500	$86,000	$90,000	
10						
11						

Figure 6-1. Range selection

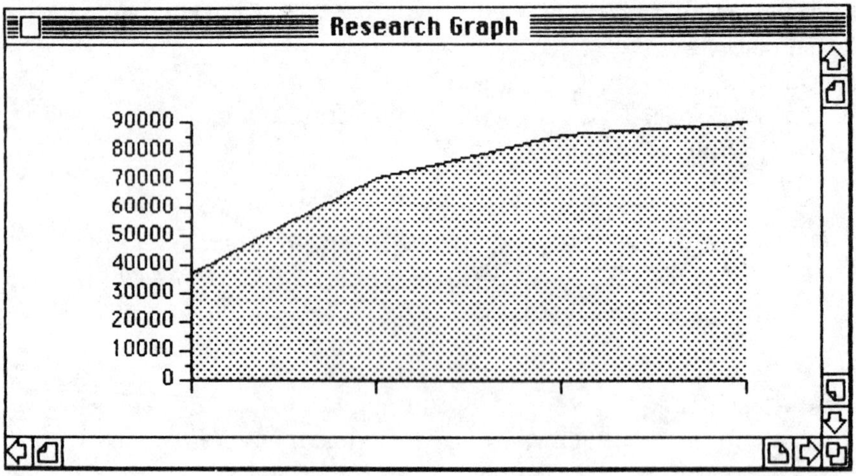

Figure 6-2. Area plot

6.04 Trap: *When you are first establishing a link between a graphics document and an underlying source document, the source document must have been the active document before the graph was opened, and it must still be open.*

In other words, if the worksheet or database containing the selected range is not lying immediately beneath the graph document, you won't be able to plot the data.

6.05 Tip: *You can easily change the way a particular plot displays your data by using the Plot Selector.*

If you choose a plot (such as a line plot) and want to plot the same data a different way (as a bar plot, for example), clicking once on the Plot Selector icon will place a row of selector icons along the plot as shown in Figure 6-3. You can tell which range the plot is graphing by looking at the address in the Reference box.

As long as the range is still selected in the document immediately beneath the graphics window (see Trap 6.03), choosing another Plot option will replot the data in

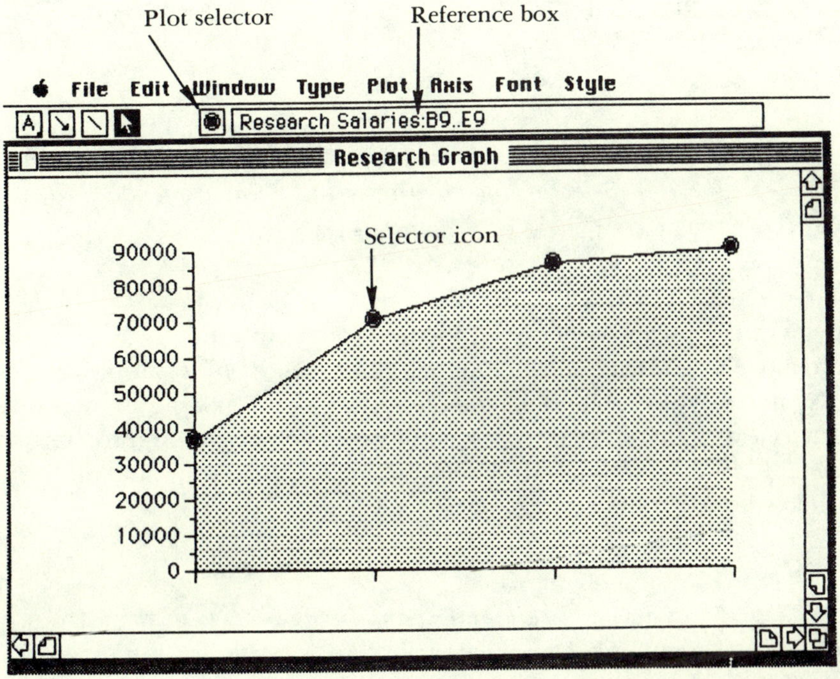

Figure 6-3. Plot selection

a new plot. You can then remove the selector icons from the new plot by clicking anywhere else in the graph.

6.06 Trap: *When plotting more than one range, you may inadvertently duplicate a plot if you don't first select a new range in the worksheet or database.*

You may select a new plot only to find you have duplicated the plot you just made. This happens when you forget to highlight a new range in the worksheet or database for each new plot. Make sure you select the new range to be plotted before you select Plot.

Sometimes you may want to represent the same range with different plots so you can choose which one does the best job and then clear the ones you don't want. Every time you select a Plot option without selecting a new range, the current range is duplicated.

6.07 Tip: *You can remove unwanted plots from your graph by using the Plot Selector and then selecting Clear from the Edit menu.*

Sometimes you may want to remove a plot from your graph entirely. First, choose the plot to remove by clicking on the Plot Selector until the plot is highlighted with selector symbols. When you have several plots, the Plot Selector highlights a different plot each time you click on its icon. When the desired plot is highlighted, select Clear from the Edit menu. If you haven't done anything else first, you can replace the plot with Undo Clear.

6.08 Tip: *Plots automatically reflect any changes made in the worksheet or database ranges they have been plotted from.*

When you create plots from data in a worksheet or database, a permanent link is established with your graph. Whenever you change the data in the worksheet or database range you have used to plot from, your graph automatically changes as well. This means you can perform graphical what-if analyses.

For example, a spreadsheet might be used to analyze future retirement income under a variety of assumptions about benefit plans, Social Security, and taxes. Once a graph is created, every time you change an assumption in the spreadsheet, the result is instantly shown on the graph.

If you include a graph in a frequently compiled report, you don't have to recreate the graph anew each time the supporting data changes. When you enter new data in the worksheet or database, your graph is updated as well. See Tip 6.10 to understand how updating depends on saving supporting graphs and documents.

6.09 Tip: *If you want to save a graph, you must first save the worksheet or database from which it was generated.*

If you create a graph with plots from ranges in a worksheet or database and try to save the graph without first saving the worksheet or database, you will get the error message "You can't save a document that depends on another that has never been saved."

To maintain the link between range and plot when the documents are saved, the source document must be saved first. The graph uses the name of the supporting document to locate the supporting data.

6.10 Tip: *You can save supporting documents on a disk other than the dependent graphs and relink the documents when the graph document is opened.*

Limited disk space may require you to save supporting documents on a different disk than the dependent graphs. This may also be necessary if you alternate the supporting document a graph is linked to. (See Tip 6.29.) Jazz allows you to do this.

When you open a graph document and the supporting document is not on the same disk, you are given a message informing you that it can't be found and that the graph depends on it. You are asked if you want to substitute another supporting document. If you click on Yes, the following dialog box appears.

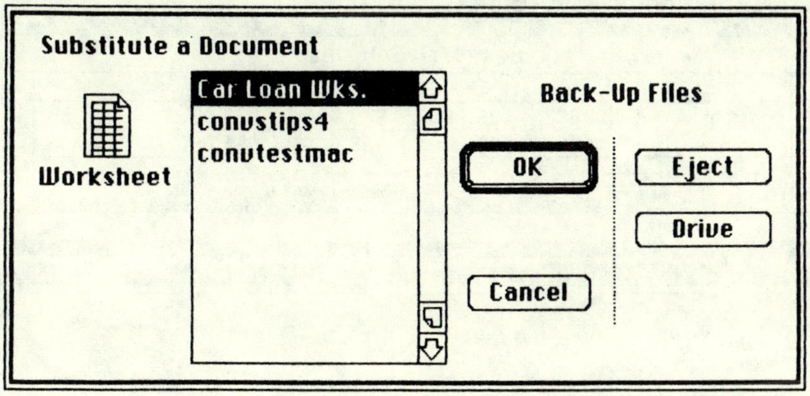

The commands available in this box allow you to eject a disk and insert the one containing the supporting document. Then you can select the file and click OK. The supporting data will be read and replotted on the open graph.

6.11 Tip: *Freeze a graph you don't wish to be automatically updated by saving the linked worksheet or database under a new name, keeping the original linked to the graph.*

You may need to make changes to a supporting document but not want the dependent graph to change. The way to do this is to save the supporting document first under its original name and then under a new name. Work with the newly named document, but leave the original name alone to preserve the graph. (To save disk space, delete data that is not part of any plots in the original documents.)

6.12 Tip: *Make it easier to select ranges for graphing by adjusting the window size so you can look at your graph and supporting document at the same time.*

Because selecting ranges and plots involves switching between the supporting and graph documents, seeing both at the same time can be handy. You can shrink each window by dragging the Size box and position the window by dragging the Title bar. Figure 6-4 shows how two such windows might be positioned.

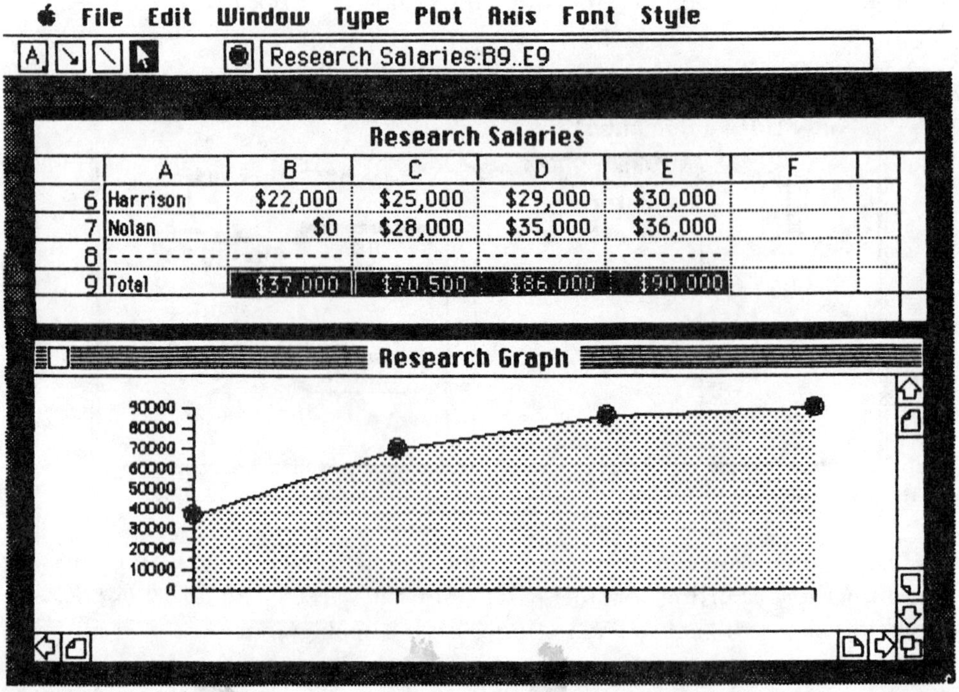

Figure 6-4. Sizing windows

When you shrink a graph window, the graph is resized so you don't have to scroll around to see different parts of it. You may need to scroll within the worksheet or database window to find the range you wish to select.

6.13 Tip: *Enhance the key parts of your graph to make it easier to understand and also more attractive.*

We'll use the following techniques to enhance the simple graph shown in Figure 6-2. The finished graph can be seen in Figure 6-5.

Labeling Values

The Axis menu contains options to let you label and format the top, bottom, left, and right sides of your graph. The Set Label command places labels beneath each data point.

Figure 6-1 showed the research staff salaries for four years, 1983 through 1986.

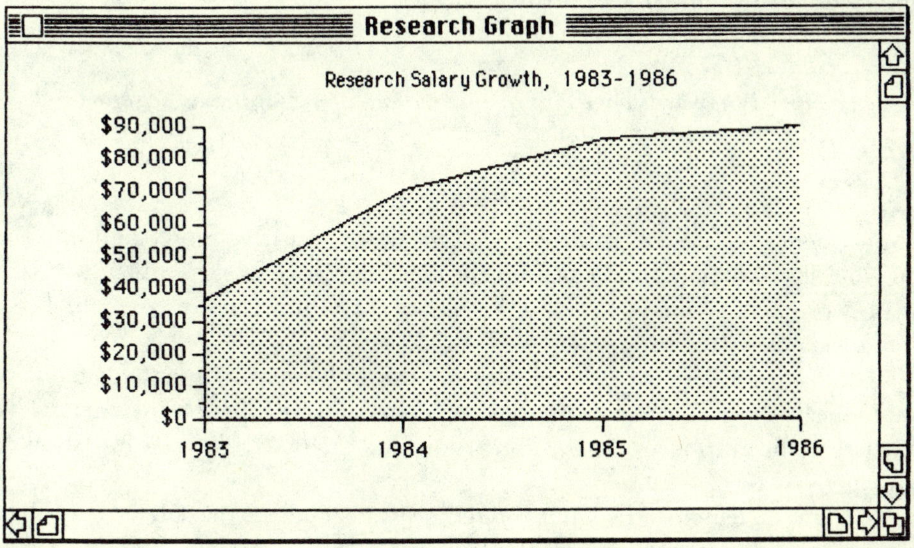

Figure 6-5. Basic enhancements

You can place these years as labels beneath the appropriate totals in the graph by selecting the range in the supporting document that contains them, making the graph document active, and choosing Set Labels from the Axis menu.

Adding a Title

Choosing a good title for your graph helps to pinpoint what you want the graph to show. In our example, you could title the graph "Growth of Research Salaries". Select Top from the Axis menu; then type the desired title. When you click on OK, the title is centered at the top of the graph.

Formatting Values

In Figure 6-2 the left axis values were not formatted as dollars. You can make them appear as currency by choosing Format from the Axis menu and then choosing Currency and zero decimal places.

You can also add arrows or insert lines to connect elements. Just click on the Arrow well or Line well in the Console and then click where you want the arrow to be placed or where the line should begin. When you place a line or arrow, dragging the pointer will lengthen or shrink it in any direction you want. Releasing the mouse button will position the line or arrow.

6.14 Tip: *When you have two or more plots in a graph, add legends to identify each plot.*

Adding legends to a graph is often necessary when you have more than one plot. Figure 6-6 shows a graph that has been created to compare sales results in two years. The only problem is that you can't tell which set of columns represents which year. Adding legends will help.

To add a legend, select Set Legend from the Style menu. Type the legends you want in the first box. Then click on the second box and type the second legend. Click anywhere in the graph to clear the borders around each box. The result is shown in Figure 6-7.

To change a legend, click on it and retype it. Legends can be deleted completely by selecting Clear Legend from the Style menu.

There are other ways to enhance the appearance of a graph. See the section "Enhancing Graphs" for some of them.

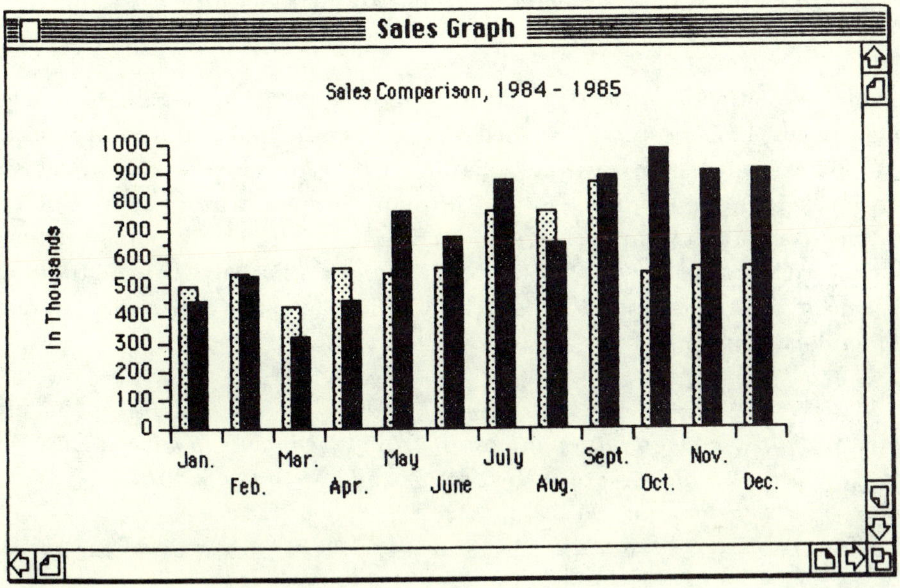

Figure 6-6. Overlapping bars

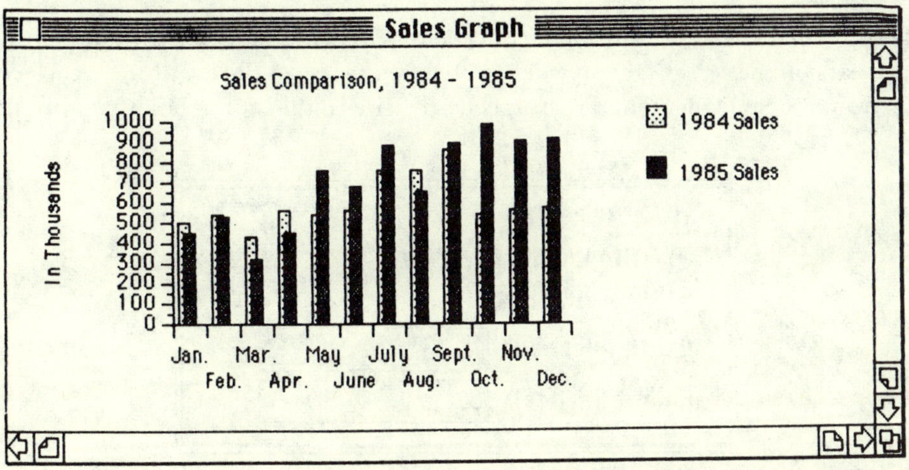

Figure 6-7. Adding legends

6.15 Tip: *If you want to restart a graph, choose Select All and Clear from the Edit menu to remove all links and formats.*

Sometimes you want to start all over. Choosing Select All from the Edit menu selects the entire graph. Choosing Clear then acts as an eraser and removes all plots and notation box contents,but leaves any axis titles, labels, fonts, styles, and formats, such as currency. It also resets the axis scales. If you just want to remove a single plot but preserve the rest of the graph, click the Plot Selector to select the plot to be removed, and choose Clear. To turn off the Select All condition, click anywhere on the graph.

The Select All command is also used to select an entire graph for copying to another document.

6.16 Tip: *Name graphs and the supporting documents in a way that reminds you of their contents and also of the fact that they belong together.*

For example, you might name a worksheet Research Salaries for the Worksheet and its graph Research Salary Graph.

6.17 Tip: *A graph will print the same size it shows on the screen.*

Choosing Print Document from the File menu will print the graph the same size that it appears on the screen. If you want to change the size of the graph, you can select Size from the Style menu and then specify the size in the dialog box that appears:

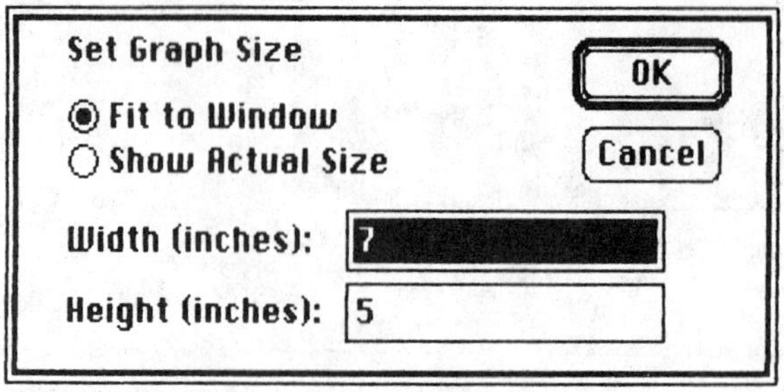

Fit to Window means the graph is always automatically adjusted to fit entirely within any window, even when the size is changed. This is very handy in allowing you to see all of the graph, even in a tiny window.

You can change the size by changing the width and height settings and selecting Show Actual Size.

The original version of the *Jazz Handbook* errs in saying that Jazz will print the size set in the width and height settings even when Fit to Window is selected. The Update pamphlet corrects this error.

6.18 Tip: *Use Tall Adjusted to print with better proportions.*

In Page Setup in the File menu you can select Tall Adjusted when preparing to print a graph. Clicking on this option prints the graph in better proportions than it appears on the screen. This is especially important in printing pie charts as true circles and not ovals. The Tall Adjusted setting also prints in a darker type.

6.19 Trap: *Setting Width and Height wider or taller than the page simply excludes part of the graph from printing.*

When you resize a graph for printing, you need to make sure it will fit on your paper. With standard 8 1/2 × 11-inch paper, a setting wider than 8 1/2 inches will begin excluding part of the graph from printing.

Working With Ranges and Plots

6.20 Tip: *Give descriptive names to the worksheet ranges you create plots from to help you work with plots more accurately.*

When you are working with plots (changing the plot type or labeling data points), the range address of the source data for each selected plot appears in the Reference box. It's a good idea to use the Range menu to assign a separate descriptive name to each source range. Seeing a descriptive name in the Reference box, such as SFSALES, is more helpful than seeing something like B10..G10. This helps you remember which plot you are working with and minimizes having to switch back and forth between worksheet and graph. If your source range gets changed by accident, you know immediately because the range name disappears from the Reference box.

6.21 Tip: *You don't have to have a supporting worksheet or database open to change the type of plot.*

Once you have created a graph and have saved the worksheet or database it is based on, you can change the type of plot by selecting it with the Plot Selector and choosing a new plot. This is handy if you want to see what the same data looks like in a new format. Remember, you won't be able to plot new data unless you open a worksheet or database.

6.22 Trap: *Deleting a linked range deletes the plot created from it.*

Remember that a plot on a graph is related to a specific range in a worksheet or database. Changes made to the data in that range will be reflected in the graph's plot. If you clear a range the plot created from it disappears from the graph. If you clear part of a range, only the remaining part is graphed. Consequently, be careful when editing a document from which a graph has been created.

6.23 Tip: *You can move a range from which a plot was generated, and the graph will still be linked to it.*

Once a range has been selected and a graph plotted from it, you can change the location of the data in the supporting document and the plot won't be removed. When you select the range a plot has been created from and cut it, it temporarily disappears from the graph. When you paste it into a new location, the plot reappears on the graph.

6.24 Trap: *If you include a blank cell or text in a range that has been plotted, your plot may look very different from what you want.*

You may unintentionally include a blank cell or text in a plotted range. In a line or bar plot, a blank cell or text causes a blank space to appear between bars or a break in the line between data points.

At times you may want to create a space in a plot. For example, if you create a bar plot of sales totals covering a period of time, inserting blanks can separate bars into distinct groups, such as daily totals grouped by week, weekly sales grouped by month, or monthly sales grouped by year.

It's important to remember that any data (including blank cells and text) that is included in a plotted range will become part of the plot.

6.25 Trap: *In graphing from a database, you can only plot values from one field at a time.*

If you select a range in a database to be plotted in a graph and select values in more than one field, Jazz will give you an error message. Unlike the worksheet, where ranges involving more than one column can be plotted at one time, the database restricts you to values in only one field at a time. (See the following Tip.)

6.26 Tip: *A selected range involving two or more columns in a worksheet will graph from top to bottom of the left column and then from top to bottom of the right column as one plot.*

Here we've selected a worksheet range that includes several rows and columns:

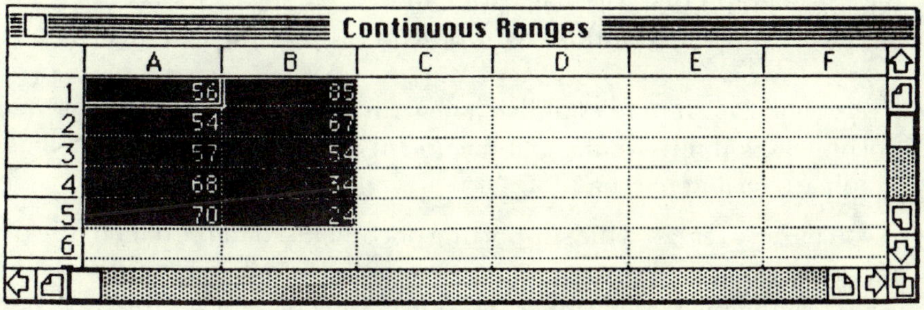

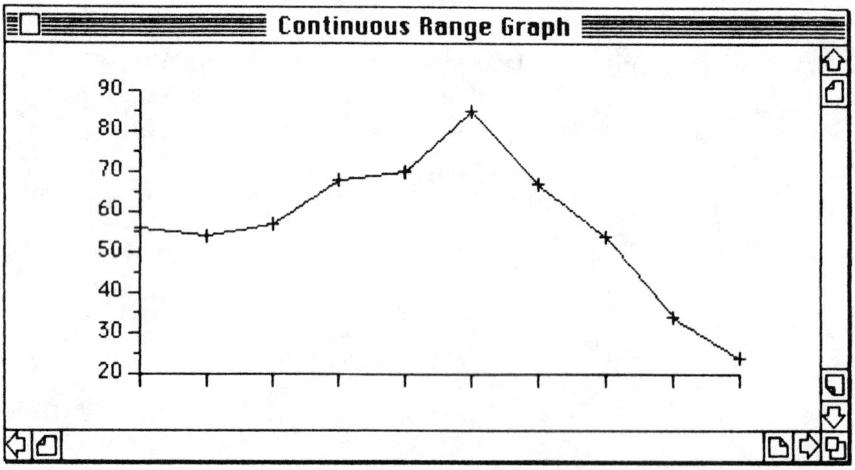

Figure 6-8. Continuous Range plot

When you plot this selection, as seen in the line plot in Figure 6-8, you can see that the data is considered as one set and plots from top to bottom of each column in left-to-right order.

6.27 Tip: *You can create a graph with plots linked to more than one worksheet or database.*

By opening several worksheets or databases and selecting one or more ranges in each, you can create a graph that uses data from all of them for its plots. There are two points to understand when working with several supporting documents:

- Every time you want to establish a new link between a plot and a range in a document, you must make that document active, select the range, make the graph active, and select a plot.
- If you haven't yet saved the supporting documents, or if the data in the plotted ranges has changed since the ranges were last saved, you need to save them before saving the graph (unless, of course, you do not want the links between the graph and the source documents to become permanent).

6.28 Tip: *If you want to create a new graph by changing one you already have, you can save time and prevent errors by using Save As to save the original graph under a new name and then make the changes.*

You might want to have several graphs of the same data, but with each graph varying in title, labeling, plot type, and so on. You won't have to recreate as much on each new graph if you save the first graph you make and then save it under a new name by using Save As. The Save As dialog box allows you to rename the graph and save it. You then have the original and a copy of the original under a new name, both connected to the same supporting documents.

Once you have the copy, you can open that document and make whatever changes you wish. In this way, you can create a whole library of similar graphics documents that differ slightly. You should, of course, give each document a name that highlights its uniqueness.

6.29 Tip: *If you create graphs from several similarly constructed worksheets or databases, you can create one "generic" graph and change the link as needed by renaming the supporting document.*

Suppose you are a financial planner and create an income projection worksheet for each client; the worksheets are identical in format but contain different data. Disk space limitations might prevent you from saving a graph for every worksheet. Not only that, but if you have several identical graphics documents and need to change a parameter (such as a title), you'll have to make the same change in all of them and avoid mistakes in the process. You can create one graph and relink it with each worksheet as needed.

To do this, first create your worksheet and the graph and save them. When you create your second worksheet, make sure the ranges you want to plot are in the same position as in the first worksheet. Save the new worksheet under a new name.

To link the saved graph to the new worksheet and thus have the new data automatically graphed, rename the first worksheet with any name you wish, and then give the new worksheet the original name of the first worksheet. When you open the graph, it will have plotted the data in the new worksheet.

In other words, Jazz "remembers" the link between each data range and its associated plot as being connected to the name of the document containing the data. When you give this name to another document, Jazz applies all the same links to that document.

Enhancing Graphs

6.30 Tip: *To remove an arrow or line you have placed in a graph, click on it first, and then choose Clear from the Edit menu.*

The original *Jazz Handbook* makes an error in saying that you can clear a line or arrow by clicking on the well. The Update pamphlet corrects this, saying that you first click on the line or arrow and then use Clear from the Edit menu.

6.31 Tip: *If you don't want legends to squeeze the graph to the left, use notation boxes.*

Figure 6-9 shows a graph of sales with two different plots identified by legends. Its appearance can be improved by using notation boxes instead of legends, as shown in Figure 6-10.

You can place a box anywhere in the graph by clicking on the Notation well in the Console and then clicking at the spot in the document. You can move the box by dragging its border; you can change its size by dragging the tiny Size box in the lower-right corner. Once you've placed the box you can enter text into it.

6.32 Tip: *Customize your graph by drawing from the full range of enhancements available to you in the Font and Style menus.*

The Font menu choices let you choose from seven fonts and seven point sizes for your text. With the style menu choices you can format text in bold, italic, underline, outline, and shadow styles. You can also choose from a wide variety of types of lines and symbols for your line plots, as well as patterns for area and bar plots. This flexibility lets you create a graph that is attractive as well as effective.

6.33 Tip: *If you want to be able to change a title's font or style, use a notation box instead of an axis title.*

When you change the font or style options, all the text and numbers in the graph change except what has been placed in the graph by using notation boxes. By using

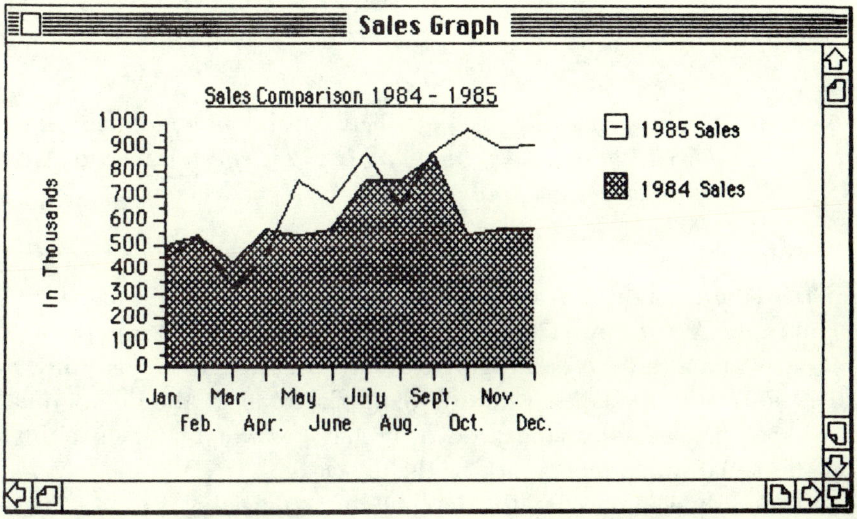

Figure 6-9. Graph with legends

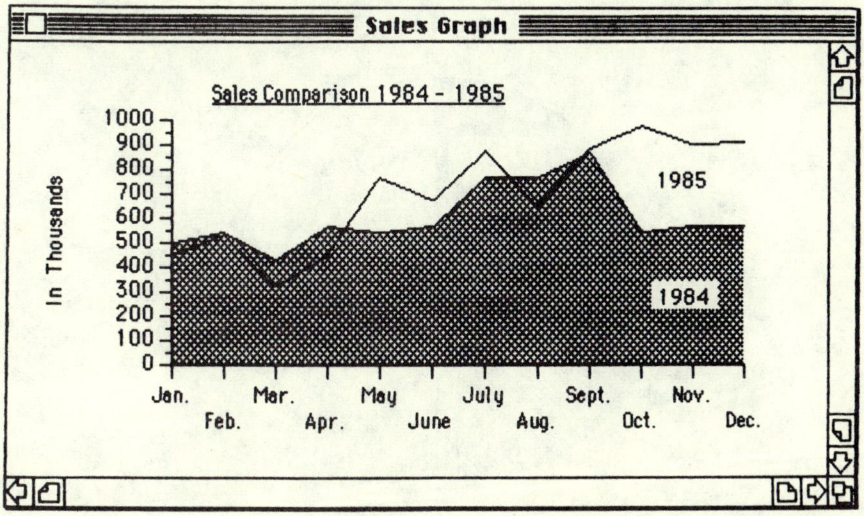

Figure 6-10. Graph with notation boxes

notation boxes you can individually control font and style, making some text bold, italic, shadowed, and so on. Only items in notation boxes can be individually "fonted" or "styled."

6.34 Tip: *You may find that placing labels directly on a plot by using the Set Point Labels command is a very effective way to add information to a graph.*

You can label the data points in a line or bar graph along the axis by using the Label command in the Axis menu. The range of labels selected in the supporting document appears along the axis (see Figure 6-10). If you had chosen Set Point Labels from the Plot menu, the labels would have appeared above the line points. This option is especially valuable in the case of a pie chart because you can use point labels to show the actual values represented by the pie wedges.

Figure 6-11 shows a pie chart that has had the actual value of each wedge added to the chart as a point label.To do this, you first select the labels in the supporting document, then select the plot in the graph document, and finally choose Set Point

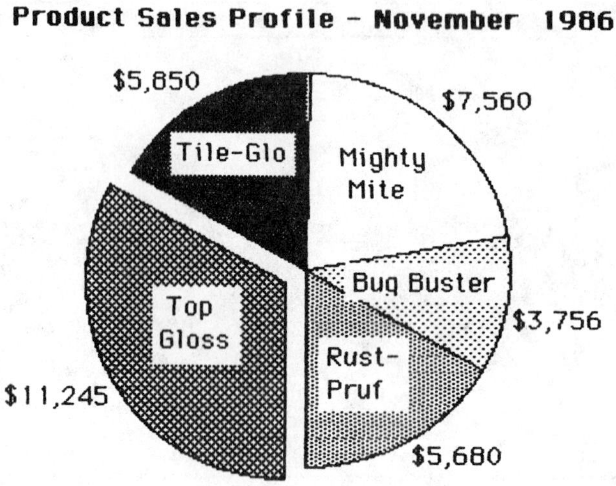

Figure 6-11. Exploded pie chart

Labels from the Plot menu. If the values in the source range change, the labels will change automatically to reflect the changes. You can add the names of the values by using notation boxes.

Printing

6.35 Trap: *You will not be able to use the Wide setting in Page Setup to print a graph sideways on your paper.*

Despite the suggestion in the original *Jazz Handbook* that the Wide option could be used to print a graph sideways on a page, it does not work.

6.36 Trap: *The Draft printing option only prints text—no plots.*

The Draft option in the Print Document menu might not ever be useful when printing graphs, as it does not print any of the plots, just the title, axis values, labels, and legends.

6.37 Tip: *You can print two or more graphs at one time by copying them into a word processing document.*

You may sometimes want to print more than one graph on a page. The best way to do this is to use Select All to highlight a graph and use Copy. The graph can then be pasted where you want in a word processing document. Graphs can be moved around in the document or changed in size by dragging their borders, but they cannot be positioned to the right or left of each other. Graphs must be positioned one above the other. You can copy as many graphs as you wish into a word processing document.

If you want the graphs to be updated automatically, use the HotView Include command instead of Copy, but remember to freeze the HotViews if you no longer need the updating. Active HotViews use a lot of RAM, leaving you less for your documents.

Another method that might serve you in certain cases is to have several graphs open at one time and adjust their windows so that they can be seen. Using the key combination of COMMAND-SHIFT-4 with the CAPS LOCK key down prints your entire screen, borders and all.

Using the same combination without CAPS LOCK depressed prints just the active window.

Using Graphs Effectively

6.38 Tip: *Make sure to use the plot type that best demonstrates the point you want to make.*

Choosing which plot type to use involves being sure about what you want the graph to say. If you ask yourself, "Why is using a chart better than using the figures by themselves?" you can focus on the fact or relationship you want to emphasize.

Each type of plot is most effective for showing certain relationships.

- *Line.* A line plot, as in Figure 6-8, is very useful for emphasizing change over time. For example, we frequently see changes in the Dow Jones Industrial average plotted by a line. The period represented could be for a day, a week, a year, or longer. We immediately understand that a line chart is showing the changes in a variable over time.
- *Bar.* A bar plot is especially useful when you want to emphasize the difference in magnitude between several different values. For example, Figure 6-12 shows total sales by salesperson for a given time period.
- *Overlapped Bar.* Overlapped bar plots accent the comparison between a pair of values. For example, Figure 6-7 compares each month's sales for two years. Having the bars overlap makes the data easy to compare. In this example, the change over time is emphasized along with the comparison. You can have as many overlapping bar plots as you want, but having too many clutters the graph and diminishes the clarity of the comparisons.
- *Stacked Bar.* Stacked bar plots emphasize the actual magnitude of each part in comparison with the actual magnitude of the total. For example, a store owner might want to show total sales dollars during a time period and also how many dollars each product contributed to that total. Figure 6-13 shows an example of such a graph.
- *Area.* The area plot, seen in Figure 6-14, is the line plot version of the stacked bar, showing changes in a variable over time and the actual magnitude of each part in comparison with the actual magnitude of the total.

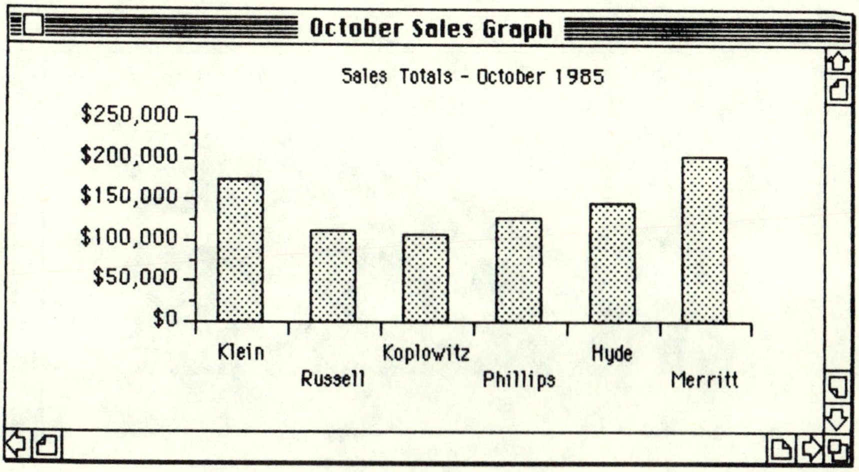

Figure 6-12. *Bar graph*

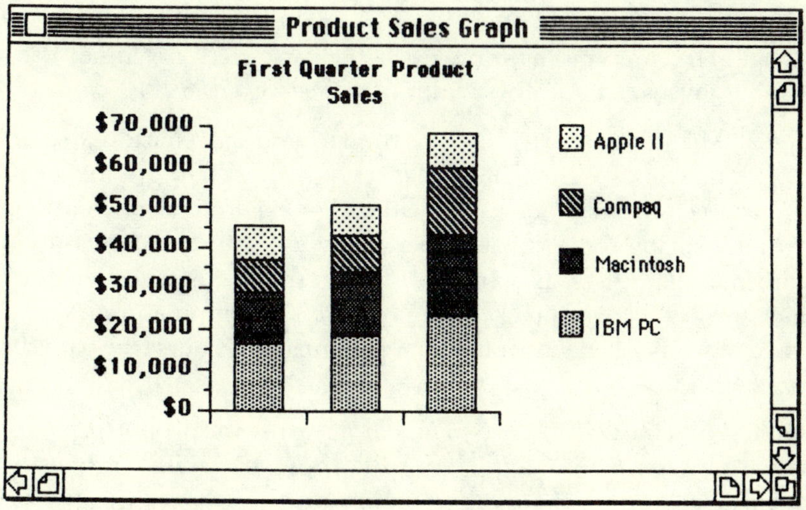

Figure 6-13. *Stacked bar graph*

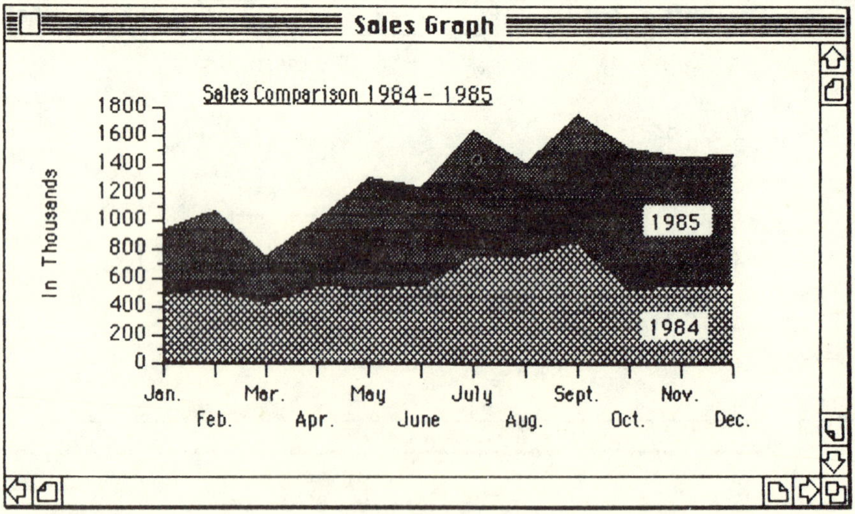

Figure 6-14. *Area graph*

- *Stock Market.* Also known as Hi-Low-Open-Close, the stock market plot graphs a range of values at one data point on the chart. Normally used to show a range of fluctuations in the price of a stock on a given day, it can also be used to show any spread of values within a range (see Tip 6.42).
- *Scatter.* The scatter chart is often referred to as an XY chart. It appears in the Jazz Plot menu as X Data and Y Data. The scatter chart graphs the relationship between two series of paired values. For example, in a scientific experiment measuring the correlation between temperature and pressure, such as temperature on the X axis and pressure on the Y axis, a scatter chart might show the degree to which pressure increases as temperature increases. The actual plot is neither temperature nor pressure alone, but is the pattern of their correlation.
- *Pie.* The pie chart is most useful for emphasizing the proportional contribution of parts to a whole, as in Figure 6-11. A pie chart will not show the actual magnitude of either the parts or the whole, though you can use Set Point Labels to place the magnitude for each wedge on the graph. When you want to see the magnitude of the whole as well as the magnitude of the contribution of parts, use a stacked bar or area chart.

6.39 Tip: *Use the View Horizontal option in the Type menu to emphasize progress toward a goal.*

The following illustration shows a worksheet recording sales totals for a group of people:

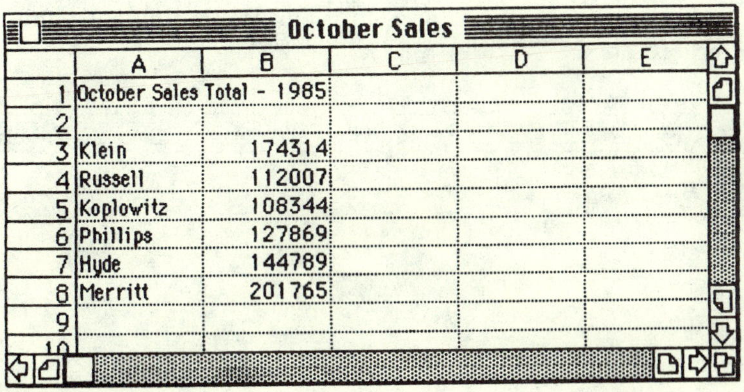

To show their relative successes, you could use a simple bar graph. However, because sales are strongly oriented to goals and every month a new challenge is given, by viewing the graph horizontally this sense of challenge is emphasized.

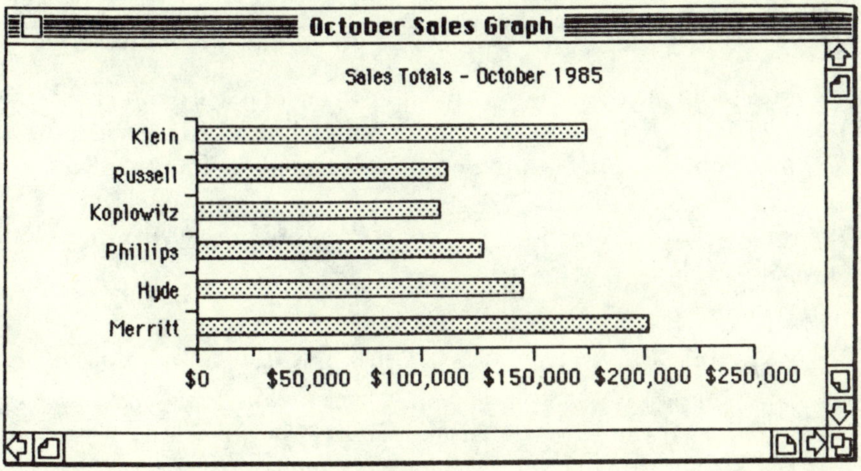

Remember, if you change a vertical graph to a horizontal one, any top axis title will appear on your right axis; you may want to delete it and enter it again at the top.

6.40 Tip: *Sometimes mixing plot types can represent your data most effectively.*

Figure 6-10 compared two years' sales data. One plot was shown with a line and one plot as an area. This highlights the contrast between the baseline 1984 sales and the rising 1985 sales.

If two line plots had been used, the graph would show the data, but it would not be as well emphasized:

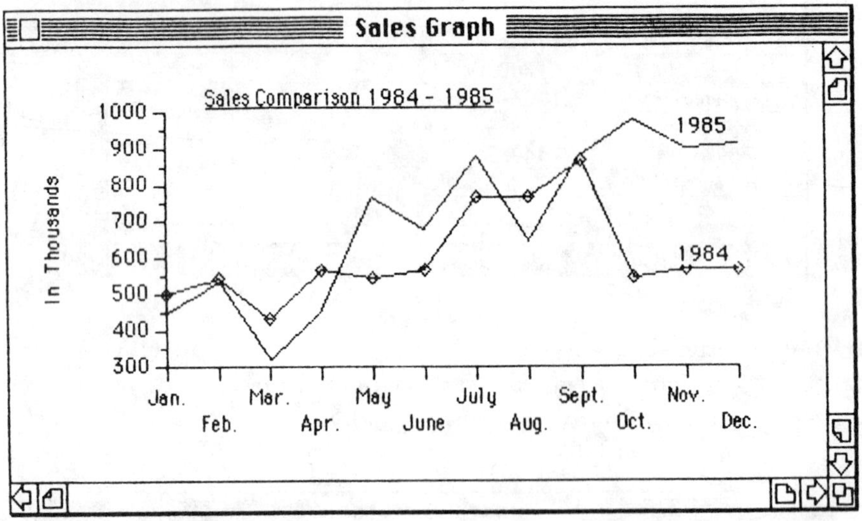

If two area plots had been chosen, the values from one year would be stacked on top of the other and the left axis would be automatically rescaled to measure the total of both years combined. This would make it harder to compare the two years (see Figure 6-14).

Thus, in this case, mixing plot types lets us make our point better than using the same plot type for all data ranges.

6.41 Trap: *When you create exploded pie plots, the Set Pie Wedges option is not available unless you use the Plot Selector to select the pie plot first.*

You can offset sections of a pie chart by "exploding" them. First, select a range in a worksheet or database. Then open a graphics document, select Pie from the Type menu, and select Pie from the Plot menu.

The next step is to create an explosion range adjacent to the data range (cells C3..C7 in the following illustration) and select it. Place a 1 in the explosion range:

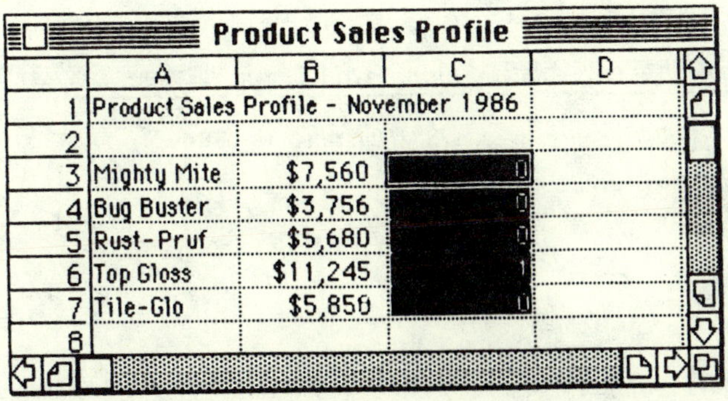

With the explosion range selected in your worksheet, switch to your graphics document. Use the Plot Selector to select the pie chart. A selector symbol will appear in the center of the pie. Choose Set Pie Wedges from the Plot menu. Figure 6-11 shows that the data with the 1 next to it in the explosion range has been exploded.

6.42 Tip: *When selecting ranges to plot in a stock market graph, make sure all the values in each range belong to the same category—for example, highs in one range, lows in another, and so on.*

Because a Hi-Low-Open-Close graph plots values falling within a range, it's natural to want to select the high, low, open, and close for each period at once. Jazz doesn't work this way.

Let's say you were plotting highs and lows for each day in a month for one stock. You would select all the data for one category (all the highs) and plot them first. Then you would select and plot another category (all the lows). It doesn't matter in what order you plot the categories.

6.43 Tip: *Show correlations between data widely separated by scale by using two plots with two different scales.*

Suppose you created a worksheet to show the correlation between the number of salespeople and total sales in each month during the year. Plotting both variables would be a good way to show the correlation graphically. However, if you create a line graph of both the sales range and the number of salespeople, you find that the difference in scale between sales in units of thousands and salespeople in units of tens causes the range of salespeople to scarcely appear on the graph.

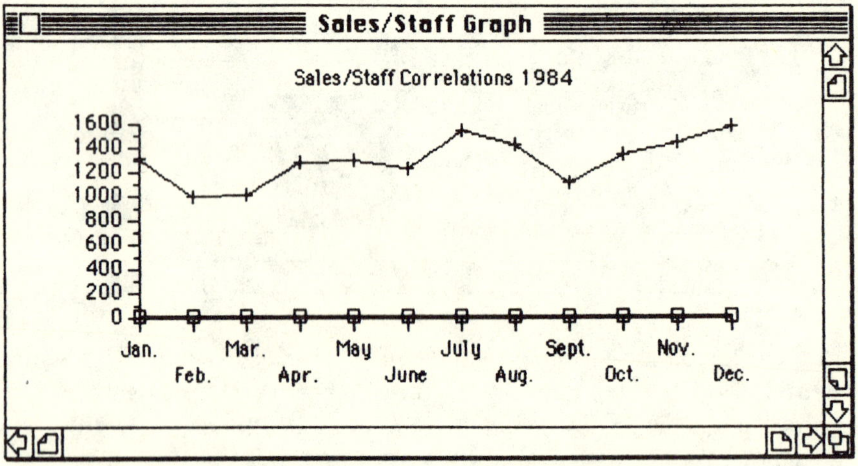

One solution is to create a separate axis on the right side of the chart that will raise the salespeople's plot to a point where it can visually be compared with sales. To do this, select the salespeople's plot with the Plot Selector. Choose Associate to Right Axis from the Plot menu, and click OK on the dialog box that appears. Jazz will correlate the scales, thus placing the plots at approximately equal levels. Figure 6-15 shows the result. By choosing Axis/Right you can reset the right axis value to separate the plots a little and make the correlations clearer, as has been done in Figure 6-15. Make sure to label the axes to make it clear which scale represents which plot.

6.44 Trap: *When you're using two or more charts to show a comparison, if you don't make the axis values the same in each, the comparison won't be emphasized.*

When you have several sets of values to plot and want to compare them, it may be necessary to create more than one graph. For one thing, too many plots in one graph makes relationships hard to see. For example, suppose you want to compare sales over time for several different products or salespeople.

If you do place each product or salesperson on its own graph and you want to be able to compare them, make sure you set the axis values the same in each graph. Because Jazz automatically creates a scale using the high and low in a range of values,

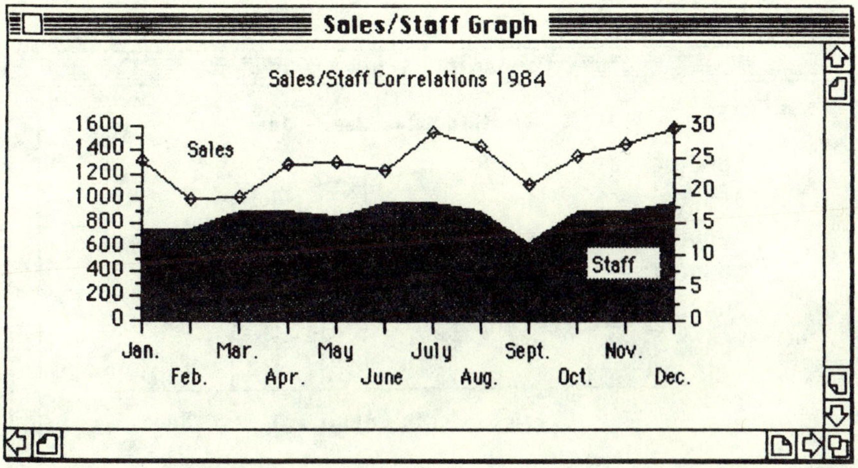

Figure 6-15. Separate scales

unless you manually set the scales the same, very different values will appear at approximately the same place on each graph, giving a distorted picture when you compare the graphs.

For example, one salesperson may have top sales of $10,000, while another may have reached $100,000. Unless you set the same axis scale in each graph, the graphs will give the appearance of the values being equal. With axis values the same, low sales will appear low on a graph and high will appear high, giving a true comparison.

6.45 Tip: *Manually set the scale to show your plots in the correct perspective.*

Jazz automatically sets a scale that spans the lowest and highest values you are plotting. In some cases this may not show your data in the correct perspective.

For example, suppose you have a standing sales goal of $100,000 for each month and you want to plot actual sales to see how they stack up. Jazz will automatically create a scale just wide enough to encompass the high and low of the sales. The largest value will reach to the top of the graph, making sales look good. You will have to keep the goal in mind to see how well sales are really doing.

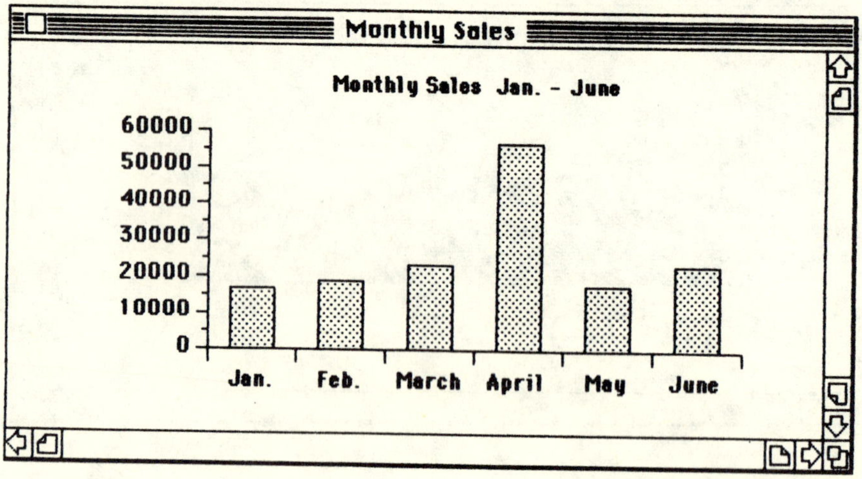

However, if you rescale the graph, the success or failure of sales is made clear. You can add a notation box to point out the goal:

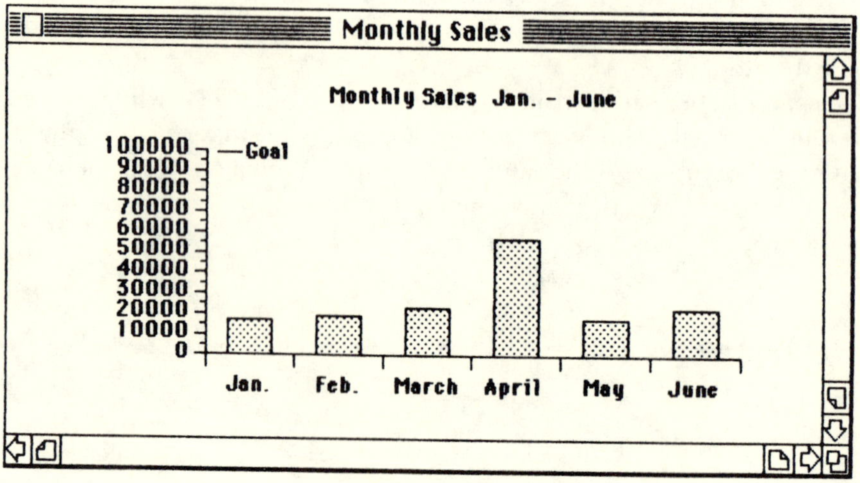

6.46 Trap: *If you manually set a scale and then plot a value higher than the scale, the plot will be cut off.*

When you override automatic axis scaling by setting a maximum scale, plotting a value higher than the scale causes the plot to be cut off the graph. You might not even notice that this has happened.

In some cases, however, you could actually turn this truncation to advantage to emphasize some value "going off the charts." For example, if sales were particularly strong, you might set the maximum scale at the level of the sales quota and then let a line plot of the sales disappear off the top of the chart.

7

Communications

Most personal computer software is designed to be used by one person on a stand-alone computer. Yet most work in the business world is done by groups of people who need to draw on information from both public and company databases and exchange information among themselves. Jazz's asynchronous Communications application lets you exchange data with computers of all types.

The first section of this chapter, "Getting Started," contains Tips and Traps you'll find useful if you're unfamiliar with communications. It contains three scenarios—communicating with an information utility, communicating with a mainframe, and communicating with another PC—that may help you become more familiar with basic communications procedures, depending on your situation. Later Tips and Traps explore methods you use to receive, capture, and send data, and suggest ways to avoid specific problems of data transmission by changing communications settings.

Getting Started

This section presents three basic scenarios with Tips that may help you get started if you've never used Jazz communications before.

Macintosh to Information Utility

7.01 Tip: *You can use Jazz to communicate with CompuServe, The Source, Dow Jones News/Retrieval, and other information utilities.*

These information utilities and many others provide a wide range of on-line services, including news, stock data, electronic mail, and user forums through which users can exchange information with each other. Each of these services requires a subscription, and many of them provide an introductory subscription for a low rate. When you subscribe, you receive a log-on ID and password, which you supply when you dial up the computer that manages the on-line service, usually called the *host computer.*

If you have a log-on ID and password, you can use a Jazz Communications document to communicate with one of these services, provided that you've also obtained a phone number through which you can access the service. You'll also need a modem, a cable connecting it to your Mac, and a phone line. (It should be a line that does not have "call waiting" or any other features that could interrupt a data transmission.) We'll use The Source as an example and briefly list the steps you have to perform (if you have any problems, consult the Tips and Traps in the sections that follow):

1. Attach your modem to the telephone port on the back of the Mac and to the phone line and plug it in. Read the manual that comes with the modem to familiarize yourself with how to set it up and how to use it.

2. Open a new Communications document.

3. Select Modem from the Settings menu, and set both the Phone Type and Modem Type. In our example, we'll use a Pulse type (rotary dial) phone and a Hayes 1200-baud modem. The last item you need to specify on this menu is the phone number of the service, in this case The Source. Many services have "direct" numbers, but many also have numbers that route you through one of the packet-switching networks like Telenet or Tymnet. In this case, we're using Telenet, so we supply the local Telenet number here. Your local number will be different (see Figure 7-1). (If you need to dial 9 to get an outside line, precede this number with a 9 followed by a

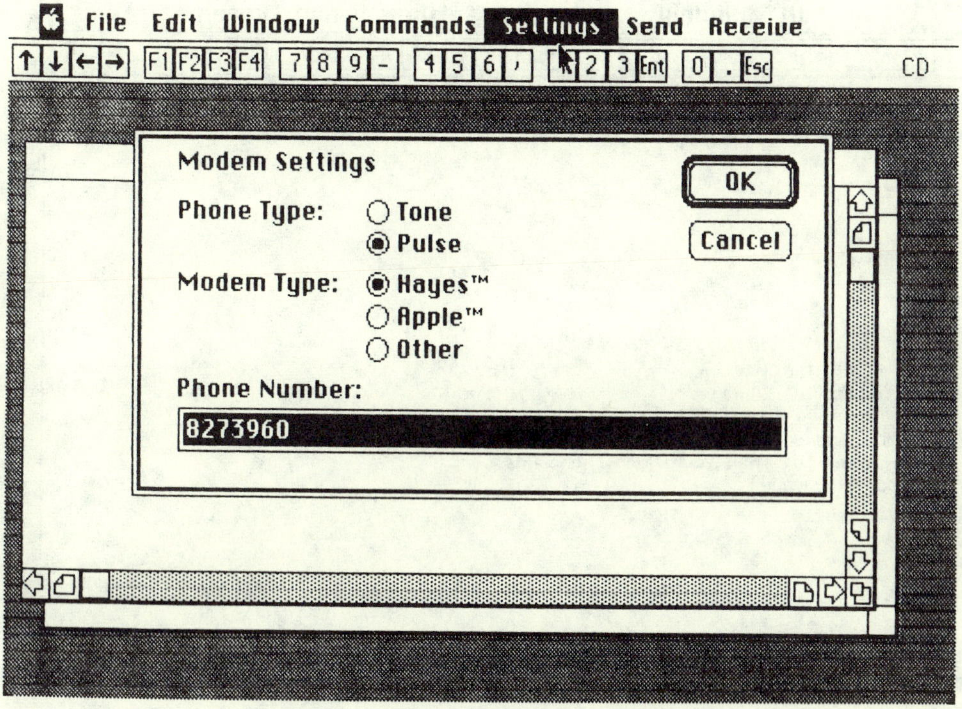

Figure 7-1. Modem settings for dialing up The Source

comma. The comma causes Jazz to pause for a moment after dialing the 9.)

4. If you have a Hayes or Apple modem, choose Dial from the Commands menu. (If not, see the "Commands" section below for a Tip on dialing.) If you've done everything correctly up until now, the host computer will answer the phone once the number has been dialed. If your modem volume is on, you'll hear a high-pitched whine. Most modems will then send you a CONNECT message. (See Figure 7-2.) If you're using Telenet (as in our example), your next step is to press RETURN twice. Telenet responds with a "TERMINAL=" prompt to which you should type **D1** and press RETURN. Telenet then gives you an "@" prompt, asking you for the Telenet network node you wish to access. The current main node for The Source is 30148, so that's what you supply. You then get a "Connected to THE SOURCE" message (Figure 7-2) and are prompted to supply your log-on ID and password. Once you do this, you'll be logged on to The Source and can access all of its services through its menus. (Figure 7-2 shows a false log-on ID and password; you would, of course, use the ones you obtained when you bought your subscription.)

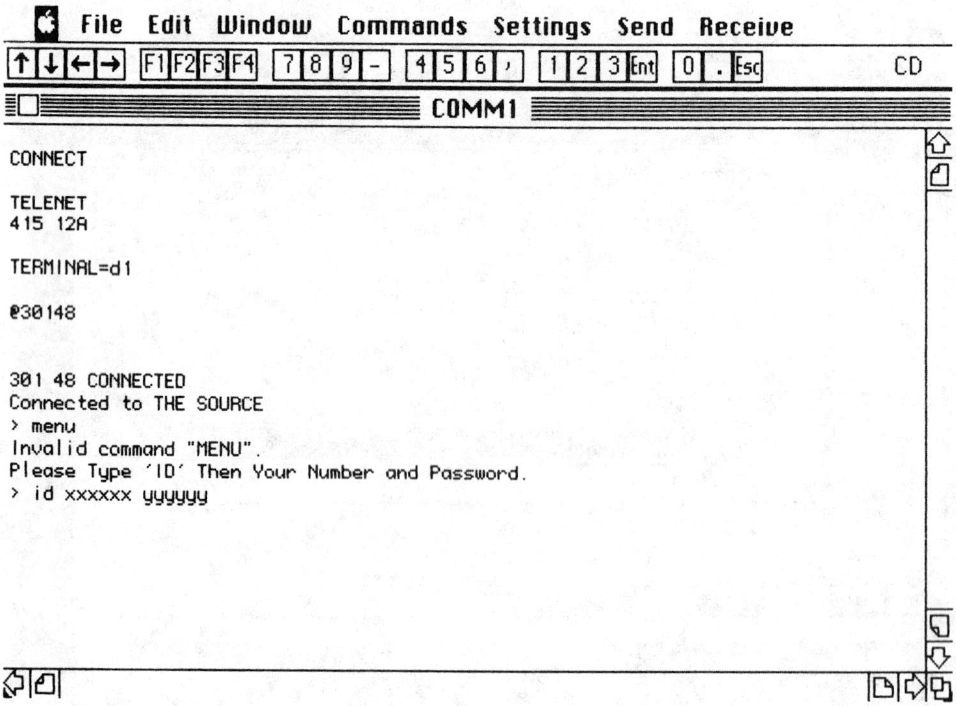

Figure 7-2. Communications screen for dialing up The Source

Macintosh to Mainframe

7.02 Tip: *You can communicate with your company's mainframe computer and both upload and download data.*

In most large organizations, the data that people want to use for analysis resides in files on mainframe computers. It's often useful to be able to select data from these files and "load" that data into Jazz for both worksheet and graphical analysis. This is called *downloading*. With Jazz you can dial up most mainframe computers and establish an asynchronous connection, in much the same way that we accessed the mainframe computer of The Source in the previous Tip. You need to find out from the people in your data processing department whether this is possible. If it is, they should be able to provide you with a phone number, log-on ID, and password. To log on, you would then follow steps similar to those we used to log on to The Source. (If you're given a direct line number, you'll be able to dispense with going through Tymnet or Telenet, as we did in the example.)

Once you establish the connection, the question becomes how you transmit the data you want from the mainframe file to Jazz. What you'll have to do first is to run (or have run for you) a mainframe job that selects the data you want and writes it out to a mainframe text file in the form of a report written to disk. Then all you have to do is prepare Jazz to capture what the other computer transmits (see the "Receiving and Capturing Data" section below for how to do this) and issue a command to the mainframe that lists that mainframe file on the screen. If, for instance, you were communicating with an IBM mainframe running the VM/CMS operating system, you'd issue a TYPE command. If the mainframe file was called SALES OUTPUT, you'd enter

TYPE SALES OUTPUT

The mainframe would then list the file to the terminal screen; you'd capture it in a Jazz document (probably a Worksheet document); and you could then work with it as you wished after a bit of preparation. (See the Tips and Traps in the section on "Receiving and Capturing Data" for details on the preparation that's necessary.) If you're using another type of mainframe system, there should be a command directly equivalent to the VM/CMS TYPE command.

Occasionally you may want to take some data that originated on the Mac and *upload* it to the mainframe so it can be stored in a mainframe file. This might be text that you want to send to another mainframe user as electronic mail, or it might be data that is going to be used later by a mainframe program. To get uploaded data into a mainframe file, you have to first start a mainframe program that can receive data from a terminal and write it to a file. Unless you have a special mainframe program for this purpose, you'll have to use one of the standard editor programs available. On an IBM VM/CMS system, the most commonly used editor is XEDIT. (Other mainframe systems have very similar editor programs. The specific details involved in using them will differ, but the general approach will be the same.)

If you issued the following commands to the mainframe, you would start XEDIT and put it into input mode, ready to receive whatever data you send from Jazz. XEDIT will write the data into the file MAIL DATA as soon as you issue a FILE command at the end of the transmission:

XEDIT MAIL DATA
INPUT

Once the mainframe editor is in input mode, you select the data you wish to upload from the Jazz document and then execute the Send Set Selection and

Send Start commands (see the "Sending Data" section below). After you've selected Send Start, you should see the transmitted data appear on your screen. When it's all been transmitted, you can choose Send Stop and then issue a command to the mainframe to write everything received to the mainframe file. With XEDIT, you do this by first issuing an extra carriage return to take XEDIT out of input mode and put it back in command mode. You can then issue a FILE command, and XEDIT saves the transmitted data into the MAIL DATA file and exits to the VM/CMS operating system.

There are several things that can go wrong in the uploading process. First of all, you must make sure the mainframe editor is set to receive the length of record you're sending, or your data will be truncated. (The default is usually 80 bytes.) Secondly, most mainframe systems interpret certain characters (usually # and @) as control characters instead of data. If you intend to upload such characters, you may need to get a mainframe expert to change the mainframe terminal settings so they'll be recognized as data.

Macintosh to PC

7.03 Tip: *You can dial up another Mac or other personal computer, communicate with its operator, and exchange data.*

The procedure here is somewhat similar to the one we followed to communicate with The Source in a previous Tip, but there are some important differences. You connect your modem in the same way (again we assume a Hayes 1200-baud modem) and open a new Communications document in the same manner, but from then on, you do several things differently. In the example you'll use here, we'll communicate with a friend who's running Lotus Symphony on an IBM PC on the desk next to yours. In such a situation, it's easy to communicate by voice to make sure that the two communications programs are set for the same parameters and are synchronized with each other. If you're physically separated from each other, things are a little more cumbersome. If you both have modems that permit you to toggle back and forth between data and voice transmission (such as the Popcom X100), the synchronization is made much easier. Otherwise, you either have to use two phone lines or switch the phone line itself between the handset and the computer.

Once you've opened a Communications document, go through the following steps:

1. Choose Settings Terminal and click on CR/LF (causing Jazz to display each line you enter on a new line on the screen), Auto Wrap (causing long lines to wrap to

the next line on the screen so you can read them), and Local Echo (causing the characters you type to be echoed back to you on your own screen).

2. Select Modem Settings and supply the phone number of the phone line attached by modem to the personal computer you're dialing up.

3. Make sure the operator of the other computer has the communications program in answer mode. This means it's ready to answer a call from another computer. (In some cases, the communications program displays a message when the phone rings or answers automatically.) Also make sure that whoever's on the other computer is using the same Connection settings that you are. (Here we've used the Jazz default of 1200 baud, 7 Data Bits, 1 Stop Bit, and Even Parity.) Since in our example the IBM PC we want to communicate with is in the same office, all we have to do is yell across the room to confirm that the other computer is ready.

4. Select Dial from the Commands menu.

5. Once you get a connection, you should be able to communicate with the operator of the other computer simply by typing on the keyboard. If you both have

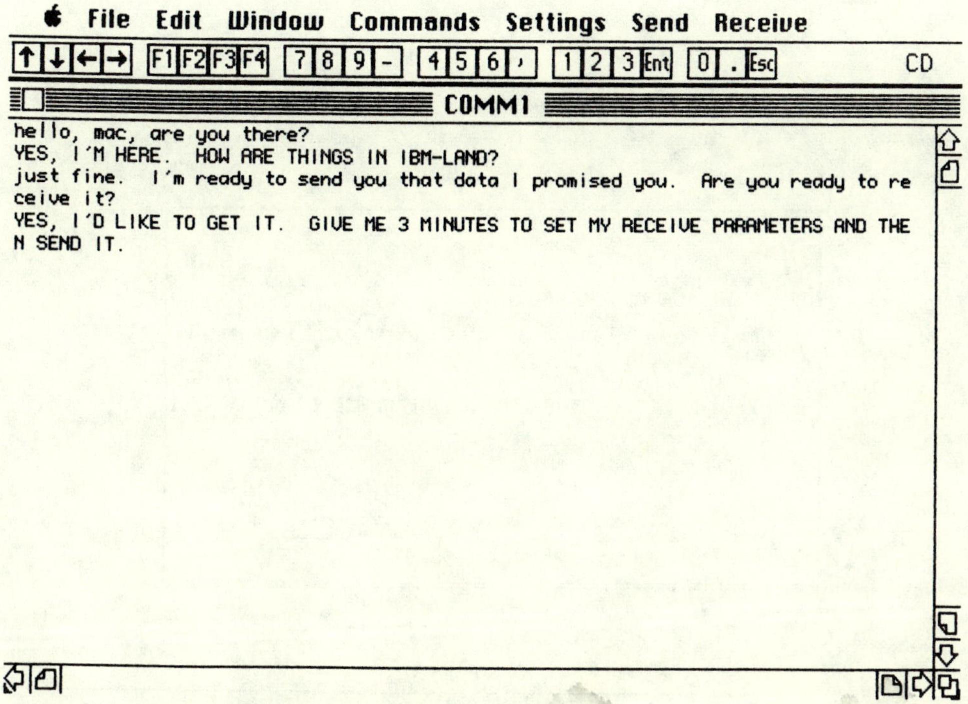

Figure 7-3. Mac side of Mac-to-IBM conversation

Local Echo on, then what each of you types should appear on both screens. When we got our connection with the IBM PC, the operator typed in "hello, mac, are you there?" We then responded. Figure 7-3 shows the dialog that followed, with the Mac messages in uppercase and the IBM PC messages in lowercase. Figure 7-4 shows that the IBM PC operator saw exactly the same dialog appear on his screen.

Once you've established a connection like this, you can transmit data back and forth between the two machines (see the sections below on "Sending Data and Receiving Data"). In our example, we wanted to get some data from the IBM PC to the Mac to take advantage of the Mac's superior ability to integrate graphic representations of data with text.

7.04 Tip: *When you want to communicate with a personal computer in the same room, you can use a direct cable connection.*

In the example in the previous Tip, we communicated with an IBM PC in the same room by having Jazz dial up its phone number. This required two phone lines and a

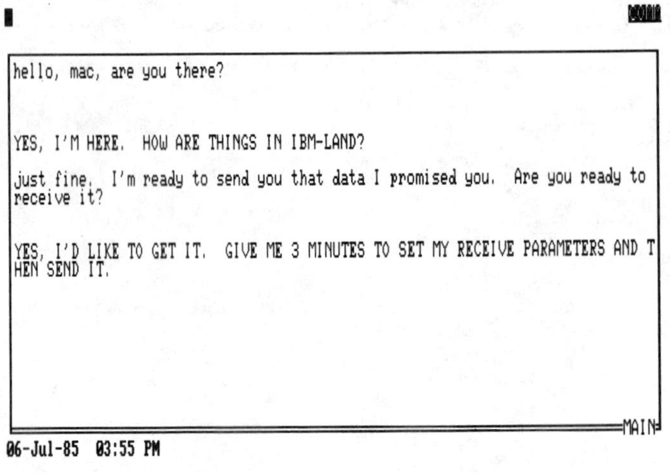

Figure 7-4. IBM side of Mac-to-IBM conversation

modem on each end and is the method you have to use if the two computers are not in the same room. However, if the two machines are literally right next to each other, you can bypass the phone lines and modems completely if you have the right kind of cable. There are several advantages to this. One is that you aren't limited by the maximum transmission speed of the modems (usually 1200 baud), so that you can transfer data very quickly. Another advantage is that you virtually eliminate the possibility of errors in transmission, which sometimes occur during phone line transmissions because of noise on the line. Finally, if you don't need modems for any other purpose, you don't need to buy them.

The cable you need for the direct connection is usually called a "null modem" or "modem eliminator." For an IBM-to-Mac connection, you'd need one with a Mac 9-pin connection at one end and an IBM PC 25-pin connection at the other. (If you were going Mac to Mac, you'd want a 9-pin connection at both ends.) In a null modem, the Send and Receive pins are crossed with each other at a special connection in the middle of the cable. This simulates what the two modems do when they're actually in the line. With the null modem connected to the serial port of the Mac at one end and to the serial port of the other computer at the other end, the two communications programs can talk back and forth and exchange data just as if they were connected by phone line. (You still need a communications program at each end so that the two machines can address the communications ports properly.) If you don't know how to make up a null modem cable, your local computer store can probably do it for you.

7.05 Tip: *Save the settings for each type of communications you do as a separate document.*

Sometimes it's quite a bit of trouble to get the settings just right for communications with another computer. Once you get a group of settings that work, save that Communications document immediately so you can open it at any later time and use the same settings. Give each document a descriptive name. For instance, if you communicate frequently with another Mac, with an IBM PC, and with The Source, you may have Communications documents called MACTOMAC, MACTOIBM, and SOURCE.

7.06 Tip: *When you have problems in a communications session, open a word processing document and keep notes on everything that occurred and everything you tried to cure the situation.*

There are so many things that can go wrong with personal computer asynchronous communications that you're certain to experience at least some difficulties. When things go wrong and you're getting more and more frustrated, it's often difficult to remember exactly what you have and haven't tried. If you keep notes on everything that happens along the way in a word processing document, it's easier to keep track of where you are in the process. If you then save those notes, they may help you if you encounter a similar problem in the future.

7.07 Trap: *If you assume that what came across your screen during a Communications session is saved with the document, you'll lose all of this data.*

Saving a Communications document saves only the settings that are part of it. If you want to capture and save part or all of the information sent to you by the other computer, you have to take additional steps, which vary depending on the circumstances.See the section on "Receiving and Capturing Data."

7.08 Tip: *If you use a modem that allows you to switch back and forth between voice and data modes, you'll find it much easier to communicate with another computer operator.*

Establishing communications with the operator of another personal computer in a remote location usually requires talking a bit on the phone in advance. It sometimes also requires talking on the phone in the middle of a communications session, especially if problems occur during the transmission. If you each have two phones, you can use one for voice and one for data. But if one or both has only one phone, things are made easier if you both have modems that let you switch between voice and data modes. The Popcom X100 is one modem that allows this.

Communications Settings

7.09 Trap: *If the next transmission from the other computer wipes out the last line on your screen, the other program is not sending a line feed at the end of each line.*

Usually the other person will have a way of telling the communications program to send a carriage return and line feed at the end of every line. This is what you want, or you'll find what shows on your screen confusing. If the cursor doesn't pop to the next line when *you* press a carriage return, you've probably left the Terminal End of Line setting at your end at the default CR, which means "issue only a carriage return when the RETURN key is pressed." If you change this setting to CR/LF, you'll issue both a carriage return and line feed every time you press RETURN. This way, neither the next line you enter nor the next line you receive will overlap the last line on your screen.

7.10 Trap: *If you don't see the entire received line on your screen, you have too small a window or the wrong Terminal settings.*

Usually you'll want to use COMMAND-W to zoom to a full-screen Communications window. Otherwise you won't see the entire text of lines either typed by you or sent from the other computer. But even if the window is full size, you may not see the whole line unless you turn Auto Wrap on. How much of a particular line actually fits on the screen before wrapping depends on the Columns Per Line and Font Size settings. If you still can't see entire lines on the screen because of these settings, you can always scroll to see what's off the screen.

7.11 Trap: *You can clear your Communications screen by changing the Terminal Columns Per Line setting.*

You may want to clear the text currently on your Communications screen either for aesthetic reasons or so you can copy what comes next into the Clipboard without its being cluttered up with old material. Changing the Terminal Columns Per Line setting will do this; once the screen has been cleared, you can set it back to what it was before.

7.12 Trap: *If you either don't see the text you're typing in a Communications window or you see it double, you have the Local Echo parameter set incorrectly.*

Most host systems (including the information services like The Source and CompuServe and your company's mainframe computer) will automatically echo back to you each character you send. This allows you to see on your screen each character you type; in this case you want to have the Terminal Local Echo setting turned off. But if you're communicating with another personal computer, it probably won't echo back to you; in this case you want to turn Local Echo on.

If you see every character you type appear twice on the screen, both Jazz and the other computer are echoing each character you type. Turn Local Echo off.

Less frequently you may find that your modem is set to echo each character. In this case it's possible to have triple echoing. If this happens, set the modem echoing off and turn Local Echo off in the Terminal Settings menu.

7.13 Trap: *If you see garbled nonsense being transmitted, your Connection Port Settings probably don't match those of the other computer.*

Your Baud Rate, Data Bits, Parity, and Stop Bits settings must match those of the other computer or the bit patterns transmitted will be interpreted differently by the two machines, and you'll see nonsense combinations of characters coming across your screen. When you're communicating with an information service like The Source or CompuServe or with another mainframe, you'll usually want to use 7 Data Bits, Even Parity, and 1 Stop Bit. When you're communicating with another personal computer, you probably want to have both systems use 8 Data Bits and No Parity; this gives you all eight bits for the encoding of data, allowing the transmission of special characters that use the eighth bit as part of their coding.

When you're either sending or receiving a file with protocol (Jazz protocol or XMODEM protocol), it doesn't seem to matter how you have the Data Bits and Parity set. Evidently Jazz automatically uses 8 Data Bits with No Parity for protocol file transfers.

7.14 Trap: *If you're actually losing characters during transmission, one computer may be transmitting too fast for the other.*

In this situation, you should turn on the Connection Flow Control setting on both ends. (Flow Control is referred to as *handshaking,* or XON/XOFF, by some communications programs.) This allows the receiving computer to stop the incoming stream of data momentarily so it can catch up. Make sure you leave the Jazz default Flow Control codes at ASCII 17 (CONTROL-Q) and 19 (CONTROL-S) unless you know for sure that the other system expects different codes, as these are the standard flow control codes used by most communications programs.

7.15 Tip: *You can establish a second communications connection through the Mac printer port at the same time that you're communicating through the telephone port.*

The printer port on the Mac is also a serial port and can therefore be used for communications. The circuitry is slightly different, however, so it is not as reliable for transmissions at 1200 baud or more over phone lines. The Jazz manual recommends using it only at 300 baud. It seems to work fine at 9600 baud with a direct cable connection between the two computers.

You establish the second communications connection by first connecting a cable with modem and telephone connection to the printer port. (If you're communicating through a direct cable link, you need the modem or the telephone.) You then open a second Communications document and choose the Connection Printer Port Setting. From this point on, you proceed as with any other Communications document.

Being able to have two Communications sessions going at once could be handy in several circumstances. Figure 7-5 shows one of them. Here we have one session going between Jazz and an IBM PC in the window at the top of the screen while we're communicating with The Source in the window at the bottom of the screen. This allows us, for instance, to receive data from the operator of the IBM PC and then upload it to The Source as electronic mail to be picked up by a third person later. (You should be aware, however, that you'll be charged for your entire time on-line with The Source, even while you're communicating with another system through the other port.)

7.16 Trap: *If you can't establish a connection with another computer in the first place, something's probably wrong with one or more of your modem settings.*

First make sure that you have the correct phone number. If you need to dial 9 or some other code to get an outside number from the phone you're using, supply that 9 followed by a comma as the first part of the Modem Phone Number setting. (The comma causes Jazz to pause for a moment before continuing transmission. Use one

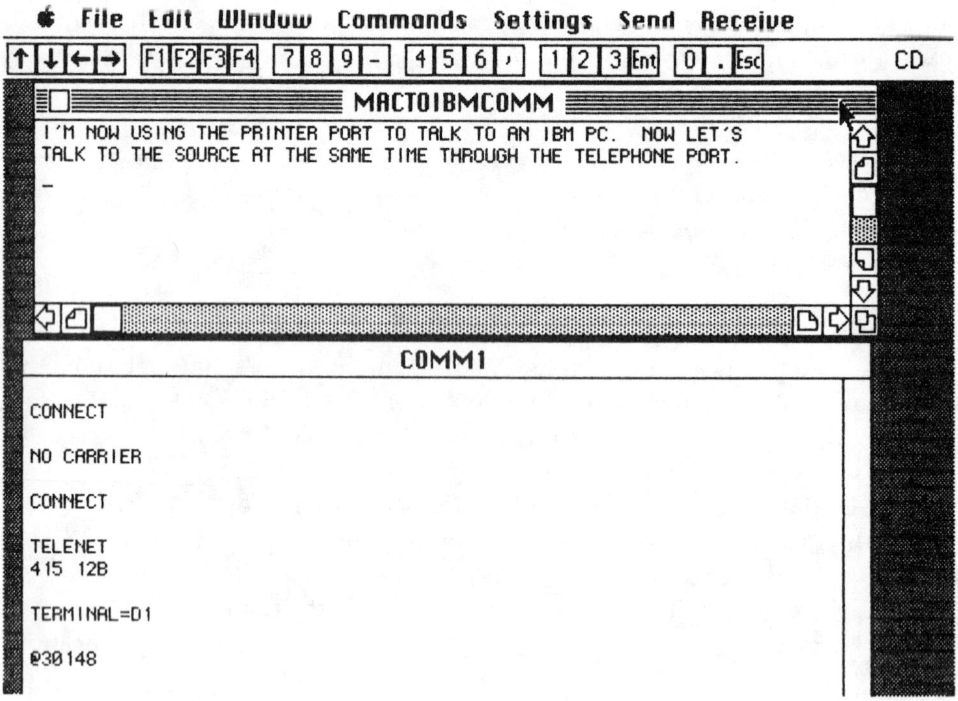

Figure 7-5. Two simultaneous communications sessions

or more commas between each separate part of the number if you need to prefix the number with access codes.)

Next, make sure you have Phone Type and Modem Type set correctly. For a rotary dial phone, use Pulse; for a touch-tone phone use Tone.

Finally, check the modem. It must be plugged in and turned on. The correct switches must be set. The cable connecting it to the Mac port must be in place on the right port, and the cable connections should be tight. If your modem has external lights, some of them should be on. When you choose the Dial command, you should see the SD (Send Data) light blink; if you don't, something may be wrong with the modem.

If you've checked all these things and you still can't establish a connection with the other computer, you may have a bad serial port, a bad cable, or a bad modem. Try switching the cable to the Printer Port, then selecting the Connection Printer Port Setting, and dialing again. Next try switching the cable or the modem if you have others available.

7.17 Trap: *If you have a modem other than Hayes or Apple, you may not be able to dial using the Dial command.*

If your modem is Hayes-compatible, as many are, it should accept the same commands the Hayes modem does. In such a case, you may still be able to use the Dial command to dial if you choose Hayes instead of Other from the Modem menu. If your modem has a non-Hayes-compatible auto-dial feature, consult the modem manual to find out the code for the auto-dial command and enter it before the phone number itself when you supply the phone number parameter. If the modem has no auto-dial feature, you'll probably have to dial the phone manually; see the modem manual for instructions.

7.18 Tip: *If your modem has an auto-answer feature and it's turned on, you won't have to choose the Answer command to cause Jazz to answer an incoming call.*

This means that you could leave your Mac unattended and ready to receive and capture data. (You do this by selecting a capture area in a document and choosing Receive Set Selection and Receive Start.) When a call comes, the modem answers automatically, the calling computer transmits, and Jazz captures the transmission into the selected area in the document.

Commands

7.19 Tip: *You can use Set Answerback together with Send Answerback to send a string of up to 20 characters at any time.*

Some computers send what's called an ENQ request when they want a response from the other computer. If Jazz receives an ENQ request, it automatically sends whatever you've specified with Set Answerback. In most situations, however, the other computer will not send any ENQ requests; you then have the option to use Set Answerback to set up any string of up to 20 characters that you wish to send automatically. Jazz will send this specified string automatically every time you choose the Send

Answerback command. You can use this feature to automatically send a log-in sequence or any other string of characters you need to send frequently.

7.20 Tip: *To stop a host transmission as it scrolls across your terminal screen, choose Send Short Break or Send Long Break.*

Suppose you're connected to The Source, CompuServe, or one of the other information services and the host computer is filling screen after screen with information you don't need. You can often stop the transmission by choosing one of these two break options.

7.21 Trap: *Forgetting to log off and hang up may result in extra telephone and other charges.*

Most host computers will automatically hang up their end of the phone after several minutes of inactivity. On some systems, however, if you forget to log off and hang up, you could stay on-line for hours and run up high on-line and telephone line charges.

Receiving, Capturing, and Sending Data

7.22 Tip: *To transmit Jazz files back and forth with another Mac running Jazz, use Send Set File or Receive Set File and select Jazz Protocol.*

This is the only protocol you can use to send Jazz Form, Communications, and Graphics documents.

7.23 Tip: *To receive Lotus 1-2-3 or Symphony worksheet files from an IBM PC, use Receive Set File and choose XModem protocol.*

The XModem protocol allows for binary file transfer with error detection and correction. Since 1-2-3 and Symphony worksheet files are binary-coded files, you must use this option rather than the Without Protocol option, which is only for text file transmission. You can use the Symphony Communications function to transmit these IBM files. You can also use any other IBM PC asynchronous communications program that observes the XModem protocol, including PC Talk III and Crosstalk XVI.

Once you've captured the 1-2-3 or Symphony worksheet file on a Mac disk, you can then convert it to Jazz format by choosing Convert from the Apple menu and clicking on the proper option. See Chapter 8 for Tips and Traps related to this conversion.

7.24 Tip: *To receive reliably any file that's not a Jazz document file, use Receive Set File with the XModem protocol.*

Since the XModem protocol has built-in error detection and correction, you'll want to use it to transmit even a text file in cases where errors in transmission are possible, as long as the other computer is running a program that observes the same protocol. Such errors usually occur because of noise on voice-grade phone lines. If the communications programs at both ends of the connection are observing the XModem protocol, they check every block of data to make sure that it was transmitted correctly. If there are errors, the data is retransmitted up to ten times until it is correct. If it is still not correct on the tenth time, the transmission is aborted.

Don't forget that the communications program running in the other computer must also be observing XModem protocol. Most IBM PC asynchronous communications programs have an XModem option, as do some minicomputer communications programs. In general, mainframe communications programs do not observe this protocol (though the CompuServe host computer does), so you probably won't be able to use it in communicating with mainframes. Thus there is currently no way of having totally error-free transmission between Jazz and most mainframes.

7.25 Tip: *You can capture received data into a Jazz document by selecting a location in that document and choosing Receive Parse Settings, Receive Set Selection, and Receive Start.*

The previous Tips in this section have dealt with the transmission of an entire file from one computer's disk to the other computer's disk. But in many cases you want to transfer data from the other system's disk or memory and capture it into a Jazz document that you already have in memory.

Suppose you have some sales data in a Symphony Worksheet (Figure 7-6)

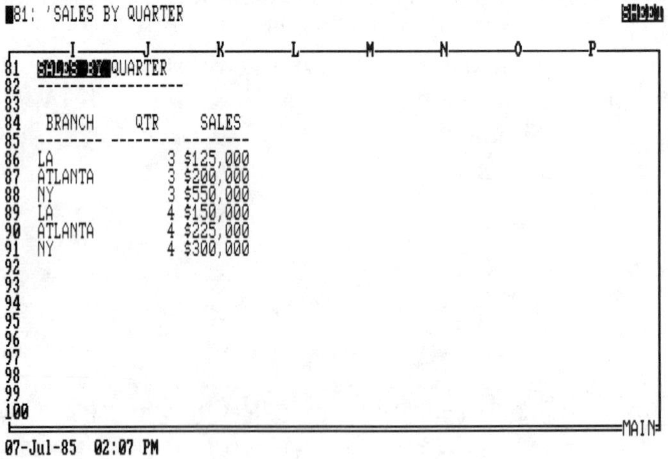

```
I81: 'SALES BY QUARTER                                                    SHEET
     ----I--------J--------K--------L--------M--------N--------O--------P----
81   SALES BY QUARTER
82   ------------------
83
84    BRANCH     QTR     SALES
85   -------- -------- --------
86   LA               3 $125,000
87   ATLANTA          3 $200,000
88   NY               3 $550,000
89   LA               4 $150,000
90   ATLANTA          4 $225,000
91   NY               4 $300,000
92
93
94
95
96
97
98
99
100
                                                                        MAIN
07-Jul-85  02:07 PM
```

Figure 7-6. Symphony sales worksheet for transfer to Jazz

that you wish to transfer directly into a Jazz Worksheet already in memory. There are several possible variations on this procedure, but here's the one that usually works best:

1. Make active the Jazz Worksheet into which you want to capture the data and click on the first cell of the area where you want it to go. Make sure you have selected only one cell, A31.

2. Select Receive Parse Settings, click on Use Column Widths, and set the width of each column to the current width of the corresponding field in the source data. (In this case, set the width for each column to 9, as shown in Figure 7-7, since that's the width of each field in the source Symphony worksheet.) This allows Jazz to break apart each line as it's transmitted and place each source field in a different target cell in the Jazz worksheet.

3. Select Receive Set Selection to point Jazz to the Worksheet cell you selected as a target in step 1.

4. Select Receive Start to put Jazz into a ready-to-receive state.

5. Transmit the data from the other computer. In this case, since you're using

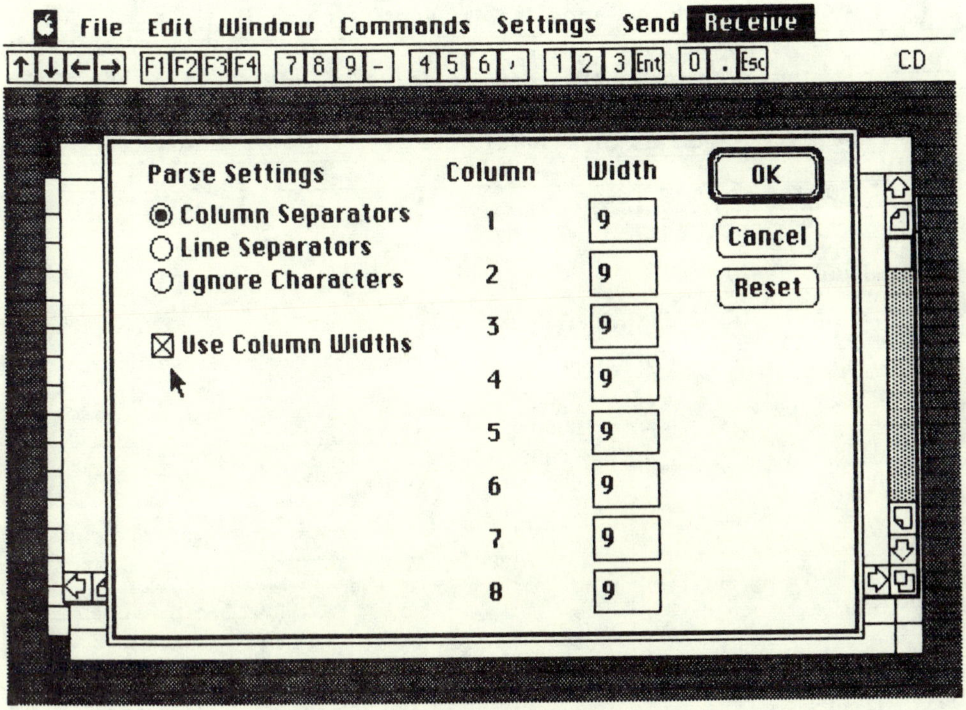

Figure 7-7. Parse Settings using Column Widths

Symphony on an IBM PC, you'd issue a Transmit Range command and specify the range I81 . . K91, as shown in Figure 7-6.

6. Select Receive Stop from the Jazz Communications menu. This allows you to make the Worksheet document active to see what you received.

Figure 7-8 shows what you get in your Jazz Worksheet as a result. Compare this with Figure 7-6 and you'll see that you got just what you wanted, with one minor exception: the "SALES BY QUARTER" title at the top lost the initial S and also got broken up in a funny way. What happened? The first thing that happened was that for some unknown reason the initial S was lost in transmission. Because this kind of thing can happen, you always have to examine carefully the results of a communications transmission. In this case it's not serious, but in cases where it affects the actual data, it could be quite serious.

The other thing that happened was that Jazz exactly followed the parsing rules we gave it in Step 2: it placed each group of nine characters in each line transmitted into a different column. This worked perfectly for all lines but the title line. Again, in

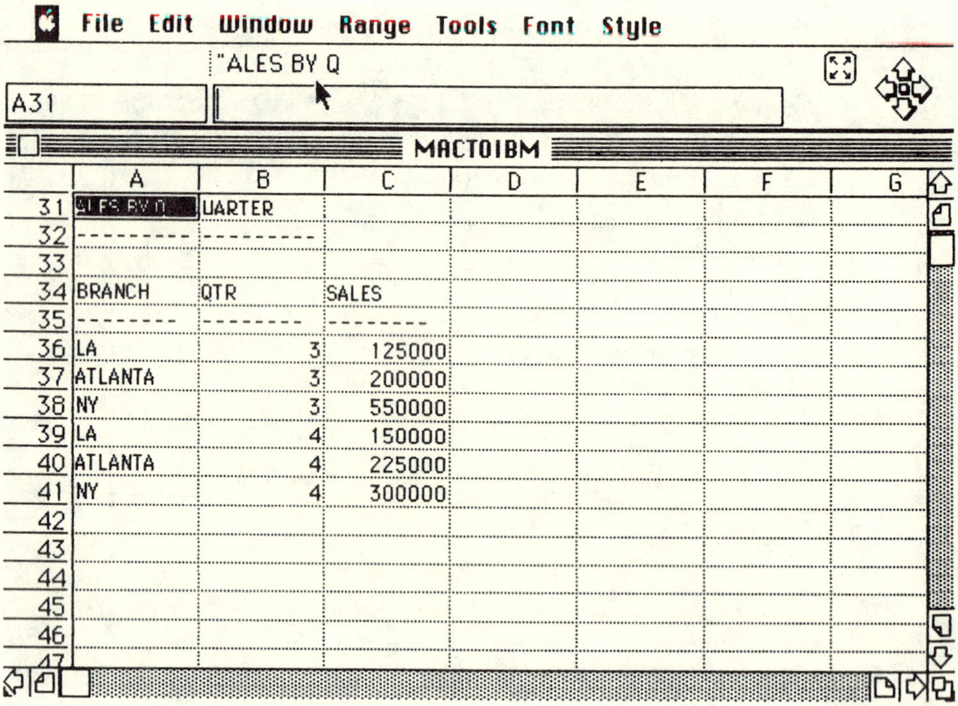

Figure 7-8. Sales worksheet transferred from Symphony using Column Width Parse Settings in Figure 7-7

this case it's not serious (since you can easily edit the title line), but in cases where the actual data got parsed in an unexpected way, it might be serious.

7.26 Tip: *For full freedom in parsing captured data, turn off all the Parse Settings and parse the captured data using =VALUE and =DATEVALUE.*

If you want to avoid the type of annoying parsing anomaly discussed in the previous Tip, you can turn off all Parse Settings by clicking on Column Separators and making sure that all the options (including Tab) are clicked off. This will ensure that Jazz does no parsing at all when capturing transmitted data into a document.

Let's try the transfer from Symphony that we tried in the previous Tip with one variation. We'll change the formatting on the Sales column in the Symphony source

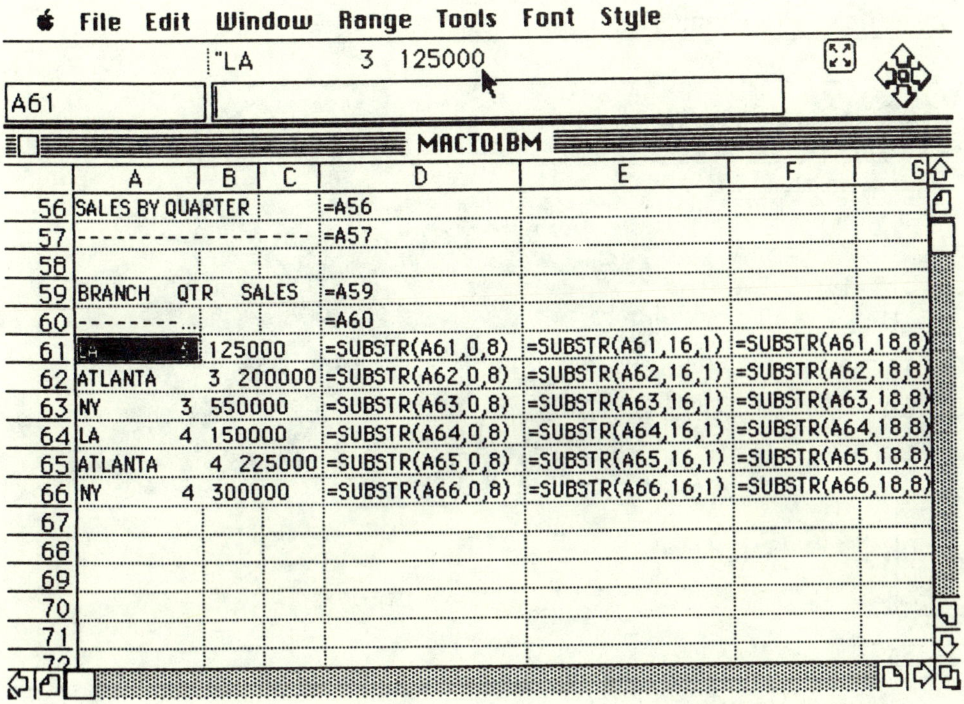

Figure 7-9. *Sales worksheet transferred from Symphony with no Parse Settings and then parsed by formula*

range (Figure 7-6) from Currency to General, so that dollar signs and commas don't display. You'll see why shortly.

This time we select A56 as the target cell in the Worksheet document and then choose Receive Set Selection and Receive Start. After we execute the Symphony Transmit-Range and choose Receive Stop, we can make the Worksheet active and see what we got. The result is shown in column A of Figure 7-9. Note that, as the Contents Box at the top of the screen shows, none of the transmitted lines was parsed by Jazz; they each went into one cell in column A as one long text label. Without parsing the numeric Sales field out of these long labels, you won't be able to do any arithmetic or graphic analysis on the Sales numbers. Note also that for some odd reason, Jazz displays the contents of the Atlanta rows as being of a different length, though in fact, they were of the same length in the source data (Figure 7-6). They're actually of the same length here, despite appearances to the contrary.

Columns D, E, and F in Figure 7-9 show in Formula Text Format the formulas that allow us to parse the long text labels in column A into their constituent fields. Figure 7-10 shows the same range (D56..F56) with the Format set back to General.

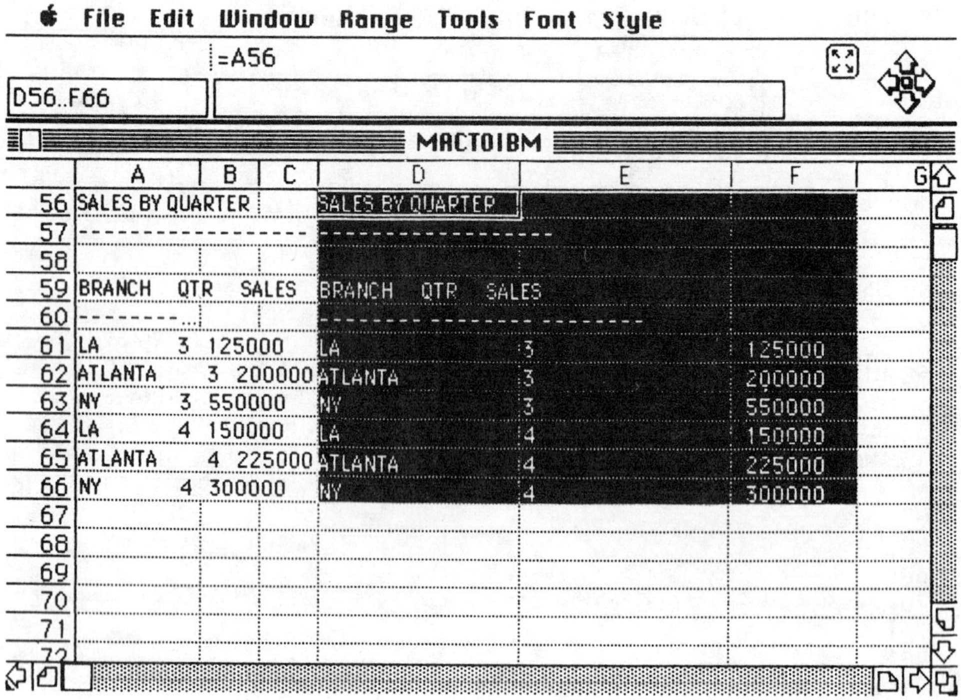

Figure 7-10. Figure 7-9 set back to General format

Apparently the fields are now separated correctly. The final step (still assuming you want to perform arithmetic on the Sales numbers in column F) is to enclose the SUBSTR formula in that column in a VALUE formula. The formula in F61 will then become

=VALUE(SUBSTR(A61,18,8)

and we'll copy this same formula to F62. . F66. If there had been dates in our data, we could have used the DATEVALUE function to convert the text representation of dates into serial date numbers in the same way.

Notice that because we set all the Parse Settings off and took full control of the process ourselves, we were able to reproduce the title in row 56 correctly (compare Figures 7-8, 7-9, and 7-10).

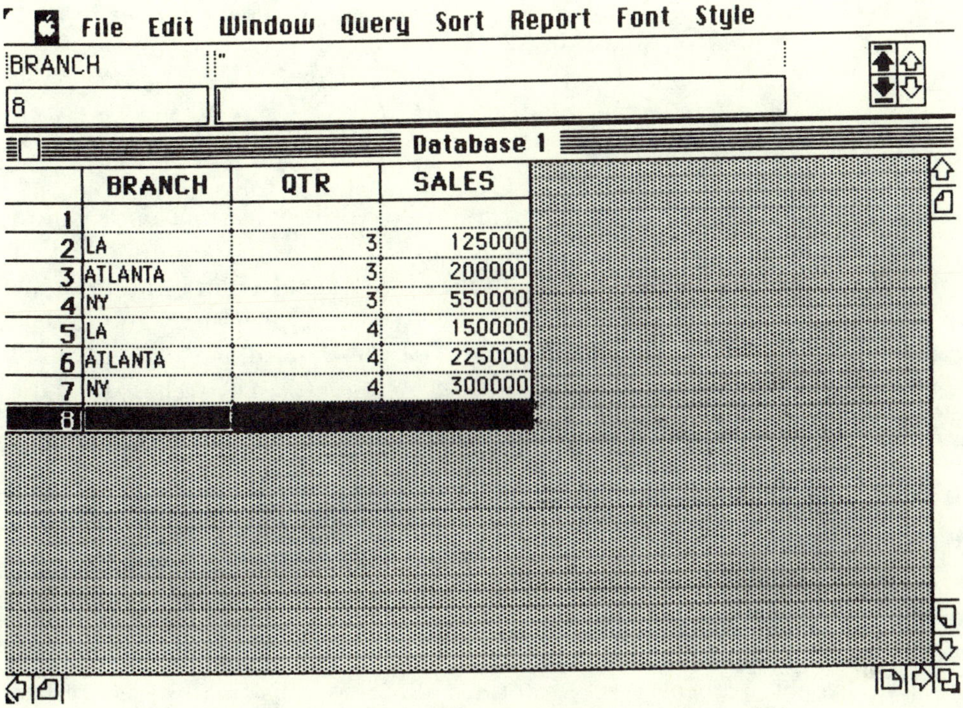

Figure 7-11. Sales data transferred from Symphony to a database

7.27 Tip: *To insert captured data into a database, click on the record number of the record below the one where you wish the insert to go and then choose Receive Parse Settings, Receive Set Selection, and Receive Start before transmitting.*

It's important to click on the record number at the left margin of the record below the one where you want the transmitted data to go. If you click on a cell in an actual database field, that's the only cell that will receive any data.

You must also set the Parse Settings properly or you won't get the right data in the right fields. Suppose we create a Jazz Database with Branch, Qtr, and Sales fields and transmit the same Symphony data from Figure 7-6 (this time excluding the title rows, which will have no meaning to the Jazz Database). If we use the Parse Settings in Figure 7-7, choose Receive Set Selection after clicking on the record number for record 1, choose Receive Start, and transmit, we get what's shown in Figure 7-11. (Don't forget that when the transmission is complete, you must choose Receive Stop before you can make the Database document active to see what happened.)

7.28 Tip: *If you select only one cell in a Database document or a range of more than one cell in a Database or Worksheet document, the subsequent transmission after Set Selection will fill only the area selected.*

In previous Tips, we've discussed how to capture everything that's transmitted into a Worksheet or Database document. But suppose you only want to capture the first part of what's transmitted. You can cut off the capture at any point by limiting the size of the selected area to the number of cells' worth of data you wish to capture. The capture will overwrite the previous contents of the selected area. When you're capturing into a Worksheet document, you need to select at least two cells to limit the capture, since a selection of only one will result in capturing everything transmitted.

7.29 Trap: *If you receive a text file using Receive Set File with the Without Protocol option, you may have trouble opening that file as a Jazz Word Processing document.*

You should be able to open a text file captured to your Mac disk in this way as a Jazz Word Processing document. However, our experience has been that when you open the document, sometimes it is empty and other times it contains only part of the text transmitted. The safest way to capture text is to open a Word Processing document and then choose Receive Set Selection and Receive Start from the Communications document menu before transmitting. What you receive will then be placed in the Word Processing document at the insertion point.

7.30 Trap: *If the document you want to receive into is not the last one active before you execute a Receive Set Selection, you'll receive into the wrong document.*

When you select Receive Set Selection followed by Receive Start, Jazz assumes that you want to capture into the last selected area in the last document that was active before you chose Set Selection. Usually this means making sure that last active document is the one into which you want to capture.

7.31 Trap: *If you forget to choose Receive Start after Receive Set Selection or Receive Set File, the capture will not take place.*

Remember that Set Selection and Set File are just preliminary and do not actually get Jazz ready for the transmission from the other computer; that does not actually happen until you choose Receive Start.

7.32 Trap: *When you're capturing transmitted data either into a Jazz document in memory or to disk, you won't capture anything unless you choose Receive Start (after Receive Set Selection) before the transmission.*

The rule here is choose Receive Set Selection or Receive Set File followed by Receive Start before the other computer has started transmitting. If you've logged on to an information service or a mainframe, you have control over this, since you're acting as a terminal to the other system. If you're communicating with another personal computer, you need to make sure that that system doesn't transmit until you're ready.

Some communications programs (such as Symphony in File-Transfer mode) will hold up a file transfer until Jazz is ready, but you shouldn't count on this. Get Jazz ready first by choosing Receive Start.

7.33 Trap: *If you inadvertently set the wrong protocol option on a Set File, you won't be able to change it without selecting Start and then selecting Cancel from the dialog box that appears.*

Once you choose a protocol option, the Set File menu option remains dimmed until you choose Start and then either execute a transfer or choose Cancel from the dialog box. There's generally a delay of a few seconds after you choose Cancel before Jazz actually cancels the transmission and un-dims the Set File menu choice. At this point, you can choose Set File again and reset the protocol option.

7.34 Tip: *Click on Cancel in the dialog box on the screen to stop a transmission in progress.*

Ordinarily you wouldn't want to stop a transmission in the middle. Sometimes, however, you may realize you've made some sort of mistake and therefore need to start over. Click Cancel and wait a few seconds for Jazz to accept it.

7.35 Trap: *Sometimes Jazz hangs up in the middle of a large file transfer.*

Why this happens is a mystery, but it's happened several times to us, always with files larger than 50,000 bytes. The way to recover from this is to click on Cancel in the dialog box, wait for Jazz to accept the cancel, and start the transmission again. If this still doesn't do it, try dividing the file in two and then transmitting each part separately.

7.36 Tip: *You can send whatever's on the Clipboard to another computer by choosing Paste from the Edit menu while in a Communications document.*

You can use this feature in place of Send Set Selection. You first Copy what you want to send to the Clipboard. You can then paste to the Communications document at any time, as long as no subsequent command replaces what's on the Clipboard. Unlike the usual method of making a selection in a document followed by Set Selection, the original source document does not have to be the one that was last active.

7.37 Tip: *You can copy part or all of the current 24 lines in a Communications window to the Clipboard at any time.*

You might want to do this if you've forgotten to select a capture point in a document and choose Receive Set Selection before transmission. By selecting that part of the screen you wish to copy and then choosing Copy, from the Edit menu, you can save any part of the current screen on the Clipboard and then paste it from there into any document. If the entire 24 lines of the current Communications screen are not visible in the window, you can scroll up or down for a few lines, but at no time can you view or select more than 24 lines. This means that anything you forgot to capture and that was subsequently pushed off the top of this 24-line screen by new text is now completely gone.

8

Data Transfer

This chapter focuses on two major areas: transferring data among Jazz applications and using Jazz with files created by other programs, specifically MacWrite, MacPaint, Lotus 1-2-3, Symphony, and Microsoft Multiplan. You should also refer to Chapter 7, "Communications," for more information on using the Jazz Communications application to transfer files to Jazz from other computers.

Transferring Data Within Jazz

8.01 ***Trap:*** *You won't be able to transfer data to another Jazz document until you select the data in the source document.*

You can transfer data in two ways: by using the Cut or Copy and Paste commands and by using the HotView command. Both require that you first select the data.

The data you select can be lines of text in a word processing document, cells in a worksheet, values in database fields or records, a graph, or even an entire document. Different selection techniques are often required.

To select a graph, for example, you choose Select All in the Edit menu. (The chapters on the Worksheet and Database environments contain specific Tips to help you choose the best selection technique for a variety of situations.)

The cut/copy and paste method and the HotView method function differently: The cut/copy and paste technique simply places data to be transferred in the Clipboard, while using HotView creates a direct link with the source document, so that when you change the data in the source document, it is updated automatically in the document you HotViewed it into.

See subsequent Tips and Traps for more information on each of these processes.

8.02 Trap: *Data you transfer by using the Cut or Copy commands will appear in the format of the document you send it to.*

For example, when you use the Cut or Copy commands to paste data into a word processing document from a worksheet or database, the data appears in the font, style, size, and format of the word processing document. The word processing document's settings override the formatting of the data being transferred, but you can edit it just as you would any other text.

Data transferred by Cut or Copy from another word processing document appears in the font, style, and point size of the document from which it came, but conforms to the margin and line spacing settings of the document you pasted it into.

8.03 Tip: *Use the HotView command to transfer data into a word processing document from another Jazz document when you want any changes in the data to be automatically updated.*

You can use HotView to transfer data from a worksheet, database, or graph to a Jazz word processing document and establish a link between them that provides automatic updating of data. This is especially handy, for instance, when you produce periodic reports with a common worksheet or graph but use data that changes with each period. When you change the data in the worksheet range, database range, or graph, the data in the word processing document changes also.

To: J.R.
From: Sales Manager
Date: Sept. 10
Re: Individual Sales Totals

Monthly Sales Report - August

Dear J.R.:

I'm happy to report a very successful August for our sales reps. I think the following results show the positive results of their efforts to expand our customer base.

The significance of their improvement can be seen in this graph comparing August sales for this year with August of last.

September is already off to a great start and we look forward to another good month.

Sincerely,

W.J.D.
Sales Manager

Figure 8-1. Sales report

Figure 8-1 shows a typical monthly sales report created with Jazz word processing. Notice that the text refers to a worksheet and a graph that are, as yet, nowhere to be seen.

The following illustration shows the actual worksheet referred to, which is currently open along with the report document.

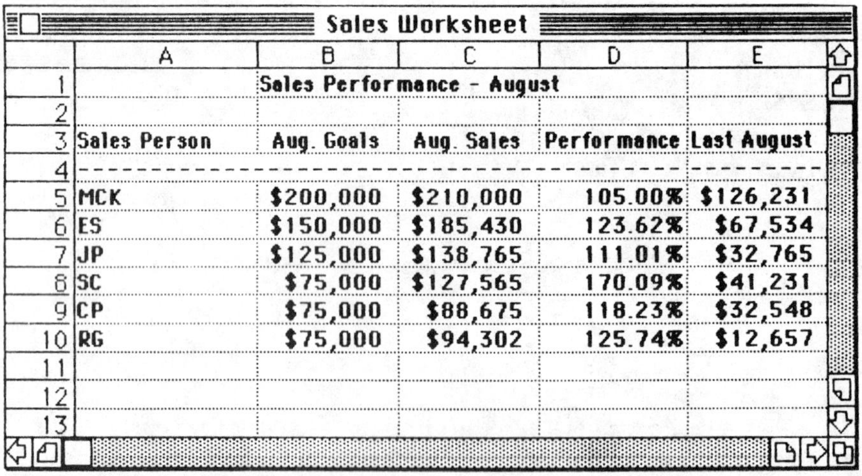

To prepare the worksheet to be transferred to the report, you can select Hide Grid from the Style menu so that the vertical and horizontal lines won't show. Then select the data to transfer, as shown in the following illustration:

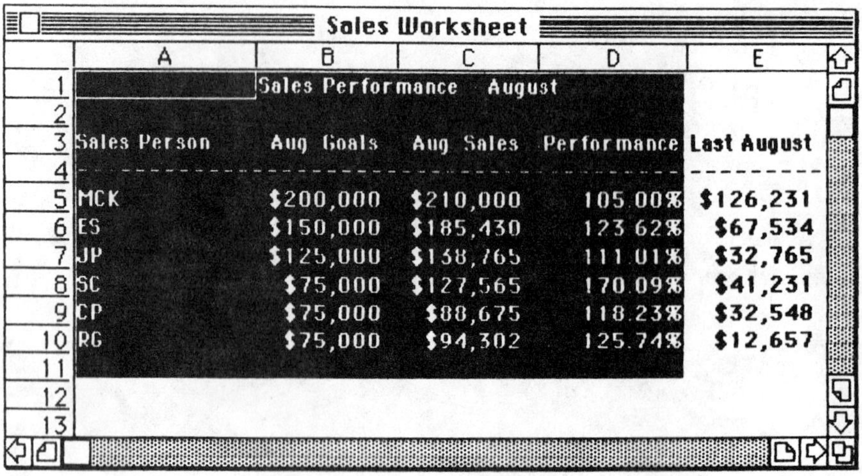

Next, switch back to the document window, place the Insertion bar at the margin following the first paragraph, and select Include from the HotView menu. This copies the worksheet selection into the word processing document, as shown in Figure 8-2.

Notice the border that is automatically placed around the selection. You can point to any spot on the border and drag the entire selection. To make the selection larger or smaller, drag the black square in the lower-right corner. You can remove the

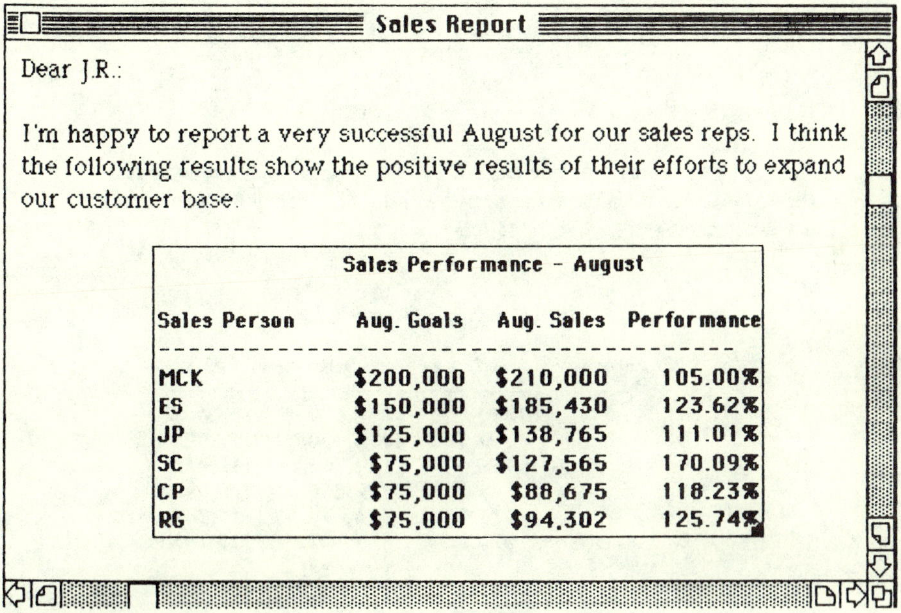
Sales Report

Dear J.R.:

I'm happy to report a very successful August for our sales reps. I think the following results show the positive results of their efforts to expand our customer base.

Sales Performance - August

Sales Person	Aug. Goals	Aug. Sales	Performance
MCK	$200,000	$210,000	105.00%
ES	$150,000	$185,430	123.62%
JP	$125,000	$138,765	111.01%
SC	$75,000	$127,565	170.09%
CP	$75,000	$88,675	118.23%
RG	$75,000	$94,302	125.74%

Figure 8-2. *Worksheet transfer*

border by clicking anywhere else in the document or bring it back by clicking within the area of the selection.

Figure 8-3 shows the result of using HotView to transfer a graph that was created from the same spreadsheet. A graph does not need to be selected, but needs to reside in the window that was previously active.

8.04 Trap: *Before you use the HotView command, make the data look the way you want it to appear after its transfer to a word processing document or you'll have to go back, change it, and transfer it again.*

Once you transfer data by Hotview, you can move it, change its size, and cut, copy, paste, or clear it as a unit — but you can't edit it in any other way. It will appear in the font, style, and point size of the worksheet or database it comes from. Line spacing or justification of the HotView material is not affected by Console settings. Because of this, make sure it looks just the way you want before you include it in the destination document. As long as the HotView is active, you can change how it looks in the word processing document by making the changes in the supporting document.

Monthly Sales Report - August

Dear J.R.:

I'm happy to report a very successful August for our sales reps. I think the following results show the positive results of their efforts to expand our customer base.

Sales Performance - August

Sales Person	Aug. Goals	Aug. Sales	Performance
MCK	$200,000	$210,000	105.00%
ES	$150,000	$185,430	123.62%
JP	$125,000	$138,765	111.01%
SC	$75,000	$127,565	170.09%
CP	$75,000	$88,675	118.23%
RG	$75,000	$94,302	125.74%

The significance of their improvement can be seen in this graph comparing August sales for this year with August of last.

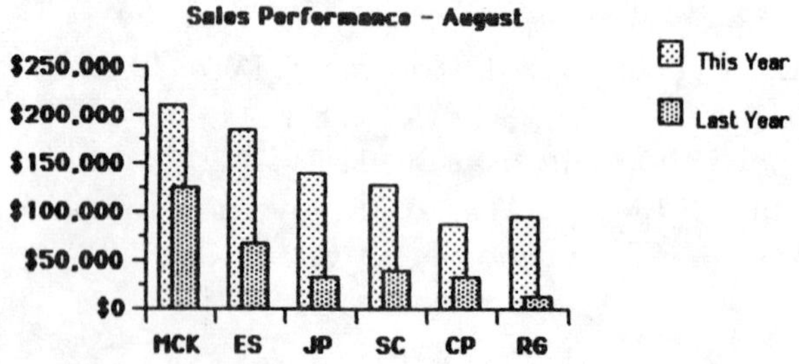

September is already off to a great start and we look forward to another good month.

Sincerely,

W.J.D.
Sales Manager

Figure 8-3. Finished report

8.05 Trap: *If you want to preserve a HotView link, you must save the supporting documents before you can save the final word processing document.*

If a word processing document contains HotViews from other documents that have never been saved, they must be saved first if you wish the HotViews to be maintained. If you don't save the supporting documents first, you will not be able to save your word processing document. You will get an error message.

You can save a supporting document on a different disk from the one that contains the HotView document. When you open the HotView document, you will get a dialog box that allows you to insert the disk containing the supporting document and reestablish the link by selecting the supporting document. See Trap 8.11 for more information.

8.06 Trap: *Unless the document containing the data to be transferred by HotView was the previous active document, the transfer won't work.*

Each open document has its own window that stands in front of or on top of those underneath it. The active document is the one "in front of" or "on top of" all the others. When you use HotView to include a selected range in a word processing document, for example, make sure that the source document resides in the window just behind the word processing document. You can make sure of this if, after selecting the source range, you make the target document active either by using the Window menu or by clicking on it.

8.07 Tip: *Use the Freeze command to prevent changes in the supporting document from appearing in the word processing document.*

You may at some point want to prevent any more changes in supporting documents from appearing in the word processing document. You can end a HotView and freeze the current values by using the Freeze or Freeze All command.

If you have several HotViews open, you can selectively freeze them. When you click on the data, the original border appears again. Freeze works on the HotView that has its border in place.

If you have only one HotView and you wish to freeze it, or if you have more than one and want to freeze them all, use the Freeze All command.

Freezing leaves the data as it is but breaks the HotView link and prevents any changes in the supporting document from being reflected in the word processing document.

8.08 Trap: *Before you freeze a HotView, make sure the data appears the way you want it, because afterward you will not be able to edit it.*

You can only change material brought into a document by a HotView by changing it in the source document. For example, while a HotView is active between a worksheet range and a word processing document, you can change the font, point size, style, or specific values by making the changes in the worksheet. Once a HotView is frozen, you cannot change the material. See Trap 8.09.

8.09 Trap: *Once you freeze a HotView, you can't make it active again.*

After a HotView has been frozen, to make it active again, you must delete it, select the range in the source document, and select Include again. In other words, you have to repeat the entire transfer process from the beginning.

8.10 Tip: *Once a HotView has made the link with one or more supporting documents, they do not have to be open for material to be updated in the destination document.*

When you create HotViews, the names of the supporting documents are saved with the word processing file. When you open the word processing document, Jazz looks for those files and automatically reads the data from the original ranges into the document, incorporating any changes that have been made. You don't have to open the supporting documents to have HotView include updates in the destination document. See Trap 8.11 for information on saving documents connected by HotViews on separate disks.

8.11 Trap: *If documents linked by HotViews are not on the same disk, a file can be opened but no updating will occur.*

Just as you need to save all documents used in a HotView for updating to occur, you also need to make sure that they are all saved on the same disk. If, for instance, you open a word processing document that depends on a database and the database is saved on another disk, you'll get this message.

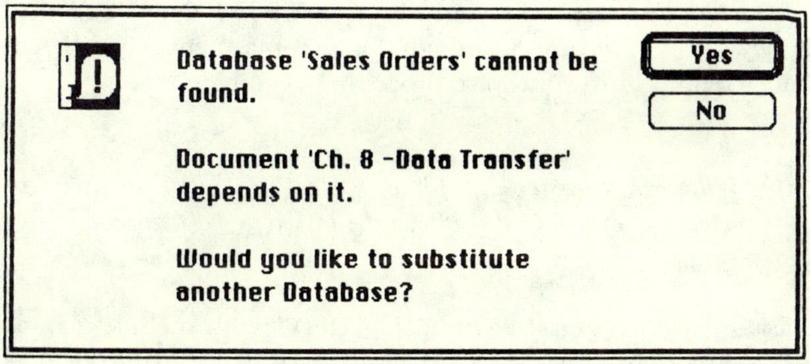

If you select Yes, you can initiate a HotView link with another database on the same disk or change disks:

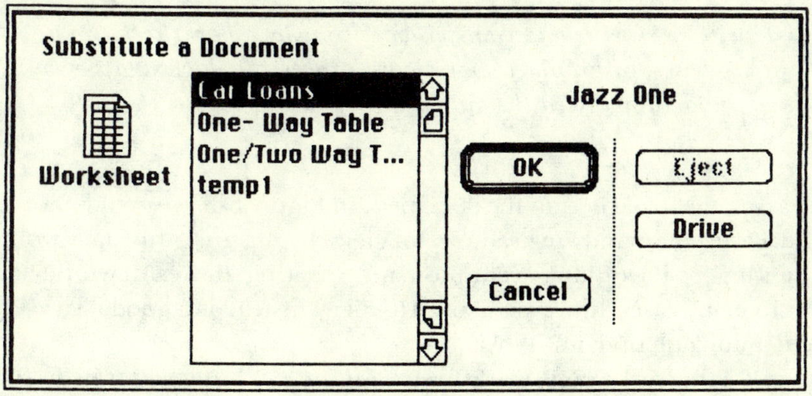

What happens when you choose another database? Whatever range was specified in the original database is applied to the newly chosen database. For instance, if your original range was A1 through A10, the material in that same range in the new database would be transferred automatically.

8.12 Trap: *You may get unexpected data in your word processing document if you edit or sort data connected by a HotView.*

When a HotView is created, it links to a specific range in the supporting document. If, for instance, you have selected records 3 through 9 in a database and sort the database on new criteria, records 3 through 9 may contain entirely different data. This new data will appear in your word processing document.

8.13 Tip: *When you transfer a graph with HotView, you don't have to select the graph first if it was the last active document.*

You don't need to select a graph before using HotView to include it in another document. As long as the graph was active before the word processing document was made active, selecting Include from the HotView menu transfers the graph at the Insertion bar. In other words, if the graph document is directly "behind" the word processing document, it will be included.

8.14 Tip: *Use HotView to transfer data from Jazz worksheets, databases, or graphs to your word processing documents even if you don't need the automatic update feature.*

In transferring the worksheet to the document in Figure 8-3, we could have used the Copy and Paste commands instead of HotView. In this case, the data would have looked the same, so if we didn't need automatic updating, the result would have been the same. In many cases, however, using HotView instead is a good idea even if you don't need automatic updates. Why?

Figure 8-4 shows the same worksheet as Figure 8-2, but it was transferred using Copy and Paste.

When you Cut or Copy and Paste to transfer data, it takes on the format of the word processing document. Because the word processing font is 12 point and the worksheet is 10 point, and because the worksheet is wider than the word processing margin settings, the data from the worksheet wrapped around and now looks different.

To: J.R.
From: Sales Manager
Date: Sept. 10
Re: Individual Sales Totals

Monthly Sales Report - August

Dear J.R.:

I'm happy to report a very successful August for our sales reps. I think the following results show the positive results of their efforts to expand our customer base.

Sales Performance - August

Sales Person   Aug. Goals
    Aug. Sales   Performance

MCK $200,000
    $210,000   105.00%
ES $150,000 $185,430
    123.62%
JP $125,000 $138,765
    111.01%
SC $75,000 $127,565
    170.09%
CP $75,000 $88,675 118.23%
RG $75,000 $94,302 125.74%

The significance of their improvement can be seen in this graph comparing August sales for this year with August of last.

September is already off to a great start and we look forward to another good month.

Sincerely,

W.J.D.
Sales Manager

Figure 8-4. Transfer using Copy

It is often easiest to use HotView to place data more accurately in a word processsing document even when automatic updating is not necessary. Also, because the HotView material retains the format of the source document, you can format it independently of the word processing document without using ruler lines. Be sure to Freeze the HotView if you don't want updating to occur. Don't forget that you can't edit a HotView in the destination document, even if you've frozen it. If you want to edit the data after transfer, use the cut/copy and paste method.

8.15 Trap: *HotViews of worksheet or database ranges will display only as much data as can fit within the margin settings of the target document.*

For example, when you use HotView to transfer data from a worksheet or database, only as much data as can fit within the current margin settings of the word processing document will be transferred. To include more, you must widen your margins and widen the current HotView by dragging its size box. See Tip 8.17.

8.16 Trap: *Although changing your margin settings will realign text, you will have to realign HotViewed data manually.*

The HotView command centers data between the current word processing document's margins. If you change the margins, the HotView data will not realign and you will have to drag its box to place it where you want.

8.17 Tip: *You can fit transferred data more accurately in your word processing document by moving, expanding, or shrinking its border.*

Data transferred by a HotView, a Cut, or a Copy appears with a black border around it. You can move it by dragging the border of the box, and you can make it larger or smaller by dragging the small black box in its lower-right corner. You can more easily resize a graph, for instance, within a word processing document by using the Size box than by changing it in the graphics document and retransferring it until you get it right.

8.18 Trap: *If you use the Cut or Copy commands, you can only transfer one field at a time from a database.*

When you want to transfer all the records in more than one field to a word processing document, it is best to use HotView and then freeze the HotView if you don't need automatic updating. If you select several fields by clicking on the field names and then select Cut or Copy, you will receive a message informing you that you can cut, copy, or clear only one field at a time.

8.19 Tip: *Use the Parse Settings option to control the placement of data being transferred to worksheet cells or database fields from the Clipboard.*

Data from other Macintosh programs as well as from Jazz can be included in Jazz worksheets or databases by copying to the Clipboard and then pasting into a worksheet or database. The problem, however, is that normally each line of text would be pasted into a single worksheet cell or database field as a "long label." Often what you really want, however, is to have (for instance) the first five characters of each line pasted into one field, the next eight pasted into another field, and so on. Or you may want to start a new field wherever you encounter one or more blank spaces in the line. The Parse Settings option in the Worksheet and Database Edit menus allow you to control all this. The default Parse Settings use the Tab character as a field separator. With this setting, you usually get long labels after pasting text from the Clipboard, so you'll probably have to change the Parse Settings to get what you want.

For example, if each item in a set of text lines to be transferred is separated by a blank, choose Blank in Parse Settings to cause each item to be placed in its own cell or field. The Parse Settings work identically in Worksheet, Database, and Communications. The Communications chapter contains an example. See your *Jazz Handbook* for details.

8.20 Trap: *Range names are lost when you transfer all or part of a Jazz Worksheet to another worksheet document.*

If you cut or copy a named range and then paste it into another worksheet, the name won't be transferred to the new document. However, when you cut and paste ranges on the same document, range names are moved to the new location. Refer to the Worksheet chapter for additional Tips and Traps on using range names.

8.21 Tip: *When you print documents containing graphs, use the Tall Adjusted option to give better proportions.*

When you have included graphs in a word processing document and you want to print it, selecting Tall Adjusted in the Page Setup menu causes the graph to print slightly wider and darker than if you select Tall.

8.22 Trap: *Having a large number of active HotViews limits the size and number of documents you can have open in Jazz.*

Using HotView to connect several documents can require a lot of RAM. By freezing unnecessary HotViews, you can free RAM so that you can work with larger documents or with more documents open at one time.

8.23 Tip: *You can merge selected information into form letters by selecting the Merge Field command from the HotView menu.*

A common use of a database is to merge data into form letters. By selecting values from one database record and merging them at the desired places in the first copy of a form letter, you set up a pattern of fields that is automatically repeated for every record you subsequently select for printing. Therefore, each copy of the letter will have different values. Here's an example.

Suppose you wanted to create a letter announcing a meeting and send it to every member of a professional group, but you wanted to make it as personal as possible. You could type one copy for every addressee or you could use your mailing list database and create a "mail merge" application. The first step in this would be to type the body of the letter, as in Figure 8-5. The first name, last name, city, state, and ZIP code of every individual would then be automatically merged into each one's own copy of the letter.

After you create your form letter in the word processing application, open the database and select the field that contains the first value to be merged. In the

---

7/5/85

Dear:

The August meeting of the Association of Data Processing Professionals will be on August 15, in the Hibiscus Rm. at the Concord Hilton and will begin promptly at 7:30 p.m. The title of this month's talk will be Micro to Mainframe Links. It promises to be a very informative evening and I hope to see you there!

Sincerely,

Michael Dempsey
Secretary, A.D.D.P.

Figure 8-5. Merge letter

following illustration, the Fname field is to be merged into the form letter shown in Figure 8-5.

Mailing List

	Fname	Lname	Street	City	State	Zip
1	Victor	Anderson	1435 Leo Way	Walnut Creek	CA	94598
2	Rich	Bosch	109 Snowpea Circle	Blackhawk	CA	94510
3	Roger	Davey	12 Black Oak Ct.	Dublin	CA	94568
4	Daniel	Dempsey	1200 Myrtle St.	Alamo	CA	94507
5	Thomas	Evans	1704 El Encanto Lane	Irwindale	CA	91706
6	Charlie	Mitchell	1504 Honeymoon Ct.	Concord	CA	94518
7	David	Overton	2667 Marina Del Rey Ct.	Brentwood	CA	94513
8	James	Peterson	1894 Merwan Lane	Walnut Creek	CA	94598
9	Roger	Siegel	2814 Monroe St.	Berkeley	CA	94705
10	James	Taylor	1230 Broadway Circle	Walnut Creek	CA	94595

When you place the cursor in the form letter where the first name is to be inserted and select Merge Field from the HotView menu, the value of this field for the first record selected (Victor) is included in the document:

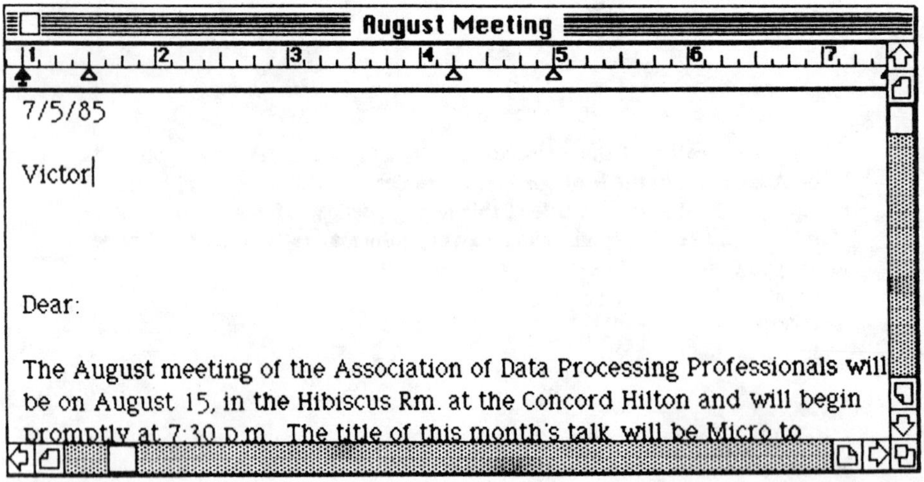

The next step is to select the next field in the database, Lname in our example, return to the letter, place the Insertion bar where the value should be inserted, and select Merge Field again. When this is done for every field we want to merge, the first copy of the letter will have values from the first record included in it, as in Figure 8-6.

When you select the desired records and choose Print Merge, one copy of the letter is automatically printed for every selected record in the database. If you forget to select any records, only one copy of the letter, containing the values from the first record, will be printed.

8.24 Tip: *Once you set up the merge fields in a word processing document using HotView, you can move or copy them and display them in any font, point, or style, but you can't edit the actual data.*

When the fields are selected and merged into a word processing document, you will be able to move the location of the merge field by adding or deleting rows or spaces, or by using Cut. You can also use Copy to duplicate the field. In this case, the field in each selected record can be merged as many times in the same copy as you want.

You can also change the font, point size, and style of each merge field to have it

7/5/85

Victor Anderson
1435 Leo Way
Walnut Creek, CA 94598

Dear Victor:

The August meeting of the Association of Data Processing Professionals will be on August 15, in the Hibiscus Rm. at the Concord Hilton and will begin promptly at 7:30 p.m. The title of this month's talk will be Micro to Mainframe Links. It promises to be a very informative evening and I hope to see you there!

Sincerely,

Michael Dempsey
Secretary, A.D.D.P.

Figure 8-6. Merged fields

displayed in a format independent from the other text. Just select the merge field in the word processing document and choose the desired format.

The only way to change the actual data, however, is to change it in the database before printing. If you select Freeze, the link with the database is broken. Once you have frozen the actual merge field data that appears in the word processing document, you can edit it, but it represents the values from only one database record or one set of worksheet cells.

8.25 Tip: *Use Query to select the specific records to be merged into form letters.*

The last step before printing a form letter containing merged fields from a database is to select the specific records for which you want to print letters. The Query command can be helpful in selecting the records. For example, you might need to send a letter reminding customers that they are late with a payment. You can use Query to select all customers with a positive amount in the Balance Due field. That way you don't have to sort the database on the Balance Due field and manually select the records by dragging the pointer.

8.26 Tip: *Before merge printing from a database, use the Show Definitions command in the HotView menu to check to see if the fields have been placed accurately in your word processing document.*

Before you choose Print Merge, select Show Definitions to see the names of the fields displayed where you have chosen to insert them, as shown in Figure 8-7. This will give you a chance to make any changes before you print.

8.27 Tip: *Before merge printing a large selection from a database, select only one record to print as a test to see if the document appears with the proper spacing.*

7/5/85

Mr. **Database 1:Fname Database 1:Lname**
Database 1:Street
Database 1:City, Database 1:State Database 1:Zip

Dear **Database 1:Fname**:

The August meeting of the Association of Data Processing Professionals will be on August 15, in the Hibiscus Rm. at the Concord Hilton and will begin promptly at 7:30 p.m. The title of this month's talk will be Micro to Mainframe Links. It promises to be a very informative evening and I hope to see you there!

Sincerely,

Michael Dempsey
Secretary, A.D.D.P.

Figure 8-7. Using Show Definition

To make sure your form letter will look the way you want it, select only one record in the supporting database and then choose Print Merge. You will see what your letter looks like in print and can make any necessary changes before making your final record selection and printing all the copies.

8.28 Trap: *If you are merging fields from more than one document, unless you make the size of each selection the same, the last value of the smaller selection will be repeated.*

For example, you might have a database containing customer names and a worksheet used to compute taxes for each customer. When you select the records from the database and the range of worksheet cells to be merged into your document, you must make sure that each record selected is matched one-to-one with the corresponding worksheet cell selected. If you select more records than cells containing the tax amounts, the last tax amount will be repeated in every copy of the document printed for the remaining names. If you select more cells containing tax amounts than records, the values in the last record will be repeated in every copy of the document printed for each remaining tax amount. See the next Tip for a way to avoid this trap.

8.29 Tip: *When you're merging data from separate documents, make sure the selection size is equal by combining all the information in one document before selecting Merge Fields and printing.*

Using the example discussed in the previous Trap, it might be easier to make sure each name in the database corresponds with the appropriate tax amount by combining all the data in one document first. The names can be copied from the database into the worksheet on the same row as the cell containing that customer's taxes. You can then clearly see the proper match and accurately select the range for merging and subsequent printing.

Using Jazz With Other Programs

8.30 Tip: *You can use your MacWrite documents in Jazz word processing by saving them as text only.*

You can use MacWrite documents in Jazz word processing if you first save them as Text Only. To do this, use the Save As option in the MacWrite File menu. You can then select Text Only and also rename the file if you want to keep the format of the original MacWrite document. Creating a text-only file removes most of the formatting and stores the document in 9-point Monaco.

When the file is saved as text only, Jazz includes it in the list that is presented when you select Open. Because most formatting has been stripped, you will need to reformat it as you wish.

When you save a file as text only, you are given the option of having a carriage return added at the end of each line or at the end of each paragraph. This determines what the text will look like when it arrives in Jazz word processing. Experiment to see what pleases you.

8.31 **Tip:** *Use MacPaint to embellish Jazz documents.*

The graphics capabilities of MacPaint allow you to enhance Jazz documents in some useful ways. For example, you can create three-dimensional graphs by editing Jazz one-dimensional graphs, as seen in the following illustration:

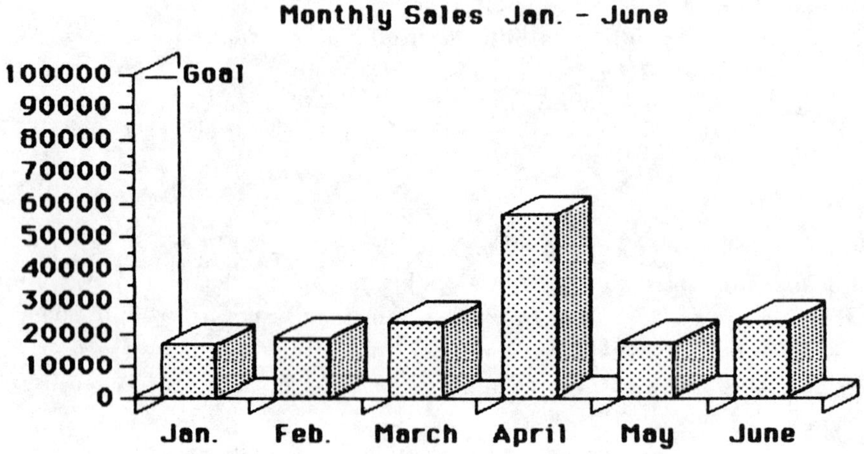

MacPaint's ability to work at the pixel level using FatBits allows complex enhancement of graphs through erasing, adding lines and shapes, adding patterns to specific areas, moving individual sections, and so on.

There are two ways in which you can place material from Jazz in MacPaint. If you have a hard disk, you can create a file that is an image of your screen. This is done by pressing COMMAND-SHIFT-3 at the same time. However, this does not work using Jazz on a floppy disk system.

If you don't have a hard disk, you will need to copy your screen to the Clipboard. Then the problem is how to paste it into MacPaint. You can either first copy MacPaint to your Jazz Start-up disk and then paste to it, or you can copy the Clipboard file to your MacPaint disk.

When you have enhanced the document, you can copy it back to the Clipboard and then paste it into a Jazz word processing document.

8.32 Tip: *You can easily convert Lotus 1-2-3, Symphony, and Microsoft Multiplan worksheet files to Jazz worksheet files.*

Using the Jazz Convert command, you can convert worksheet files created with other programs so that you can use them with Jazz. Lotus 1-2-3 and Symphony files and Microsoft SYLK files can be converted to Jazz worksheet documents. You can't convert 1-2-3 or Symphony graphs or forms, but you can convert a worksheet that contains the graph or form data and then cut or copy and paste it into a database or word processing document. Before a file can be converted, it must first be stored on a Macintosh disk. Microsoft Multiplan files can be used directly if they have been saved in SYLK format. The SYLK format (Symbolic Link) is an ASCII representation of data that can be directly accessed by Microsoft and other Macintosh programs or telecommunicated to other computer systems.

Before you can convert Lotus 1-2-3 and Symphony files, you will have to transfer them to the Macintosh environment by using any standard IBM PC communications program (such as the Symphony communications utility) that observes the XModem protocol. If you have access to an IBM and Macintosh at the same location, you can use a direct cable connection and eliminate the need for modems and phone lines. Refer to Chapter 7 for additional information on telecommunicating files from IBM to Macintosh.

Once your file has been transferred to a Macintosh disk, select the Convert command and respond to the dialog box by clicking on the appropriate document type. When Jazz has completed the conversion process, the Save As dialog box appears, and you name your document.

Jazz preserves most of the original file's settings. (Refer to the *Jazz Handbook* manual for a list of settings that Jazz does not preserve.) Macros in 1-2-3 and Symphony worksheets will be transferred to Jazz as text, but are not functional. All 1-2-3 and Symphony formulas are converted to their Jazz equivalents.

We thoroughly tested the Convert utility and found it to be error-free.

8.33 Trap: *If you don't save your Microsoft program files in SYLK format, they can't be accessed by Jazz.*

If your Microsoft files haven't been saved in SYLK format, Jazz won't be able to convert them to Jazz files. If you have a library of existing Microsoft program files saved in Normal format, you'll need to resave them in SYLK format before converting. Open one file at a time and resave it, specifying SYLK format.

8.34 Trap: *If you remove the Convert file from your disk, you won't be able to select the Convert command.*

You can remove the Convert file from your start-up disk to leave more room for document storage. However, when you want to convert a file, make sure that you are using a start-up disk that contains the Convert file. Without this file, the Convert command can't be selected from the Apple menu. If you've removed the Convert file, you can always copy it back from your original start-up disk.

8.35 Trap: *Be careful when converting 1-2-3 files containing formulas that reference label cells; you may get unexpected results.*

While 1-2-3 assigns a zero value to cells containing labels, Jazz does not always do so, and consequently, some formulas referencing label cells return ERR (error). One instance is when formulas reference individual cells, not ranges, requiring Jazz to perform arithmetic on individual cells:

Worksheet 1

	A	B	C	D	E	F
1			Sales 85	Sales 86		
2		North	$2,460	$3,075		
3		South	$3,320	$2,085		
4		East	$5,485	$5,590		
5		West	$11,050	$13,800		
6			---------	---------		
7		=SUM(C1..C5) >	$22,315	ERR	< =D1+D2+D3+D4+D5	
8						

The Formulas and Functions chapter explains how to solve this problem once you've converted a 1-2-3 worksheet to Jazz.

8.36 Trap: *Because Jazz calculates numbers to more decimal places than 1-2-3 or Symphony, formula results may be different after a file is converted.*

Formula results may be slightly different when you convert 1-2-3 or Symphony files to Jazz worksheets because Jazz stores formula values with greater precision (more decimal places). This may not be apparent if the display format of the formula cell in Jazz specifies a limited number of decimal places. However, if a formula compares two values, such as in an IF function, the logical test may fail strictly as a result of unequal calculation precision. The solution is to reenter formulas in Jazz, using the =ROUND function to round off values to a fixed number of decimal places before making the comparison. Refer to the Formulas and Functions chapter for additional Tips and Traps on using the =ROUND function.

Trademarks

The following names are trademarked products of the corresponding companies.

Apple®	Apple Computer, Inc.
CompuServe®	Compuserve, Inc.
Corvus OmniDrive™	Corvus Systems, Inc.
CrossTalk™	Microstuf, Inc.
Dow Jones News Retrieval	Dow Jones & Co., Inc.
Hayes®	Hayes Microcomputer Products, Inc.
IBM®	International Business Machine Corporation
Lotus™	Lotus Development Corporation
Macintosh™*	Apple Computer, Inc.
MacPaint™	Apple Computer, Inc.
MacWrite™	Apple Computer, Inc.
Microsoft®	Microsoft Corporation
Multiplan™	Microsoft Corporation
1-2-3™	Lotus Development Corporation
Popcom®	Prentice Co.
Symphony™	Lotus Development Corporation
Telenet™	Telenet Communications Corporation
The Source℠	The Source Telecomputing Corporation
Tymnet®	Tymshare, Inc. (McDonnell Douglas Information Systems Group)

*Macintosh is a trademark of Macintosh Laboratory, Inc., and is being used with expressed permission of its owner.

Index

D

L

M

N

O

P